ZEW Economic Studies

Publication Series of the Centre for
European Economic Research (ZEW),
Mannheim, Germany

ZEW Economic Studies

Further volumes of this series can be found at our homepage:
springeronline.com/series/4041

Oliver Heneric · Georg Licht
Wolfgang Sofka (Eds.)

Europe's Automotive Industry on the Move

Competitiveness in a Changing World

With 86 Figures
and 81 Tables

Physica-Verlag
A Springer Company

Zentrum für Europäische
Wirtschaftsforschung GmbH

Centre for European
Economic Research

Series Editor
Prof. Dr. Dr. h.c. mult. Wolfgang Franz

Editors
Oliver Heneric
Dr. Georg Licht
Wolfgang Sofka
Centre for European Economic Research (ZEW)
L7,1
68161 Mannheim
Germany
heneric@zew.de
licht@zew.de
sofka@zew.de

The content of this book was a subject of a Report prepared under the responsibility of the Austrian Institute of Economic Research (WIFO) for the European Commission's Enterprise Directorate General. Original Report: © European Communities, 2004

Adapted by the Centre for European Economic Research (ZEW)
Authors: Thomas Cleff (University of Applied Sciences, Pforzheim), Oliver Heneric (ZEW), Georg Licht (ZEW, chapter responsible), Stefan Lutz (ZEW), Wolfgang Sofka (ZEW), Alfred Spielkamp (University of Applied Sciences, Gelsenkirchen), Waltraud Urban (WiiW, Vienna)

The information and views set out in this book ly entirely with the authors and do not necessarily reflect those of the European Commission.

Cataloging-in-Publication Data
Library of Congress Control Number: 2005927785

ISBN 3-7908-1590-X Physica-Verlag Heidelberg New York

Physica-Verlag is a part of Springer Science+Business Media

springeronline.com

© Physica-Verlag Heidelberg 2005
Printed in Germany

Cover design: Erich Dichiser, ZEW, Mannheim

SPIN 11431541   43/3153-5 4 3 2 1 0 – Printed on acid-free paper

"An American can have a Ford in any color so long as it is black."
Henry Ford

Main
BookTitle:
1/20
VII

Preface

The automotive industry is a major pillar of the modern global economy and Europe is one of the key players. It has a unique role to play in Europe in employment, manufacturing, R&D, transportation and investment, and there are crucial challenges and opportunities ahead. We shed light on a broad range of issues – globalisation and restructuring, trade and foreign direct investment (notably in China and Russia), innovation, regulation, and industry policy – and put a special focus on the new member states. While change may be inevitable, progress is not. This book shall serve as a map to all stakeholders: business executives, policy makers, investors and scholars.

The contents originate from the 8th European Competitiveness Report 2004 project of the European Commission. They document the contribution made at the Zentrum für Europäische Wirtschaftsforschung (ZEW) – Centre for European Economic Resarch – in Mannheim, Germany, in cooperation with several external researchers. We as editors wish to mention and sincerely thank the many persons and institutions who have helped us in this effort. Special thanks go to the contributors: Thomas Cleff (Professor at the University of Applied Sciences in Pforzheim, Germany), Stefan Lutz (then researcher at the Centre for European Economic Resarch, Mannheim, Germany), Alfred Spielkamp (Professor at the University of Applied Sciences in Gelsenkirchen, Germany) and Waltraud Urban (Vienna Institute for International Economic Studies in Vienna, Austria). We are also grateful to Eva Anderson, Thomas Eckert, Martin Hoffmann, and Tzvetana Kaicheva for their assistance at every stage of producing this book.

Mannheim, Germany, March 2005

Oliver Heneric
Georg Licht
Wolfgang Sofka

Table of Contents

Book Title:

1 Introduction

L62

Oliver Heneric and Wolfgang Sofka   (Europe)

Europe is on the move. Automotive mobility is part of European everyday life: on the job and during vacation, with friends or family, from Poland to Portugal. The importance of the European automotive industry runs much deeper. The automotive industry is one of Europe's key industries. There can hardly be any doubt about the important role of this sector as an engine for employment, growth and innovation in Europe. Given its importance, menaces and barriers to its competitiveness cannot be neglected. A number of challenges such as new technologies, overcapacity, the need for cost reductions and sluggish market growth are currently at the top of manufacturers' and suppliers' agendas. Besides, the industry has undergone major structural and organisational changes, most notably eye-catching mergers such as the one by DaimlerChrysler as well as the abortive acquisition of BMW and Rover. However, there are still a number of issues which need to be considered with regard to the present and future of the industry:

- What is the impact of reorganisation in the industry?
- What are the consequences of reorganising the value chain for the innovation capabilities in the automotive sector?
- Are there new players on the market or just new markets?
- What is the impact of the EU enlargement on the European automotive industry?

The purpose of this report is to draw a broad picture of the *European automotive industry – competitiveness, challenges and future strategies.* The intention is to offer an overview of the industry and its sources of competitiveness as well as the challenges it faces and to outline policy implications.

Today the term "competitiveness" is widely used in various contexts and with sometimes ambiguous definitions. In its most general form competitiveness is defined here as the ability to defend and/or gain market share in open, international markets by relying on the price and/or the quality of goods. This ability is affected by a wide range of factors, frameworks and conditions. Hence, one has to look at a multitude of indicators to assess competitiveness ranging from production costs to technological and organisational innovation, from the regulatory framework to macroeconomic conditions. Given this variety competitiveness cannot be expressed in a sole number or ranking. Instead, our approach is to compare a wide set of indicators internationally and assess their development over time, too.

The research framework, and subsequently methods and data, rests upon six chapters which determine the competitiveness of the European automotive industry. Following this introduction chapter the analysis sets the stage by presenting the economic importance, the industry structure and the major players in the automotive industry. Chapter 3 focuses both on international and domestic markets as an indicator and source of competitiveness. Chapter 4 pays closer attention to the innovation aspect of competitiveness while the following part highlights the same context with regard to the impact of regulation. Eventually, the report closes with a summary of major results and conclusions.

The new member states (NMS) are already an important part of Europe's automotive system. The report emphasises their special role wherever appropriate. Besides, for stylistic reasons the report occasionally uses the term "motor vehicle industry" instead of automotive industry[1], both terms are considered synonyms and should not be interpreted as factually different.

The report comprises the following chapters:

The European Automotive Industry in a Global Context

By means of a detailed analysis of different economic indicators the economic activity of the automotive industry is described. The report covers key data which highlights the importance of this industry and its dynamic developments. The chapter provides industry specific indicators such as value added, employment as well as capital stock and investment. The significance of the automotive industry indicators is emphasised by drawing comparisons with other sectors and countries dynamically over time. An industry profile carries the chapter forward. The purpose of this section is to present both the market players and the industry itself. The industry is divided into *car, truck and bus* segments. Each segment is analysed in a *global and a European context.* The underlying indicator of this analysis is the output of the manufacturers which is measured in terms of production units. The global view describes the distribution of output volume between America, Europe, Asia and Africa.

The European view covers the EU member states and as far as possible the new member states as well. A ranking of the leading manufacturers is given for each segment. The section also includes a description of the *supplier* industry and its important role for manufacturers. Different supplier strategies and a ranking of the top supplier firms highlight their crucial role in this industry. A deeper analysis of the suppliers is provided later in the report. Furthermore, the document contributes to discussion of the internationalisation strategy of the automotive companies. The

---

[1]   Passenger cars are motor vehicles with at least four wheels, used for the transport of passengers, and comprising no more than eight seats in addition to the driver's seat. Light commercial vehicles are motor vehicles with at least four wheels, used for the carriage of goods. Mass, given in tons (metric tons), is used as a limit between light commercial vehicles and heavy trucks. This limit depends on national and professional definitions and varies between 3.5 and 7 tons. Minibuses, derived from light commercial vehicles, are used for the carriage of passengers, comprising more than eight seats in addition to the drivers seat and having a maximum mass between 3.5 and 7 tons. Heavy trucks are vehicles intended for the carriage of goods. Maximum authorised mass is between 3.5 to 7 tons. They include tractor vehicles designed for towing semi-trailers. Buses and coaches are used for the carriage of passengers, comprising more than eight seats in addition to the driver's seat, and having a maximum mass between 3.5 and 7 tons. The industry includes also component suppliers.

discussion points out the *globalisation* trend in the industry and the closely connected restructuring process among manufacturers and suppliers. Besides pointing
out mergers and acquisitions, the demonstration of the spread of intra-industrial
connections represents the current picture of the automotive industry. Finally, the
chapter tackles the issue of capacity utilisation.

Competitiveness: A Market Perspective

This chapter starts by focusing on measuring competitiveness of the European
automotive industry on international markets. World market shares and revealed
comparative advantage (RCA) numbers are presented to assess competitive performance and potential. The subsequent section emphasises foreign direct investments (FDI) as the second major instrument in internationalisation strategies both
on a country and firm level. Additionally, the chapter analyses two specific promising emerging markets, China and Russia, in more detail. Finally, the chapter
turns to the European home market to identify sources of competitiveness from
domestic demand. Apart from market size and growth special attention is paid to
market segmentations and brand esteem in the passenger car and commercial
vehicles segment.

Innovation and Competitiveness

Competitiveness can hardly be described as a static concept. Innovation and R&D
activities pave the way for future success. Those projects reflect a company's
assessment of its future prospects and its willingness to exploit market opportunities by investing in new technologies. Necessarily, the chapter starts with a broad
examination of productivity. Subsequently, we focus on skilled labour, R&D expenditures as well as patents and emphasise the relevance of innovation patterns
and research networks in the automotive sector. While innovation is often confined to technical innovations we extend this view towards organisational aspects
especially in the automotive value chain.

Regulation and Industrial Policy

The automotive industry is more and more affected by regulation at the EU level.
In general, this regulation can foster competitiveness on the one hand by increasing competition within the sector and may induce new innovation trajectories. On
the other hand regulation also might pose a threat as it can be seen as a major
driver of additional costs and may point innovation activities into dead ends where
global demand will not follow. This chapter points out the importance of the
transportation system as well as its social costs and the major elements of regulation initiatives which affect the automotive industry. This section highlights specific regulations e.g. Block Exemption or end of life vehicle as well as the efforts
of the industry to take the environmental challenges into account. Therefore, the
report provides a deeper look at the sustainability endeavours of the automotive
industry.

Challenges and Opportunities for the European Automotive Industry

Consequently, the report reaches its final stage: the *SWOT Analysis*. The SWOT Analysis provides a systematic overview of strengths (S), weaknesses (W), opportunities (O) and threats (T). It is a well established and straightforward concept which is helpful in matching an industry's resources and capabilities to the competitive environment in which it operates. The aim is to conclude from each section mentioned above the strength, weaknesses, opportunities and threats of the European automotive industry. To extend the scope of this analysis into the future while still providing meaningful results an additional scenario analysis is conducted to highlight major connections and interactions among SWOT factors in a best and worst case scenario. These steps lay the groundwork for the formulation of implications and policy issues.

2 The European Automotive Industry in a Global Context

L 6 2   L 11 L 25

Oliver Heneric, Georg Licht, Stefan Lutz, and Waltraud Urban

2.1 Economic Importance

2.1.1 Overview

The automotive industry is one of Europe's biggest industries. It contributes about 6% to total manufacturing employment and 7% to total manufacturing output in Europe making it a major driver of the European economy. Employment in the EU motor vehicle industry amounts to 1.9 million employees and annual value added produced is about EUR 114 bn. The US automotive industry produces about the same volume (in value added at current exchange rates). However, employment figures are only 60% of the European level thus exhibiting a significantly higher level of labour productivity per employee. Japan's automotive production volume is about 65% of that of the EU-15 or the US; with only 56% of the US employment level, the Japanese industry boasts even higher labour productivity levels than the US.[2] However, labour productivity growth has been consistently higher in the EU-15 since the early 1990s, so that European automotive manufacturing productivity is in a continuous process of catching up with the US and Japan. Catching up has continued since 1995, contrary to evidence about a relative European slowdown since the mid-90s in total manufacturing. However, the relative sizes of the three big regions of automotive production have not changed very much during the last decade or so.

In addition to its own size, the automotive industry generates more economic activity through various backward (to supplier industries) and forward linkages (to customers). A comparison of total production, value added, production volumes and imports for the EU-15, the USA and Japan, puts imports and value added, respectively, at roughly a quarter of total production. This is evidence for upstream inputs of up to two times the volume of value added in the automotive industries. Inspection of input-output tables supports these findings. E.g. in Ger-

---

[2] Employment figures in automotive industry vary significantly according data source. E.g. OECD/STAN data reports about 950,000 employees for the USA whereas US BLS (the original data source) reports around 1.2 million employees. Similar differences can be found with respect to Japan. Even more, there seem to be differences with regard to the (detailed) definition of what belongs to the automotive sector, and it seems that in some countries different definitions of the sector are employed with regard to output figures (production value, value added, etc.) and labour input figures. Hence, one should be extremely cautious when comparing productivity figures (level) across countries.

many, backward linkages provide products worth about EUR 1.3 for every euro in final demand for automotive production.

Probably due to differences in outsourcing behaviour along the value chain, the domestically generated value added component in total vehicle production has increased in the EU-15 while it was about stable in Japan and fell in the US. This might have been exacerbated by a relatively high decrease in total manufacturing relative to GDP in Europe and the introduction of domestic content requirements following NAFTA in the US.

It is noteworthy that the EU-15 automotive industry is highly concentrated with Germany alone accounting for close to half of total value added generated. The six largest national industries, i.e. Germany, France, the United Kingdom, Italy, Spain, and Sweden account for over 90% of total value added generated.

Nevertheless, since the total manufacturing sector is shrinking relative to the service sector in advanced economies, i.e. total manufacturing is less than one third of total domestic product, the automotive industry accounts for less than 2% of GDP in the USA, Japan and the EU-15. Likewise, the automotive industry provides less than 1.5% of total employment in these regions. Hence its importance follows to a large degree from linkages within the domestic and international economy.

While the automotive industry is not a high-tech industry in the strict sense, it is a major driver of new technologies and of the diffusion of innovations throughout the economy. Almost 20% of all R&D in manufacturing is undertaken by car manufacturers. Its close links to many other manufacturing sectors (such as chemicals, plastics, electrical and electronic parts, etc.) contribute to the rapid diffusion of new technologies. Moreover, the industry is an important demand source for innovations from other industries, including high-tech sectors such as ICT.

Finally, motor vehicles are one of the most important consumer goods in terms of total household expenditures. As motor vehicles are the largest durable consumer goods in terms of expenses (next to housing), demand for motor vehicles is highly correlated with and contributes to general growth and business cycle movements.

2.1.2   Value Added

The automotive industry contributes about 6% to total manufacturing employment and 7% to total manufacturing output in Europe. Employment in the EU motor vehicle industry is in excess of 1.9 million and annual value added produced in excess of EUR 114 bn.

Table 1. Value added in motor vehicles in EU, USA, Japan

		2000	2001	2002
EU-15	EUR mn	117,154	118,156	114,170
USA	USD mn	120,400	109,334	120,800
	EUR/USD	1,086	1,118	1,062
	EUR mn	110,866	97,794	113,748
Japan	JPY bn	8,129	8,753	9,254
	1000 JPY/EUR	0.1078	0.1215	0.1253
	EUR mn	75,408	72,041	73,855

Source: VDA, International Auto Statistics 2003. OECD/STAN and own calculations.

Total value added produced in the motor vehicle industry in the EU-15 was about the same in 2002 as in the USA – roughly EUR 114 bn at current exchange rates. A similar calculation for Japan puts that the country's motor vehicle value added about 35% lower at EUR 74 bn.

Within the EU, the largest national motor vehicle industries by percentage of total EU-15 value added in 2002 were Germany (45%), France (17%), the United Kingdom (11%), Italy (7%), Spain (7%) and Sweden (6%). Together, these six countries account for about 93% of motor vehicle production within the EU-15.

Table 2. Value added in motor vehicles in the EU by country in 2002

Year	EUR mn	% of EU total
Austria	2,223	1.95
Belgium	2,774	2.43
Denmark	345	0.30
Finland	344	0.30
France	19,047	16.68
Germany	51,490	45.10
Greece	75	0.07
Ireland	145	0.13
Italy	7,967	6.98
Luxembourg	n/a	n/a
Netherlands	1,766	1.55
Portugal	968	0.85
Spain	7,665	6.71
Sweden	6,840	5.99
United Kingdom	12,521	10.97
EU-15	114,170	100.00

Source: VDA, International Auto Statistics 2003.

Value added[3] in motor vehicles as a percentage of value added in total manufacturing has been stable since 1991 in Japan and the EU-15 but increased signifi-

---

[3]   Source: OECD/STAN data.

cantly in the US. In 1991 it was about 8% in Japan, 4% in the US, and 6% in the EU-15. Up to the year 2000, this percentage grew to 9% in Japan, 8% in the US and 7% in the EU-15.

Within the EU, motor vehicles are most prominent as a percentage of manufacturing value added 2002 in Sweden (15%), Germany (13%), France (10%), Spain (7%), Belgium (7%), Austria (6%), UK (5%) and Italy (4%). All other EU member countries have percentage rates of below 4%.

This supports the notion of an industry concentrated in a few countries. Since in the EU-15 as a whole, automotive value added accounts for less than 2% of total GDP, it follows that it is rather negligible in about half the EU countries. More precisely, this ratio is less than 0.5% in Denmark, Finland, Greece, the Netherlands and Portugal. Note that it is also less than 0.5% in the US.

2.1.3   Employment

In the year 2002, the motor vehicle industry employed 1.91 million workers in the EU-15, 1.15 million in the USA, and 0.65 million people in Japan, respectively. From 2000 to 2002 employment in the USA decreased by about 12%, whereas it fell more moderately in EU-15 (by 2%) and in Japan (by 5%).

Since the ratios of value added and employment suggest much higher labour productivity levels in Japan and the US than in the European Union, the relative employment dynamics of the US and the EU indicate a slowdown in the catching-up process of the European auto industries since the turn of the millennium.

Table 3. Employment in motor vehicles in EU, USA, Japan (thousands)

	1999	2000	2001	2002
EU-15	1,901	1,944	1,933	1,907
USA	1,312	1,313	1,212	1,151
Japan	705	683	664	646

Source: VDA, International Auto Statistics 2003. OECD/STAN and own calculations.

Employment in the motor vehicle industry as percentage of employment in manufacturing[4] in Japan, the USA and the EU-15 increased by about one percentage point from 1991 to 2000. The highest percentage in both years was in Japan, where it grew from about 6.5% in 1991 to 7.5% in 2000. This is followed by the EU with an increase from 5.5% to 6.5% during the same period. The USA exhibits the lowest levels over the same period, moving from 4.5% to 5.5%. However, since industrial production is only a fraction of total production in these three regions, this translates into less than 1.5% of total employment in the respective economies. Between 1995 and 2000, this percentage remained roughly stable at 1.4% in Japan, 0.7% in the USA, and 1.1% in the EU-15. The table also shows that the automotive industry is in a critical situation in all three regions. Since

---

[4]   Source: OECD/STAN data.

2000 a significant drop in the number of employees can be observed in the US. Also, Japan and the EU show a trend towards lower employment figures in recent years. However, looking at the long-run trend employment in the EU automotive industry is still increasing.

Within EU-15, 45% of employment in vehicle manufacturing was in Germany in the year 2002. Other major employers are France (14%), the United Kingdom (11%), Italy (9%), and Spain (8%).

Table 4. Employment in the motor vehicle industry in the EU by country 1999-2002 (thousands)

Country	1999	2000	2001	2002
Austria	28.2	29.1	30.7	30.2
Belgium	52.7	53.9	53.2	51.0
Denmark	8.1	7.5	7.1	6.5
Finland	7.3	7.5	7.2	7.1
France	273.9	277.3	276.8	273.2
Germany	835.5	855.6	867.6	866.6
Greece	1.7	n/a	n/a	n/a
Italy	181.0	178.8	175.8	163.9
Ireland	3.3	3.4	3.7	3.5
Luxembourg	n/a	n/a	n/a	n/a
Netherlands	28.0	28.0	26.8	26.8
Portugal	24.4	28.2	20.9	20.0
Sweden	72.3	77.5	79.1	80.6
Spain	159.5	165.6	161.9	158.5
United Kingdom	224.7	231.3	222.4	219.2

Source: VDA, International Auto Statistics 2003.

Within the EU, percentages of manufacturing employment in the motor vehicle industry in the year 2000 are largest in Germany (11%), Sweden (10%), Belgium (8%), Spain (7%) and France (7%). These numbers have increased since 1991 by about half to one percentage point in all those countries with the exception of France, where that percentage rate remained stable.

A similar picture emerges when looking at individual EU countries' employment as a percentage of total employment in the respective national economies. In the year 2000, this percentage was the highest in Germany (2.4%), Sweden (1.8%), Spain (1.3%), Belgium (1.2%), France (1%), and Italy (0.75%).

2.1.4   Production, Backward and Forward Linkages

In addition to its own size, the automotive industry generates more economic activity through various backward and forward linkages. A first indicator of backward linkages is the ratio of total production to value added, since the difference between production and value added are inputs. Generally, value added in motor vehicles is about one quarter of total production in motor vehicles.

Measured in current USD and using OECD purchasing power parities[5], production in motor vehicles[6] has remained roughly constant in Japan at about USD 250 billion. In the US production increased from USD 200 billion in 1991 to USD 400 billion in 2000. In the EU-15, production increased during the same time frame from USD 300 billion to USD 550 billion.

Between 1991 and 2000, value added as a percentage of total production in motor vehicle manufacturing[7] has been between 20 and 30% in Japan, the USA and EU-15. While this percentage has increased in Japan (25% to 27%) and the USA (22% to 30%), it has dropped in the EU-15 (30% to 22%) from the beginning to the end of that time period.

In comparison, between 1995 and 2000, value added as a percentage of total production has increased by about 10% in Japan while it fell by about 10% each in the US and the EU-15. Since automotive value added as a percentage of manufacturing total was slightly increasing in all three regions, the different directions of trends seem to reflect general trends in manufacturing.

The explanation for the different movements in value added relative to production in Europe and the US might therefore be found in two recent developments. Firstly, outsourcing has recently been developed to a higher degree in the EU than in the US. Secondly, the introduction of domestic content requirements in the US following the ratification of NAFTA may have contributed to the observed trend in the USA.

This gives a first rough estimate of backward linkages, i.e. production of inputs demanded by motor vehicle manufacturers. Since a part of these inputs are foreign imports, they have to be subtracted to obtain the domestic backward linkage effect. As imports account for approximately 25% of total production on average, this results in a backward linkage effect of a magnitude of 2. Consequently, each dollar, euro or yen of value added in motor vehicles demands approximately two more dollars, euros or yen of domestic inputs for production. A similar effect would be expected for employment relationships.

A more precise way of quantifying the magnitude of backward linkages is through input-output tables. We restrict the analysis to the latest available input-output tables for Germany (published by the Statistical Office in December 2003) as EU-wide input-output tables are not available. Figure 1 shows the impact of a EUR 1 increase in final demand for cars on production values and imports (in EUR) of goods produced by the automotive sector itself and other sectors. It is important to bear in mind that the coefficients presented there also account for indirect effects including the additional demand for cars as response to an increase in the induced output of other sectors. The interpretation is straightforward. The main impact of an increase in final demand for cars is visible in the automotive sector where the production of automotive products (including parts) increases by EUR 1.4. Not surprisingly, an increase in the demand for cars has a large impact

---

5   Note that this results in European production being relatively higher when compared to using industry association data with current nominal exchange rates.
6   Source: OECD/STAN and own calculations.
7   Source: OECD/STAN and own calculations.

on steel production, the metal working industry, high-tech manufacturing (i.e. mechanical and electrical engineering, measurement and control, electronics, etc.), chemical products and rubber.

Fig. 1.   Backward linkages of final demand for automotive products in Germany

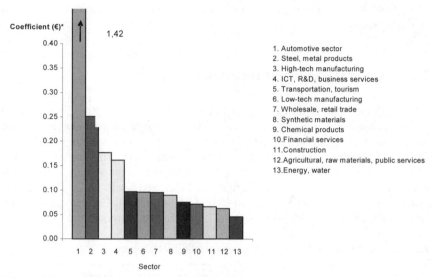

1. Automotive sector
2. Steel, metal products
3. High-tech manufacturing
4. ICT, R&D, business services
5. Transportation, tourism
6. Low-tech manufacturing
7. Wholesale, retail trade
8. Synthetic materials
9. Chemical products
10. Financial services
11. Construction
12. Agricultural, raw materials, public services
13. Energy, water

* The coefficient shows the impact of a EUR 1 increase in final demand for cars on production values and imports (in EUR).
Source: ZEW calculations using data from the Federal Statistical Office Germany.

Surprisingly, there are strong links between car production and several service sectors namely business services (including R&D and IT services), financial services, transport and trade. In sum, service sector output is raised by nearly EUR 0.5. Low-tech sectors are also linked through the supply chain to the automotive sector, however. These links through the value chain also demonstrate the importance of the automotive sector as an engine for growth and employment. Although this data only refers to the German automotive sector, the results probably hold for other EU countries as well. In a recent study Garel Rhys (2000) reports various estimates linking employment in the automotive industry and the rest of the economy. He concludes that one should expect an "employment multiplier" between the automotive sector and the rest of the economy in the magnitude between 1:0.6 and 1:1.4. These estimates are in line with the estimated link which indicates a 1:0.9 relation between automotive and other products and other sectors. However, note that this link is not a national one. Given the international nature of the automotive value chain the reported numbers also show a large potential for linking the European economies (from which the bulk of automotive part imports stem) through the car industries value chain.

At first glance, domestic production and employment effects through forward linkages outside of vehicle manufacturing seem to be rather insignificant. However, the structure of the input-output tables masks major downstream effects for

the automotive repair and maintenance services industries, since these services are
contracted through final users of vehicles. Domestic demand for these services
originates from the total stock of new and used vehicles owned by domestic firms
and consumers and is fuelled by the about 25% of total turnover demanded by
domestic consumers and firms. Another major downstream effect within the EU-
15 is given by intra-EU exports, which are in the order of magnitude of 35% of
total production.

2.2   Capital Stock and Investment

Motor vehicle manufacturing is an investment-intensive industry. This is borne
out by consistently high levels of investment in fixed capital like plants and
equipment. The aggregated level of investments in the motor vehicle industries of
the EU-15 countries was EUR 30.5 bn in the year 2001. The largest investing
national industries were in Germany (39% of EU-15 motor vehicle industry investment), France (21%), United Kingdom (14%), and Spain (7%). The German
motor vehicle industry alone invested EUR 11.6 bn in 2001. Germany and France
together contributed roughly 60% of total EU-15 industry investments.

Table 5. Investment levels in the motor vehicle industry by country in 2001

	EUR mn 2001	% of EU-15 total 2001	ECU mn 1995	% of EU-15 (1) total 1995
Austria	424	1.39	215	1.27
Belgium	926	3.03	n/a	-
Denmark	44	0.14	62	0.36
Finland	35	0.11	43	0.25
France	5,129	16.81	3,649	21.48
Germany	11,642	38.16	6,565	38.65
Ireland	31	0.10	n/a	-
Italy	4,209	13.79	1,957	11.52
Luxembourg	n/a	-	n/a	-
Netherlands	162	0.53	n/a	-
Portugal	224	0.73	307	1.81
Spain	2,874	9.42	1,143	6.73
Sweden	1,041	3.41	710	4.18
United Kingdom	3,771	12.36	2,335	13.75
EU-15	30,512	100.00	(1) 16,985	(1) 100.00
Japan	n/a	-	12,497	-
USA	n/a	-	15,813	-

(1) No comparable data available for Belgium, Ireland, Luxembourg and the Netherlands.
Hence EU-15 figures exclude those countries.
Source: VDA, International Auto Statistics 1999 and 2003.

The investment rate, i.e. investment relative to value added[8], ranged between 7 and 38% for individual EU countries in the year 2001. Similarly, investment per worker employed in 2001 varied between 3 and 18 EUR/employee. By both measures, the lowest investment levels were those in Finland (note that these are values from one year earlier, though).

Highest investment rates were achieved in Spain (38%), Portugal (32%), the United Kingdom (29%), and France (29%). Highest investment levels per employee were exhibited by France, Spain, and the United Kingdom (all three close to 18%). The latter three countries seem therefore to have been major contributors to the recent productivity increases in the European automotive industry.

Trends in investment activity[9] in the motor vehicle industry are, again, similar to trends in total manufacturing. Investment levels as percent of value-added and production tend to remain stable.

Table 6. Investment ratios in the EU motor vehicle industry by country in 2001

	Investment per person employed (in EUR)	Investment per value added (in %)
Austria	13.2	18.8
Belgium	10.9	18.0
Denmark	9.0	17.8
Finland	3.2*	6.9*
France	17.9	29.3
Germany	13.5	20.3
Greece	n/a	n/a
Ireland	8.0	19.5
Italy	10.7	26.5
Luxembourg	n/a	n/a
Netherlands	6.0	9.2
Portugal	12.0	31.6
Spain	17.8	37.9
Sweden	15.0	23.4
United Kingdom	17.5	29.4

*) Value for the year 2000.
Source: Eurostat, New Cronos, March 2004.

2.2.1 Special Focus on the New Member States

The new member states (NMS) are small but highly specialised road vehicle producers in the European context. The automotive industry is also growing much faster in these countries than in the old member states (OMS). A new automotive industry 'axis' is emerging, comprising the Czech and the Slovak Republics,

---

8   Source: OECD/STAN and own calculations.
9   Source: OECD/STAN data.

Southern Poland and Western Hungary, based on skilled workers, low labour costs and large potential demand. Although this will enhance the international competitiveness of the EU automotive industry, global overcapacities may lead to companies moving out of the OMS.

2.2.1.1   The Relative Size of the NMS Automotive Industry

When comparing production values in the NMS with those in the OMS, one has to take into consideration the still undervalued currencies of the NMS. Converting output with purchasing power standards (PPP) instead of market exchange rates brings the share of the NMS automotive industry in EU-25 production up from 5% to 10%, the truth may be somewhere in the middle. The share in EU-25 employment is 11% (Table 7).

Table 7. Overview of number of establishments, production and employment 2002 in motor vehicles, trailers and semi-trailers (NACE 34)

	No of enterprises	Production[1]					VAD[3]			Employment[2]		
		EUR millions		% of manuf.	% of EU-25		EUR millions		% of manuf.	People (thousands)	% of manuf.	% of EU-25
		at exch.rates	at PPP		at exch.r.	PPP	at exch.r	at PPP				
Cyprus	46 [3]	18.3	24.6	0.6	0.0	0.0	7.5	10.1	0.8	0.4	1.0	0.02
Czech Rep.	385 [3]	9.093.6	17663.5	16.2	1.7	3.2	1620.7	3148.1	10.9	87.0	8.4	4.08
Estonia	20	74.0 [3]	145.5 [3]	2.2 [3]	0.0	0.0	24.3	47.8	2.5	1.5 [3]	1.2 [3]	0.07
Hungary	399	6.813.6	12901.3	14.5	1.2	2.4	1166.3	2208.4	10.1	36.1	4.8	1.70
Latvia	21	10.7 [3]	23 [3]	0.3 [3]	0.0	0.0	5.8	12.4	0.4	0.6 [3]	0.4 [3]	0.03
Lithuania	32	9.0 [3]	21 [3]	0.1 [3]	0.0	0.0	1.2	2.7	0.1	0.3 [3]	0.1 [3]	0.01
Malta	16	3.1	5.6	0.1	0.0	0.0	1.3	2.3	0.2	0.1	0.2	0.00
Poland	1092 [3]	7.242.3	13708.4	6.4	1.3	2.5	2044.5	3869.9	4.5	78.0	3.5	3.66
Slovak Rep.	74	2.939.8	6976.2	17.2	0.5	1.3	321.4	762.7	8.2	18.2	4.8	0.85
Slovenia	144 [3]	1.329.9	1888.9	9.7	0.2	0.3	133.6	189.8	3.3	7.0	3.0	0.33
NMS-10	2229	27.534.2	56612.4	10.3	5.0	10.3	5326.6	10951.9	6.2	229.1	4.4	10.76
EU-15[4]		520.000.0		10.7 [5]						1.900.0	6.9 [5]	
EU-25		547.534.2		10.7						2.129.1		

VAD = value added, PPP = purchasing power parity. 1) at current prices; 2) employees only; 3) 2001; 4) Eurostat (2004: 240), rounded values; 5) year 2000.
Source: wiiw Industrial Database; Panorama of Czech Industries, Eurostat, New Cronos, SBS.

2.2.1.2   'Big' and 'Small' Producers

In terms of production value and employment, the 'Big Three' automotive producers among the NMS are the Czech Republic, Poland and Hungary – followed by the Slovak Republic and Slovenia (See Table 7 and Figure 2). However, in terms of the *number of vehicles* produced, Slovakia ranks third, before Hungary, indicating a lower unit value of cars produced in the former than in the latter country.

Comparing individual countries, the automotive industries in the Czech Republic, Hungary and Poland – and probably Slovakia in the near future as well – are similar in size to that of Austria and the Netherlands and rank in the lower middle field of European automobile producers, while the other NMS belong to the group of minor producers in the EU, such as Denmark, Finland, Greece and Ireland.

Specialisation

Although rather small in the overall European context, the automotive industry plays a very important role in these NMS and is a major driver of their economies. The most specialised NMS countries are the Czech Republic, Slovakia and Hungary.

In 2002, the share of the automotive industry in total manufacturing output reached 17.2% in Slovakia and 16.2% in the Czech Republic and 14.5% in Hungary (see Table 7 and Figure 3). In these countries, the share of the automotive industry is in fact higher than in the big West European car producing countries, such as France, Italy, UK and Spain, ranging between 5 and 14%, except Germany (17%).

Fig. 2.   Motor vehicle production in the old and in the new member states (2001/2002) in EUR mn

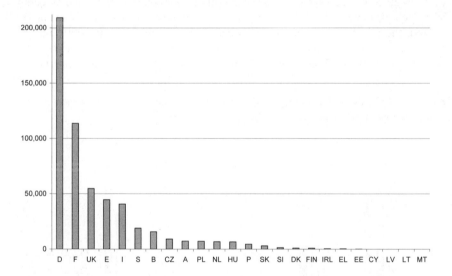

Source: Eurostat, New Cronos, SBS, Panorama of Czech Industries 2003.

However, while the automotive industry is the most important manufacturing sector in the Czech and the Slovak Republics, indicating a clear specialisation in this field, it ranks just third in Hungary, with the electrical equipment and the food industry taking the lead there. Notably, in Slovenia where the automotive industry is very small in absolute size, it nevertheless has a relatively high share in manufacturing (9.7%), while in Poland, which ranks second in car production after the

Czech Republic, the role of the industry is relatively small (6.4%), due to the large size of the overall economy.

Comprising many assembly plants, the value added shares of the automotive industry in the NMS are typically lower than the production shares, but the investment shares are generally higher, driven by foreign direct investment and pointing to the dynamic development of the industry. Employment shares are relatively low due to the capital intensive character of the industry (see Figure 3).

2.2.1.3 A Small but Fast-Growing Automotive Industry

The automotive industry in the NMS is small measured by EU standards, but has been developing very dynamically and much faster than in the old member states and also faster than total manufacturing in the NMS. This outstanding growth can be attributed to the high inflow of foreign direct investment (attracted by skilled and cheap labour which makes the industry internationally very competitive), by investment promotion by local governments, and the expectation of expanding domestic markets.

Between 1995 and 2002, average annual growth of output (at constant prices) reached an impressive 28% in the Slovak Republic, 25% in Hungary, and 20% in the Czech Republic, surpassing average manufacturing growth in these countries by 15 to 20 percentage points per annum. Only minor automobile producing countries such as some Baltic states showed below average growth in this sector. In Poland, the automotive industry developed rapidly until the year 2000, but has performed poorly ever since (Figure 4 and Figure 5). This is partly due to specific problems such as the Joint Venture between Daewoo and the Polish government

Fig. 3.   NMS automotive industry: VAD, production, employment and investment percentage in total manufacturing, 2002

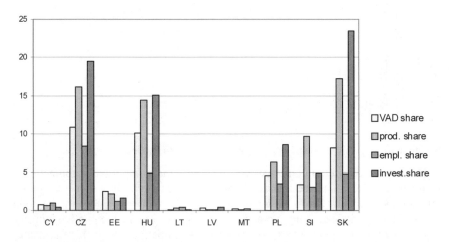

Source: See Table 7 and Eurostat, New Cronos, SBS.

and the indirect impact of the 1997/1998 Asian economic crisis, but there are signs of overall weakness in the automotive industry in Poland as well – probably linked to demand which has developed less well than expected and a relatively high wage level compared to other NMS competitors.[10]

Fig. 4.   Industrial production index for the automotive industry (NACE 34) in major car producing NMS

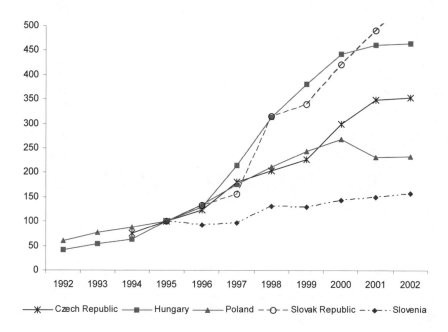

At constant prices 1999, national currency; 1995=100.
Source: wiiw Industrial Database; Panorama of Czech Industries, Eurostat, New Cronos, SBS.

Output in the vehicle industry is also decelerating in Hungary, although it is important to bear in mind that 2002 was a bad year for the automobile industry all over Europe due to a fall in overall demand which hit the car industry in particular. The recent data indicating very high production growth in Lithuania must be interpreted with care as the level of production is very low and fluctuates strongly; this is probably due to changes in the classification of automobile parts which can, for example, be assigned to the automobile industry one year and the electrical industry (wires, electronic components) or the plastic & rubber industry (bodies,

[10]   The production of Fiat Auto declined from 340,630 cars in 1999 to 178,044 in 2002. Production of FSO Polonez (Daewoo) came down from 18,891 cars in 1999 to just 1,444 in 2002 – the number of trucks produced fell from 7,625 to mere 350 during the same period (Ward, 2003).

components) the next. But there is no doubt that the supplier industry is developing rather well in Lithuania[11].

Fig. 5.   Industrial production index for the automotive industry (NACE 34) in secondary car producing NMS

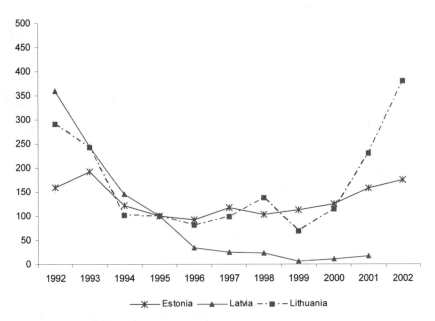

At constant prices 1999, national currency; 1995=100.
Source: wiiw Industrial Database; Panorama of Czech Industries, Eurostat, New Cronos, SBS.

2.3   Industry Profile

2.3.1   Automotive Production

The automotive industry is a key strategic industry within the European economy. A considerable number of the leading automotive companies have their origins in Europe. The industry is characterised by large internationally owned manufacturers and suppliers as well as a number of small and medium-sized companies which meet the criteria of component suppliers (tier 1 to tier 3, see below). Manu-

---

[11]   Lithuania produces mainly bodies (NACE 34.2) and parts (NACE 34.3), but is supplying a wide range of components for the automobile industry from other industries, in particular electrical equipment and plastic parts (Ekonomines Konsultacijos ir Tyrimai UAB, 2002).

facturers and suppliers in this sector constitute a key source of R&D and innovation. A major labour force consisting of almost two million people is employed in the manufacturing sector alone. At the same time, Europe is also the world's largest automotive market. Exceeding half of worldwide turnover, Europe reveals its extraordinary position within this industry. In the following, the automotive industry will be described in terms of its segments and players. In order to obtain an overview of the industry, we describe the car, truck and bus sector. Each sector will be discussed in a global and European view. The major league of operating companies will be presented in terms of output for each sector. We also add a digest of the supplier industry to point out its importance for manufacturers. For the purpose of this study, the European automotive industry is defined as the production of light vehicles, heavy-duty vehicles i.e. trucks, including the manufacture of parts, systems and technical units (in statistical terms, the industry corresponds to NACE 34) taking place within the EU-15, and as far as is possible EU-25.

The following definitions[12] provide an overview of the automotive related terms. These terms are used throughout the report.

The Original Equipment Manufacturer (OEM) or manufacturer is a company that manufactures and/or assembles a final product. For example, a car made under a brand name by a given company may contain various components, such as tires, brakes or entertainment features, manufactured by several different "vendors", but the firm doing the final assembly/manufacturing process is the OEM.

Supplier industry is structured in several groups of so-called component suppliers i.e. each component affects different parts along the value chain. Therefore the following distinction is widely used:

Tier 1 supplier is a component manufacturer delivering directly to final vehicle assemblers, responsible for the finished assembly, product development and continued technology innovation. Tier 1 suppliers work hand-in-hand with automobile manufacturers to design, manufacture and deliver complicated automobile systems and modules, such as significant interior, exterior or drive train units. Tier 1 suppliers in turn purchase from tier 2 and tier 3 suppliers, which rank below tier 1.

Tier 2 suppliers: These companies produce value-adding parts in the minor sub-assembly phase. Tier 2 suppliers buy from tier 3 and deliver to tier 1.

Tier 3 suppliers are suppliers of engineered materials and special services, such as rolls of sheet steel, bars and heat treating, surface treatments. Tier 3 suppliers rank below tier 2 and tier 1 suppliers in terms of the complexity of the products that they provide.[13]

Therefore the value chain could be described as follows. The starting point is the supplying industry which delivers parts to the OEM. After the production process which is more and more closely connected between OEM and suppliers, the retail channel forwards the products to the final customer.

---

[12]   See Plunkett's Industry Almanac.
[13]   See Plunkett's Industry Almanac.

Fig. 6.   Automotive value chain

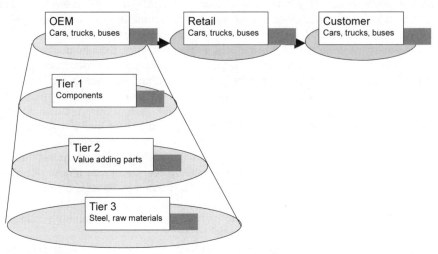

Source: ZEW.

Taking a global view of the market (Figure 7) and its global production, it is possible to consider Europe[14], America[15] and Asia-Oceania[16] as the three pillars of the automotive industry. Each of these regions has a share of almost one third of global production volume.

Europe – which accounts for a market share of 33.8% benefits from the positive contribution of the Eastern European market. While Africa plays a minor role, America (31.8%) and Asia-Oceania (33.9%) are the counterparts of Europe.

The manufacturers of the global vehicle production reflect this general pattern. A closer look at the TOP 10 manufacturers reveals that these are based in the three regions of America, Europe and Asia with companies from the USA, Germany, France, Japan and Korea. The strong European representation in this automotive league is emphasised even further if account is taken of the very close cross-ownership affiliation between Renault SA and Nissan Motor Co. (see Table 10).

---

[14]   Europe is defined as EU-15 plus the new member states (EU+10) and others.
[15]   America is defined as USA, Canada, Mexico, Brazil and others.
[16]   Asia-Oceania is defined as Australia, South Korea, Japan, China, India and others.

Fig. 7.   Global vehicle production 2002

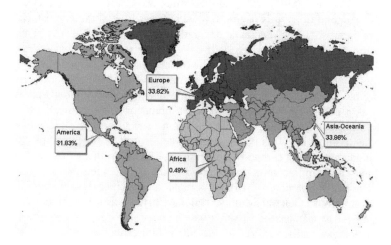

Source: OICA.

Table 8.   Global vehicle production by manufacturer (cars and trucks) – output in units

		2002	2001	2000
1	General Motors[17]	8,276,000	7,786,000	8,494,000
2	Ford Motor Co.[18]	6,973,000	7,008,000	7,424,000
3	Toyota Motor Co.[19]	6,309,616	5,848,094	5,888,260
4	Volkswagen AG[20]	5,023,264	5,107,945	5,156,455
5	DaimlerChrysler AG[21]	4,471,900	4,424,200	4,677,894
6	PSA/Peugeot-Citroen SA	3,262,100	3,136,300	2,877,400
7	Hyundai Motor Co. [22]	2,913,726	2,517,719	2,545,958
8	Honda Motor Co.	2,900,787	2,651,661	2,485,213
9	Nissan Motor Co.	2,690,295	2,466,995	2,605,155
10	Renault SA[23]	2,343,954	2,375,084	2,444,370

Source: PricewaterhouseCoopers Global Automotive Financial Review 2002.

---

[17] Includes Holden, Opel, Vauxhall and Saab.
[18] Includes Aston Martin, Jaguar, Land Rover and Volvo Car Corp.
[19] Includes Daihatsu and Hino.
[20] Includes Audi, Bentley, Bugatti, Lamborghini, Rolls-Royce, Skoda, Seat and Volkswagen.
[21] Includes Chrysler group, Freightliner, Mercedes-Benz, Setra, Smart, Sterling, Thomas Built Buses and Western Star.
[22] Includes Hyundai Motors and Kia Motors.
[23] Includes Dacia and Samsung Motors.

Most manufacturers recovered in 2002 after the sales problems experienced in 2001 as a result of an unstable world economic situation. Comparing these companies by financial conditions, it is useful to have a closer look at the companies' earnings before interest, taxes, depreciation, and amortisation (EBITDA). This earnings measure is of particular interest in cases where companies have large amounts of fixed assets which are subject to heavy depreciation charges (such as automotive companies) or in the case where a company has a large amount of acquired intangible assets on its books and is thus subject to large amortisation charges (such as a company that has purchased a brand or a company that has recently made a large acquisition). EBITDA is often used to compare the profit potential between companies. This business ratio intended to be a measure of the amount of cash generated by a company's operations. Figure 8 reflects that the top ten of the automobile manufacturers got a very unequal trend taking the last couple of years. The profit potential of Toyota is remarkable. Their development is more or less continuous. General Motors, DaimlerChrysler and Ford did have some more problems to manage the situation which ended in pacing up and down. This development is not really mirrored by the output figures in Table 8.

Fig. 8.   Earnings before interest, taxes, depreciation and amortisation (EBITDA) by the top ten automotive manufacturers in 1995-2006, in USD mn

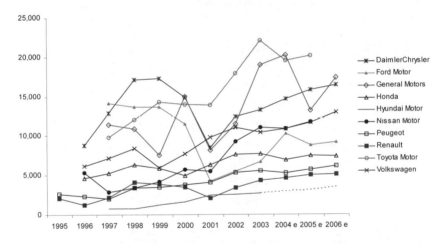

Source: ZEW calculation using annual reports and financial statements; estimates after 2003.

Global vehicle production consists of passenger cars, commercial vehicles and buses. In the following, each of these constituents will be analysed in a global view as well as in a more European context.

Fig. 9.   Global car and truck production: world market shares of production in 2002

Cars

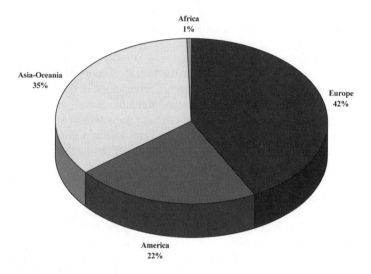

Trucks

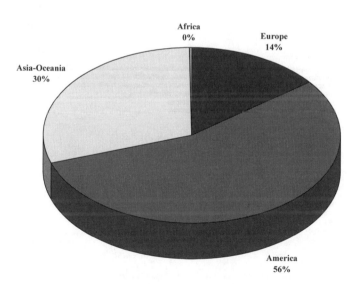

Source: OICA.

2.3.2   Manufacturers

2.3.2.1   Cars

The car[24] sector is strongly dominated by the European market. With a share of 42% of world production, Europe leads the triumvirate followed by Asia-Oceania with 35% and America with 21%. There are a number of different reasons for Europe's leading position one of which is the historical roots of the industry. Today at least 14 automotive company groups are represented in the market. Eight of these (BMW, Daimler; Fiat, PSA, Porsche, Renault, Rover and Volkswagen) originate in different European countries. Global production of cars increased by 3.1% in 2002 at a volume of 41,115,585 units. Traditionally the automotive industry measures company output in terms of motor vehicle production. The capability of different companies can be usefully reflected by their output performance. From a worldwide perspective the Japanese company Toyota is the leading top car manufacturer (Figure 10). In 2002 the company led the field producing more than 5 million units – followed by well known companies such as GM, VW, Ford, Honda and PSA. However, the significance of car production in Europe is illustrated by the fact that more than 15 million units, i.e. 37% of world production, originate in Europe. Taking all manufacturers into account, it is apparent that companies from China and Russia also appear on the list. Although these companies do not have anything like the major impact exercised by the leaders, they do underline the strategic focus on these emergent markets even if these companies are operating as partners for strategic alliances with firms such as GM or VW.

Fig. 10.   Ranking of car manufacturers 2002 – output in units

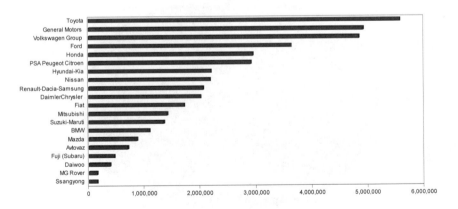

Source: OICA; the typical unit perspective prevents some high value but low volume producers like Porsche (66.803 units in 2002) from appearing in the figure.

---

[24]   Passenger cars.

Fig. 11. Car production in Europe – market share of production 2002, in %

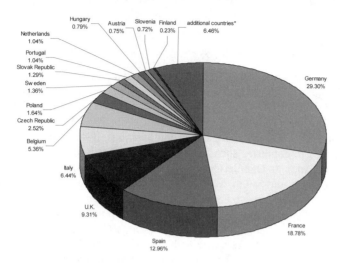

· Russia, Romania, Uzbekistan, Ukraine, Serbia

Source: OICA.

European passenger cars production is as follows: More than two thirds of the European market is accounted for by four countries. Germany has the biggest market share with 29% followed by France with 18%, Spain with 13% and the UK with 9%. As a result Germany plays an important role in this industry by providing the location of the majority of key European manufacturers. The sector is one of the largest employers in Germany. With approximately 866,000 people working in the industry (NACE 34), the automotive sector has a very strong labour force. Furthermore, output of German manufacturers totalled[25] 5,469,309 units in 2002 i.e. 5,301,189 passenger cars, 212,358 light trucks, 123,968 medium/heavy trucks and 9,745 buses. DaimlerChrysler, Volkswagen, BMW and Porsche are all companies with a German origin. Foreign brands such as Ford, Opel (GM) or Mitsubishi with plants in Germany are also driving forces behind the industry in Germany. One important factor is the new investment in East Germany. Six manufacturers (BMW, DaimlerChrysler, Mitsubishi, Opel, Volkswagen and Neoplan) have established assembly plants in this region. The automotive industry is also a key industry in France and the country's 21 assembly plants produce upwards of 3 million units. The sector employs 273,200 people. Even foreign brands such as Toyota or Mercedes-Swatch produce for the European market in France.[26]

---

[25] Passenger cars, light trucks, medium/heavy trucks, buses.

[26] These figures should not be used to derive direct productivity differentials between Germany and France. Both countries are characterised by very different production structures and the recoverability of various stages of the value chain are different as

Spain and the UK profit from investment from foreign manufacturers. In both countries global manufacturers have established assembly plants which have had a positive impact on an upcoming supplier industry as well.

2.3.2.2 Trucks

The commercial vehicle sector also reflects the dominance of the big three – America, Europe and Asia-Oceania (Figure 12). The global perspective indicates in contrast to the car sector that America takes the biggest share of the market with 56% of production volume followed by Asia-Oceania with 30%. Europe is number three with just 14%. One reason for the strong positions of America and Asia are the long distances in countries such as the USA, Brazil, China or India. As a result, manufacturers such as DaimlerChrysler – which has a number of different assembly plants in North and South America – are endeavouring to benefit from these markets. DaimlerChrysler also has an investment in Asia in FUSO, an Asian commercial vehicle manufacturer. A closer look at the top manufacturers shows the strong position of American and Asian brands. DaimlerChrysler has also profited from the merger with Freightliner, originally an American commercial vehicle company which holds different brands in this sector and is therefore a strong player in this market.

Fig. 12.   Ranking of truck manufacturers – output in units 2002, in %

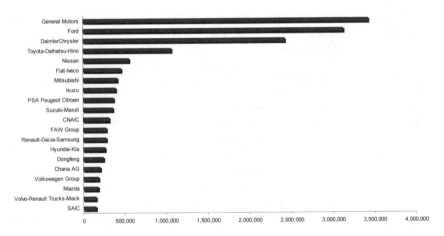

Source: OICA.

Asian companies are relatively more important in truck production than in car production with a couple of manufacturers outside of Japan. A small group of Chinese companies also play a significant role in this market. The company Dongfeng, for example, is the number three behind First Automotive Works (FAW) and

well. A closer look at the gross value added of NACE 34 in 2002 shows that Germany takes a lead with EUR 51.5 bn compared with France's EUR 19.1 bn.

Automotive Industry Corp in China. Among other things they are involved in joint ventures with Nissan, Peugeot and Kia which enable them to provide the commercial vehicle market with more than 240,000 units, or more than the output of Volkswagen or Volvo in this segment.

The EU distribution of truck production is similar to car production. As in the car section, four countries play a major role by producing commercial vehicles. In this case Spain, France, Germany and Italy have the biggest output in terms of units. The supreme position is taken by Spain with more than 580,000 units which determine a share of 24%. It is important to note that the majority of this output is accounted for by light commercial vehicles which are up to 3.5 t where French manufacturers have an extraordinary position. Manufacturers such as PSA, Renault, GM and DaimlerChrysler have established assembly plants in Spain. The leading company is PSA which produces 40% of Spain's entire commercial vehicle output. Production is not designated for the domestic market; 85% of all commercial vehicles are exported to the "rest of the world". Nevertheless, France takes the second position with a share of 17%, which is more than 400,000 units, followed by Germany with 14% corresponding to an output of more than 300,000 units. Italy with a share of 12% is dominated by the local industry of the Fiat-Group which comprises Fiat itself and the commercial vehicle manufacturer IVECO.

Fig. 13.   Truck production in Europe – market share of production 2002, in %

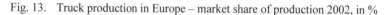
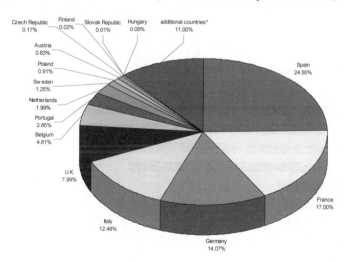

Source: OICA.

2.3.2.3 Buses

The bus sector (including minibuses and coaches) reveals a different picture compared with cars and commercial vehicles. This market is strongly characterised by

Asian manufacturers. The region of Asia-Oceania, and China in particular, constitutes a huge market for buses. China has a share of 70% of output i.e. a production volume of more than one million units in 2002.

Fig. 14.   Global bus production – market share of production 2002, in %

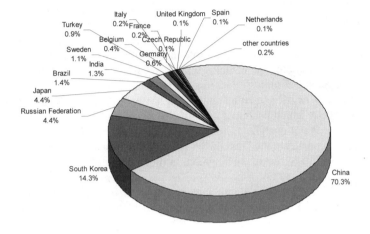

Source: OICA.

Fig. 15.   Ranking of bus manufacturer – output in units, 2002

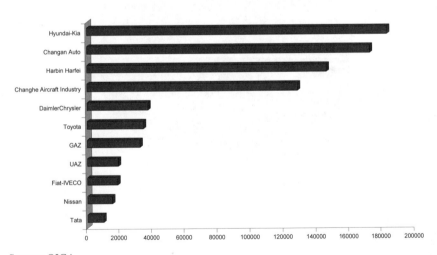

Source: OICA.

Number two in this market is South Korea with a share of 14%. Interestingly, the Russian Federation is number three in this market. Russia steps ahead of European countries with a share of 4%. The Western European countries, headed by Sweden, trail behind.

This picture is underlined by the top manufacturer (Figure 15). The majority of the big bus manufacturers originate in Asia and primarily supply this region only. The biggest player is Hyundai and its affiliate Kia which has the highest output. The companies Changan Auto, Harbin Harfei and Changhe Aircraft Industry dominate production in China. DaimlerChrysler with its brands Evobus and Mercedes-Benz are strong in Europe. Furthermore one third of DaimlerChrysler bus production takes place in Brazil, which emphasises the importance of South America.

2.3.3   Special Focus on Manufacturers in the New Member States

The NMS have become an important field of activity for the EU automotive industry, with major European vehicle producers and suppliers establishing assembly and production plants in the region. In 2002, 83% of the 1.2 million vehicles produced in the NMS were produced by affiliates of EU companies, whereby the Volkswagen group enjoys a clear lead (720,000 vehicles) followed by Fiat (178,000 vehicles) and Renault (126,000 vehicles); for more detail see the yearly updated ACEA EU-15 Economic Report. With the big investments planned by Hyundai in Slovakia (200-300,000 vehicles) and the consortium Toyota/PSA Peugeot Citroen (300,000), the share held by European producers is set to fall somewhat but will remain high nevertheless. The picture in the supplier industry is similar. Motor vehicle manufacturers in the NMS produced 2.1% of the number of vehicles made worldwide, equivalent to 7.3% of EU-15 production and 6.8% of a fictive EU-25 in 2002.

Comparing the two broad product categories, namely *cars* and *trucks* (including buses), car production is dominant and production of trucks and buses plays a significantly smaller role in the NMS than in the OMS, having a share of total motor vehicle production of about 1% and accounting for just 0.1% of world production and 0.6% of EU-25 production in this field. The biggest producers of trucks and buses in the region were the Czech Republic (5,765 units) and Poland (4,163 units) in 2002. The production of trucks and busses has been far more prominent in the past in all NMS, but most existing local enterprises did not survive the transformational recession and foreign investors have shown little interest so far in investing in this particular segment of the automotive industry.

2.3.4   Suppliers

The supplier industry represents a vital element of the automotive sector. Enormous opportunities were created in the early 1990s by the new wave of Japanese transplants in Europe. Toyota, for example, took advantage of a multiplicity of component suppliers in UK to establish an assembly plant in Burnaston, Derby. New production facilities continue to represent business opportunities for suppliers today in East Germany and the new member states. Over 700 suppliers are now located in Germany, the importance of which is underlined by the fact that these 700 suppliers include more than 50% of the top 100 group of suppliers. An analysis of the supplier industry in the new member states (EU+10) will be given later in this report. Value chains are also subject to a number of changes. The dramatic changes in the value chain of the automotive sector mean that manufacturer and supplier partnerships are now indispensable. Suppliers in this sector are assuming more responsibility for different parts of the value chain and this is indicative of the major roles these companies now play in the production process. This particular point will be stressed later in the report in a discussion of upcoming production trends.

A closer look at the distribution of different parts of the value chain in the automotive sector reveals that, in some cases, suppliers assume the lion's share of responsibility for production. This underlines the point of strategic options for these companies. According to a study of VDA/CAR focusing on the growth potential of the supplier industry, there will be at least three windows of opportunities: growth in terms of

• access to new markets,
• increased vehicle value, i.e. innovations in electronics,
• benefits from manufacturer's outsourcing strategies.

The changes referred to above represent sophisticated challenges for suppliers which demand major input in terms of manpower, R&D expertise, etc. Globally operative manufacturers demand globally operative suppliers, which also need to be able to finance their assembly plants all over the world. According to the top 100 league of suppliers, all of these companies are international operating firms with turnover of at least EUR 940 mn which indicates that growth in terms of new markets and innovation could be met by this industry.

The twenty biggest supplier companies fall into three geographical groups dominated by America, Europe and Asia as represented by the countries USA, Germany, France and Japan. The German supplier industry is reaping major benefits from growth potential in this area. The new business locations selected by German suppliers in the last five years (1997-2002) have a very strong focus on globalisation. Special attention should be paid to the new member states mainly in Eastern Europe[27] (Figure 16). 26% of all new locations were in Eastern Europe which strengthens the importance of this region. The rest of Europe and especially Germany is still a dominant region for business in the supplier industry.

---

[27]   Poland, Czech Republic, Slovakia, Hungary.

Table 9. Ranking of suppliers in the automotive industry by turnover in 2001

	Company	Country	Turnover, EUR bn 2001
1	Delphi	USA	28.7
2	Bosch	D	23.2
3	Visteon	USA	19.6
4	Denso	J	17.9
5	Lear	USA	15.0
6	Johnson Controls	USA	15.0
7	Magna Int.	CDA	11.6
8	Continental	D	11.2
9	TRW	USA	11.1
10	Faurecia	F	9.6
11	Aisins Seiki	J	9.3
12	Dana	USA	8.5
13	Valeo	F	8.1
14	ZF Friedrichshafen	D	7.8
15	Yazaki	J	6.8
16	Arvin Meritor	USA	6.4
17	Thyssen Krupp Automotive	D	6.2
18	DuPont	USA	5.7
19	Siemens VDO Automotive	D	5.7
20	Michelin	F	5.1

Source: AP.

It should be also pointed out that the supplier industry is traditionally much more local than OEMs. There also appear to be traditional links between US OEM and US first tier suppliers, French OEMs and French first tier suppliers, and between German OEMs and German first tier suppliers. As a rule Japanese OEMs prefer to use suppliers from their own conglomerates. These traditional links are in decline because of the discernible globalisation trend. OEM globalisation also poses a challenge for suppliers and, as a rule, big suppliers seem to be at an advantage when it comes to developing global activities. Large US and German based suppliers consequently enjoy a number of size-related advantages. In line with this argument increasing M&A activities are also observable in the supplier industry (see Sturgeons and Florida, 2000, for more details).

Fig. 16.   New supplier locations (1997-2002)

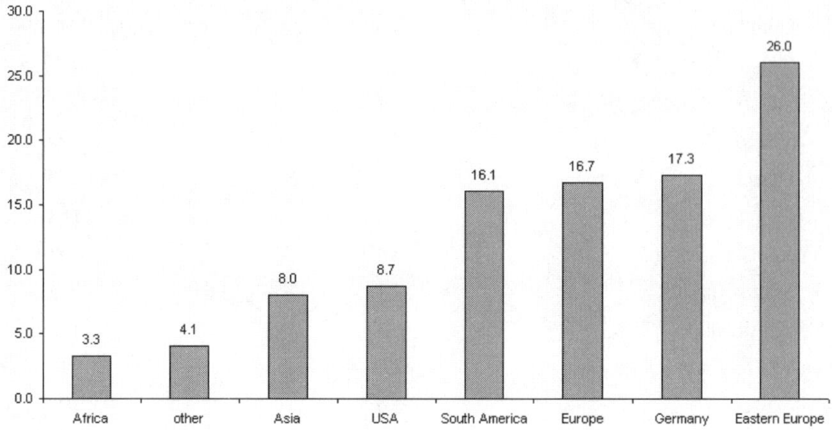

Source: VDA.

2.3.5   Special Focus on Suppliers in the New Member States

In the NMS, the distribution among the three important *sub-sectors* of the automotive industry representing different stages in the production chain, namely *vehicles* (NACE 34.1), *bodies for motor vehicles* (34.2) and *parts and accessories* (34.3), is on average quite similar to that in the OMS, with vehicle production taking the largest share (around 80%), followed by parts and accessories (around 20%) and bodies for motor vehicles accounting for just a few percent of total production. There is considerable variation across countries, however, with parts production playing a particularly small role in Slovakia (9%) and a relatively big role in the Czech Republic (45%), partly reflecting the special provisions made in the Skoda-VW deal concerning local supply, but also showing a certain specialisation of the Czech Republic in this field as well.[28] Notably, the production of parts and accessories has gained relative importance over the last couple of years in all NMS indicating that suppliers are hot on the heels of producers. Refer to the site map of important producers and suppliers in the NMS below (Figure 17). In addition, NMS profit from the ongoing reorganisation of the value chain by OEMs as well as by large first and second tier suppliers which outsource parts of their value chain to benefit from local cost advantages.

---

[28]   In Lithuania, the dominant role is played by the production of bodies for motor vehicles.

Fig. 17.   Production shares of vehicles and parts, 2001/2002

Figure 1

Production shares of vehicles and parts, 2001/2002

☐ vehicles (NACE 34.1 + 34.2)   ▨ parts (NACE 3.43)

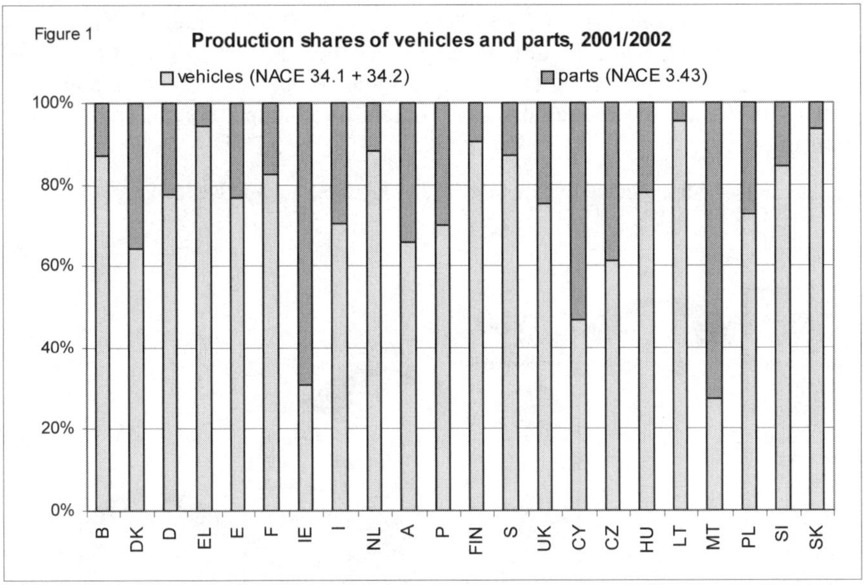

Source: Eurostat (2004); Panorama of Czech Industries 2003; VAD; Eurostat, SBS.

2.4   Globalisation and Restructuring

The international automotive industry is characterised by rapid changes. Mergers and acquisitions among manufacturers and suppliers are changing the global environment. Even the forecast that a major share of future demand will be generated by developing countries is of crucial importance for all multinationals. The design of international strategies is based upon the interplay between the comparative advantage of countries and the competitive advantage of firms (Kogut, 1985). For this reason, the automobile industry has been characterised by two ongoing developments over the last decade: globalisation and restructuring, both of which are closely related. Global output of automobile products has generated more exports and increased competition. A global profile i.e. selling and producing in all different segments all over the world, is a business prerequisite in today's world. Despite the benefits which globalisation offers, this process nonetheless poses business challenges for all the companies involved. Manufacturers and their affiliates respond to globalisation and restructuring with organisational changes. The restructuring process was designed to reduce the share of value added by automobile manufacturers. Many companies were unable to cope with the challenge of building up assembly plants and retail structures in different countries. For example, the internationalisation strategy of Japanese companies had an impact on the European market. In the late sixties and at the beginning of the seventies, Asian manufacturers began supplying the European and US market. Over the last three decades, the number of companies came down from 36 in the 1970s to 31 in the 1980s. This trend continued in the 1990s with the number of automobile manufacturers falling to 22. Since the turn of the century there have been only 14 automotive companies on the market (Figure 18). Some companies were unable to meet globalisation and restructuring demands, others were simply bought up by bigger companies.

Fig. 18.   Restructuring in the European, U.S. and Japanese automotive industry[29]

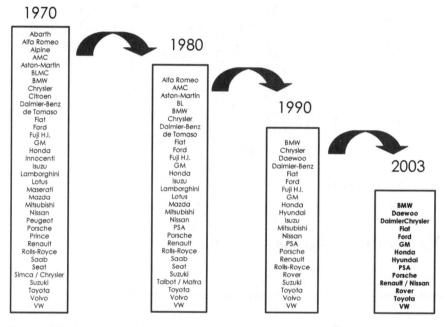

Source: AP.

Despite the reduction in the number of car manufacturers, competition in regional and local markets has increased as larger companies have established a presence on all markets.

Competition forces manufacturers to be present in all kind of markets, including regional markets, and market niches. Takeovers serve both strategies. A closer look at automobile manufacturers clearly reveals that these firms are being transformed from automobile companies into automobile groups (Figure 19). The various companies now affiliated with these groups (GM, Volkswagen, Ford, DaimlerChrysler, Toyota or Renault-Nissan) are meeting the different requirements of

---

[29]   A truly global perspective should certainly include producers from China, India and Russia. Given the focus of this study and the lacking availability of comparable historical information, narrowing the scope to the major producing areas Europe, Japan and the USA should provide useful insights.

regional market or market niche strategies. Ford, for example, acquired a number of firms for this purpose. The benefits derived from different regions such as Asia and Europe were generated by involving Mazda, Volvo and Rover. A market niche such as luxury cars was integrated into the company portfolio with the acquisition of Jaguar. The same pattern is recognisable in other automotive groups. DaimlerChrysler adopted a clear focus on regional strategy to tap the Asian market and established a distribution grid with companies like Mitsubishi, Hyundai and Kia to cover the whole region.

Fig. 19.   From automotive companies to automotive groups – extract of major groups

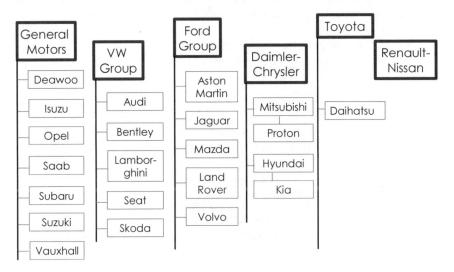

Source: ZEW/AP.

Today global corporations can use a diverse array of organisational mechanisms to integrate dispersed operations (Govindarajan and Gupta, 2001). At the present time merger & acquisitions are still a prevailing topic. Particularly with regard to the latest deals in the automotive sector, manufacturers and suppliers are taking the path of growth to ensure the options of new markets and niches. An interesting deal among manufacturers is the financial involvement between Renault SA and Nissan Motor Co Ltd. After Renault acquired a 44% share in Nissan two years ago, Nissan is now in the process of buying a 15% stake in Renault which will accelerate them into the top ten league of global automotive manufacturers. GM is pursuing a regional market strategy by acquiring Daewoo.

The supplier industry is also taking advantage of merger and acquisitions (M&A) strategies to meet the demands made by manufacturers i.e. innovations and increased product responsibility. In this context it is interesting to note that a number of deals are being made between first and second tier suppliers. This could be interpreted as a first tier strategy to back up preliminary stages of the value chain. In fact this is apparent in the acquisition of Varta AG, a German battery manufacturer, via Johnson Controls Corp, one of the biggest first tier suppliers worldwide. Company size is becoming increasingly important for achieving and guaranteeing further R&D capability. First tier suppliers are very keen to play their role in the industry with a global presence.

The motivation of mergers and acquisitions is manifold. The possibility of market access as well as fulfilling the product portfolio could be an incitement for preparing a financial involvement which sometimes ends with a merger or an acquisition. The event of M&A in the automobile industry is characterised by individual strategic reasons. It is not really predictable but there is sometimes an indication which has a lot to commend it. On the basis of the multifaceted linkages between different manufacturers it could be expected that some companies will recognise a strategic fit by taking over another manufacturer or supplier.

Table 10. M&A transactions 2002 – manufacturer

Target	Target Nation	Buyer	Buyer's Nation	Deal value (USD mn)	% Acquired
Daewoo Motor Co – Certain Assets	KOR	General Motors (& affiliates)/ Daewoo Creditors	INT	2627	100
Renault SA	FRA	Nissan Motor Co Ltd	JPN	1959	15
Nissan Motor Co Ltd	JPN	Renault SA	FRA	1620	7.6
General Motors Corp	USA	Undisclosed Investment Bank	USA	1160	5.7
Ferrari SpA	IT	Mediobanca (net 24%)/ Commerzbank (net 10%)	IT/D	760	34
Dmax - diesel engines	USA	General Motors Corp	USA	422	20
Maruti Udyog Ltd	IND	Suzuki Motor Corporation	JPN	285	4.2
Tianjin Automotive Xiali Co Ltd	CHN	First Automotive Works	CHN	171	51
Aixam	FRA	Norbert Dentressangle SA	FRA	129	100
Yantai Bodyshop Corp	CHN	General Motors/Shanghai Auto	US/CHN	109	100

Source: PricewaterhouseCoopers.

Multinational companies have a long history of leveraging their geographic roots to their competitive advantage (Doz et al., 2001). These roots or links have taken different forms. Links within the automobile industry go far beyond equity deals and a glance at all the affiliations which actually exist between automobile manufacturers reveals a complex system of varying forms of relationship which span the entire sector. These links may take the following forms:
- Equity
- Joint venture
- Interchange or buy-off of products
- Marketing or distribution agreement
- Technology or R&D agreement
- Assembly agreement.

Table 11. M&A transactions 2002 – supplier

Target	Target Nation	Buyer	Buyer's Nation	Deal value (USD mn)	% Ac-quired
TRW Inc	USA	Northrop Grumman Corp	USA	11,7	100
Edscha AG	D	Carlyle Management Group/Edscha Manage-ment	USA	605	98
Teksid SpA	IT	Questor/JP Morgan PE/PE Partners/AIG	USA	453	100
Donnelly Corp	USA	Magna International Inc	CAN	389	100
Varta AG (Auto Batteries Div)	D	Johnson Controls Inc	USA	308	100
FTE Automotive GmbH	D	Hg Capital Ltd	UK	198	100
Conti Temic Microelec-tronic GmbH	D	Continental AG	D	188	40
Unisia Jecs Corp	JPN	Hitachi Ltd	JPN	184	83.3
Cie Financiere Michelin	CHN	Michelin SA	FRA	175	6.3
Aetna Industries & Zenith Inc.	USA	Questor Management Co	USA	145	100

Source: PricewaterhouseCoopers.

The outline of the entire system of interrelationship within the automotive sector would go beyond the scope of this study. Therefore the example of the Italian manufacturer Fiat should give the impression of the huge grid of linkages in this sector.

The Case of Fiat and Its Different Types of Linkages with Other OEMs and First tier Suppliers (Source: AP)

GM has a 10% stake in Fiat. The Italian manufacturer has an option to sell the remaining 80% to *GM* by 2009. Both firms have pooled together their logistic activities in Argentina. *GM* took over the Mexican distribution of Fiat and Alfa Romeo in 2003 and started to assemble cars in Thailand.

Fiat is involved in a joint venture with *Ford* in the UK where they build commercial vehicles together with Iveco Ford Truck Ltd. Both companies have a share of 48%. A second joint venture concerning the commercial vehicle sector is built up with *GAZ*, to cover the Russian market. As a result, Fiat is also involved in a joint venture with the Russian manufacturer *AvtoVAZ*. The object of production is the assembly of drive propulsion systems. In the range of new diesel engine for commercial vehicles Fiat is also taking part in a R&D agreement with *Nissan*. *DaimlerChrysler* participates in a R&D agreement with Fiat with the aim to develop a new common rail injection pump for turbo diesel engines.

Bertone had an assembly agreement with Fiat. They produced open-topped Fiat Puntos[30] and create the design concepts for the new small car model and the Alfa

---

[30]   The contract concerning the production of Punto expired.

Romeo coupé. *Fuji* supplies the automatic transmission. According to the joint venture with *GM*, Fiat carries out some purchasing operations for *Fuji* and *Isuzu*. The Canadian supplier company *Magna Int* provides all Fiat Pandas with all-wheel power trains.

Fiat and *Peugeot* have finalised a strategic alliance for the production of light commercial vehicles. Both of them have also been affiliated with the Moroccan assembly manufacturer Somaca. Fiat and *Peugeot* have a 20% stake and *Renault* has a 8% stake. The Italian company *Pininfarina* has concluded an assembly agreement with Fiat for different models and also undertakes some design projects for the manufacturer.

Fiat is planning a R&D and assembly agreement with *Suzuki* for the production of an SUV (Sports Utility Vehicle) by 2004.

2.5   Capacity Utilisation and Structural Overcapacity

In a worldwide perspective the current output of the car industry is well below the production frontier. Several features of the competition in automotive markets contribute to the phenomenon of overcapacity. On the one hand overcapacity is a transitory feature depending mainly on the cyclical variation of demand for cars. On the other hand overcapacity is often seen as a more permanent feature in the automotive industry. Short-run fluctuations and long-run under-utilisation of existing capacities are quite distinct phenomena and highlight the different aspects of car markets.

First of all, the car sales in Europe show cyclical variation. A cyclical downturn of the car market induces an increase in the number of unsold cars which leads to a greater price competition and more attractive terms for de luxe equipment. If cyclical variation affects a whole set of regional markets it will also reduce the number of produced cars and hence cause a temporary under-utilisation of capacity. During the last fifteen years capacity utilisation rates in the car industry have shown quite similar developments for most European countries (EU-15 only; see Figure 20). The most distinct features of the European automotive production are the dramatic decline of capacity utilisation in the first half of the 1990s and the revival of capacity utilisation until the year 2000. Since then capacity utilisation declines gradually and it is not clear whether we will see an upturn of the average capacity utilisation rate in Europe in the near future. We can also see from this figure that even in the boom periods 1989-1990 and 1999-2000 capacity utilisation rate amounts to 90%.

The lower half of the figure shows the capacity utilisation rates by country. There is a distinction between large countries and smaller countries with a significant production of cars or production of parts. The figure suggests that variation is more pronounced in those countries with a large final production of cars. Moreover, the general trends are quite similar in all countries although there are significant differences. The most obvious one is that the Italian car industry shows a lower degree of capacity utilisation than the other European countries. Even in the boom period in the late 1990s the Italian automotive industry realised a capacity utilisation rate which is below the rate of Germany, the leading car producer, during the slump in the early 1990s. Hence, there seems to be a structural overcapacity there as well. Finally, we should note that even in extreme boom periods capacity utilisation rates never approach 100%. Therefore, one should not consider 100% as the full capacity utilisation rate. Capacity utilisation rates close to 100% (say 90-95%) can already be taken for full utilisation of capacity.

These figures refer to the automotive industry as a whole comprising car and truck manufacturers as well as suppliers. Separate data on capacity utilisation rates for final producers and suppliers are not available from DG ECFIN. National level data reveal that as a rule the capacity utilisation rate for final assembly of car is significant lower than for the manufacturing of parts (1st, 2nd, 3rd tier suppliers). Hence, overcapacity is primarily a problem of car makers. Accordingly, overcapacity can be linked to market strategies of car makers and idiosyncrasies of final car production.

When setting up a final assembly plant car makers have to assess the market potential for the model(s) produced in the assembly. The planning of plant capacity normally takes considerable time before a new model enters the market or – in emerging markets – before the market potential for a new model can be estimated accurately. The marginal costs of an ex-post capacity increase are much larger than the cost of the ex-ante capacity increase.[31]

In addition, the cost of extended delivery times which are the result of lower capacities are especially large in market segments which are fiercely competitive and the possibilities of product differentiation between companies are relatively low. In this way, it is more reasonable to build plants based on more optimistic variants of sales forecasts. Therefore one should expect lower capacity utilisation rates for plants with standard cars than for the luxury car or the SUV segment of the market.

Given the fierce competition in global automotive industry an additional argument arises when looking at the capacity utilisation in emerging markets. Looking at the distribution of market shares on national car markets it becomes obvious that there are lasting effects of being a "local" company. Hence, there is a widespread believe that being the first to produce locally and to reach a significant market share very early will have lasting effects on reputation. As a consequence of strategic interaction between companies, the overall capacity of new plants in emerging markets often exceeds current and near-future market potential quite dramatically.[32] Presently, this is quite obvious in the case of expansion plans of

---

[31]   Admittedly, there is the possibility to change from a two-shift to a three-shift and vice a versa, which gives some ex-post flexibility. However, changing the number of shifts also induces different unit labour costs.

[32]   See Sturgeon (1997) for a more detailed discussion of this argument. As a striking example Sturgeon and Florida (2000) report an average capacity utilisation rate in transplants in Vietnam of around 10%.

Fig. 20.   Capacity utilisation in EU-15 car industry – 1st quarter 1988 to 4th quarter 2003

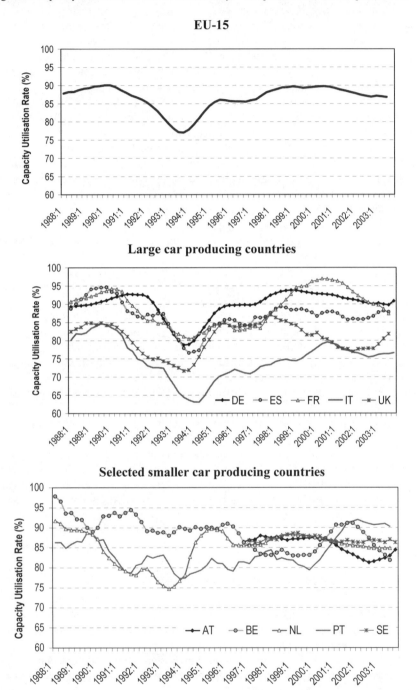

Remark: The original quarterly capacity utilisation rate is smoothed by a moving average filter using 3-quarter lags and leads. The original data does not show any evidence of seasonal variation. Other filters (e.g. Hodrick-Prescott) do not lead to different conclusions. Data on capacity utilisation are gathered by a group of economic research institutions as part of the regular business cycles surveys. National data are harmonised and published by DG ECFIN.
Source: DG ECFIN 2004-05-26.

automotive producers in China. So, the strategic objective to gain a first mover advantage in new markets seems to be another driver of overcapacity in global automotive markets.

Hence, one should expect larger over capacities in emerging markets, as illustrated by figure 21 which refers to the boom year 2000 in order to eliminate the impact of the current downturn in major markets. The figure shows that the capacity utilisation rate was quite high in North American plants and EU-15 plants. Significant overcapacity was present in Eastern Asia, Latin America and other countries but also in Eastern Europe.

Fig. 21.   Capacity utilisation rate for car assembly plants in major regions during the 2000 boom

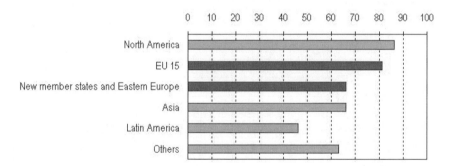

Source: Reinaud (2001).

More precisely, overcapacity is less likely a problem in higher priced market segments where competition is less fierce than in the standard car segment. Low capacity utilisation in Asian plants can be attributed to different reasons. Japan, the leading car market shows a slow growth during the 1990s. Moreover, export sales of Japanese plants face additional competition in US and Europe from the new Japanese transplants in both regions. As a result structural overcapacity arises. Similar arguments refer to Korea which was also severely hurt by the 1997-98 Asian crises.

Eastern Europe faced a rapid expansion of production capacities in the last decade. Capacity utilisation in the standard car segment is far below the capacity utilisation in EU-15. A recent study of PwC AUTOFACTS (2004) estimates capacity utilisation for car plants in Poland remaining at about 50%, and at 40% in Slovakia in 2004. The study forecasts average capacity utilisation to remain at this level in Poland and a strong increase in Slovakia (70%). However, even in the long run capacity utilisation rates in the new member states are expected to be below capacity utilisation in most of the EU-15 countries. Low production costs in the new member states and the existing potential for further decreases in unit labour costs in car production will increase competition in EU-15 markets. The impact of excess capacity will put the traditional car producing locations in EU-15 under pressure as well. Besides, as suppliers open up additional production facilities in the new member states they encounter similar dangers.

More recently, capacity utilisation rates for major assembly facilities seem on the rise again. PwC AUTOFACTS estimates a slightly increasing capacity utilisation rate for car assembly plants in the EU. On average capacity utilisation is expected to rise to around 78% in 2004 (77% in 2003; 76% in 2002). However, this increase is the result of capacity reduction, and not of an increasing demand, and new capacity will enter the market in the new member states soon. There is a close link between capacity utilisation and profitability. As a rule of thumb, car makers break even when capacity utilisation rates reach 80% with some variation between plants. The close relation between profitability and capacity utilisation is evident from the figure 22.

Fig. 22.   Capacity utilisation rate and profit margin in European assembly plants in 2003 by automotive groups

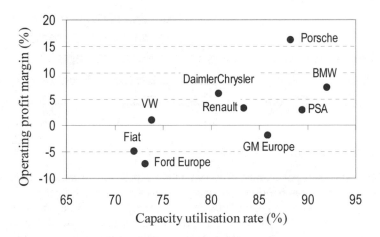

Source: PwC AUTOFACTS / Automotive News Europe June 2004.

Figure 22 shows a wide variation in capacity utilisation and also profitability between car makers in Europe. This group-level data also reflects what was evident from the industry level capacity utilisation rate above. Fiat shows capacity utilisation below European average whereas the French and some German car makers are above average. The wide variation in capacity utilisation again makes us suppose that overcapacity is to a lesser extent a problem for European plants than for other locations outside of Europe. However, some European plants show low capacity utilisation rates, and hence we should expect that with a sluggish market there will increasingly arise a discussion where to reduce capacity. It is well-known in the industry that capacity reductions are made only when a low capacity utilisation stays for some years and when it is expected that even new models will probably not lead to increased capacity utilisation.

In summary, when looking at the overcapacity issue in global automotive industry one has to separate cyclical developments from structural explanations. In a global perspective capacity utilisation in EU-15 is high. However, sluggish market development in major car markets together with a rapid expansion of production capacities in emerging markets as well as transplants in developed car markets will fuel the overcapacity problem. This will lead to stronger competition especially in traditional segments of the car market and increase the pressure on production costs and hence stimulate the search for product innovation to escape from fierce price competition in the standard car segment. Additionally, it will stimulate the search for cost reduction via new production technologies and organisational innovations. The overcapacity will stimulate competition within automotive groups between different local production units but also the cooperation between brands within and between groups. The re-organisation of the industry which will also take place within the EU will probably increase the competitiveness of the EU car industry since the EU offers both low cost production possibilities and a large potential for innovation. However, the process of reduction of capacity takes time. Normally, capacity adjustment in the form of plant closures will only take place when a low degree of capacity utilisation stays for some years. So, despite the existing overcapacity in EU-25 the capacity of EU car assembly plants is only gradually adjusted downwards in Western Europe. Hence, we expect some reduction of capacity in the coming years.

2.6   Conclusion

Europe is a very big and important market for all the market players. The fact that eight companies have their roots in Europe is highly significant. Car production is still dominated by Europe. A closer look at the biggest manufacturers shows that European companies such as Volkswagen, DaimlerChrysler, PSA and Renault play a dominant role among the world's largest automotive enterprises.

In some automotive segments such as trucks or buses, manufacturers have concentrated production in regions such as America and Asia. In terms of buses China is becoming increasingly more important than other countries. Public transport is developing rapidly in this country, and this represents a strong demand advantage. The major players in this segment are exclusively from Asia. The truck segment is strongly dominated by the American market. GM and Ford take the worldwide lead in truck production.

The biggest opportunities remain in the hands of Eastern Europe. Despite their recent membership of the European Union, Eastern Europe is still the region with an accelerated automotive industry growth. New assembly and production plants have been installed in these countries. Not only are manufacturers setting up in Eastern Europe, the preliminary value chain is moving as well, i.e. the whole supplier industry is taking advantage of this region.

Globalisation offers a lot of possibilities for multinational companies and regions. These regions – Europe, America and Asia – find themselves in tough competition for the best assembly locations. Certain countries such as China attract manufacturers both owing to the advantageous production conditions and new markets – largely untapped to date – which they offer.

3 Competitiveness: A Market Perspective

(Eu, Russia, CEEC)

Georg Licht, Wolfgang Sofka, and Waltraud Urban[1]

L11

3.1 Overview   L6* F23 P23

The concepts of competitiveness and competitive advantage have traditionally been discussed on a firm level base. National competitiveness has long been solely treated as the result of factor-based comparative advantages. Among others, Porter (1990) has pushed this approach towards a competitive advantage of nations by demanding that "a rich conception of competition includes segmented markets, differentiated products, technology differences, and economies of scale."

The following analysis uses both frameworks as scaffolding. At first, it focuses on the performance of the European automotive industry on international markets, both in terms of trade and foreign direct investment. This follows the simple rationale that markets (in this particular case international markets) are the single most efficient mechanism to filter and condense decentralised information from all relevant sources. Put simply, the market participants that perform best on the world market must be competitive (in the absence of trade distorting measures). This concept fits nicely with the definition put forward by Scott and Lodge (1985): "national competitiveness refers to a country's ability to create, produce, distribute and/or service products in international trade while earning rising returns on its resources." While this aspect reflects mostly comparative advantages the following section on the home market introduces the points that Porter mentioned above by moving from comparative to competitive advantages.

3.2 International Markets

Operating globally has become almost a prerequisite of success for the automotive industry. It allows automotive companies not only to open up new sales opportunities but also enables them to tab into scarce pockets of regional expertise to attain competitive advantage. Figure 23 focuses on the sales motive and illustrates the varying importance of overseas markets for European car manufacturers. It also highlights how crucial especially the North American markets are for European premium quality manufacturers.

Fig. 23.   New passenger car registrations in NAFTA and Japan as ratio of Western European registrations in 2002 for major European brands

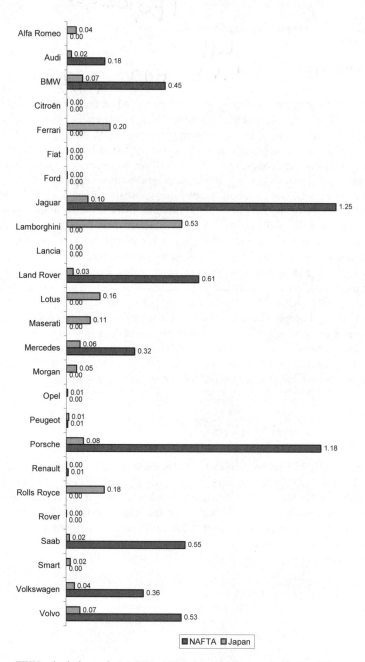

Source: ZEW calculation using ACEA, VDA data; Ford covers only Ford Europe.

A brand perspective is also helpful in assessing market shares for passenger cars. While production of most automotive producers in the world is spread over various countries in their value chain the brands are still considered to reflect some national identity. The following figure shows the market shares of major brands in a geographic and historically dynamic context.

Fig. 24.   Brand segmentation in new passenger car registrations or sales in EU-15, Japan and USA 1998 and 2002[33]

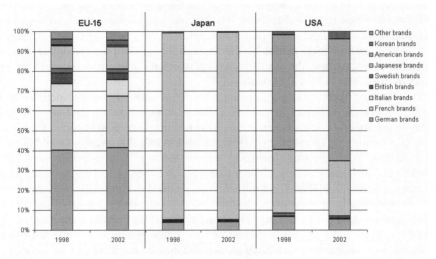

Source: ZEW calculation using VDA data; no comparable data available for the new member states.

In Europe (EU-15) only slight shifts in the composition of the market shares between 1998 and 2002 are visible. The market is dominated by European brands. German and French brands hold by far the largest shares and were even able to expand their market presence while Italian and British market shares declined. Japanese brands are the largest external players on the European markets considerably in front of Korean brands. Albeit the market shares of both Asian brand groups remained almost static compared to 1998. It should be mentioned that this is strictly a brand and unit perspective. While this presentation gives the big picture it could very well be that the distribution in prices and hence sales among brands is somewhat different. Still, this is a suitable solution due to the lack of other applicable data. Also, it should be mentioned that the large American manu-

---

[33]   German brands (Audi, BMW, Ford, Mercedes, Opel, Porsche, Smart, Volkswagen); French brands (Citroen, Peugeot, Renault); Italian brands (Alfa Romeo, Ferrari, Fiat, Lamborghini, Lancia, Maserati); British brands (Ford, Jaguar, Land Rover, Lotus, Morgan, Rolls Royce, Rover, Vauxhall); Swedish brands (Saab, Volvo); Japanese brands (Daihatsu, Honda, Isuzu, Mazda, Mitsubishi, Nissan, Subaru, Suzuki, Toyota); American brands (Chrysler, Ford, General Motors); Korean brands (Asia, Daewoo, Hyundai, Hyundai Prec., Kia, Ssangyong); other European brands (Seat, Skoda).

facturers serve the European markets, mostly through their European branches and hence brands (e.g. Opel). Therefore, traditional American brands may be absent from the European markets, the US manufacturers are not.

The Japanese brands control almost the complete Japanese market. Only some German brands make recognisable inroads into that market. Their share remains relatively stable between 1998 and 2002. In the US market American brands hold the largest shares and even expanded them compared to 1998. Japanese brands hold a sizeable stake of that market, still their market share has diminished. German brands hold the third largest share of the US market although their share has slightly declined compared to 1998. To the contrary, Korean brands have gained considerably in the US between 1998 and 2002.

The notion of a home market bias in demand for cars will we elaborated shortly in more detail. At first, the channels through which these international markets are served (trade and FDI) will be analysed.

The following sections stress two major forces in international competitiveness: Trade and Foreign Direct Investment (FDI). Common sense would suggest that implementing one of those internationalisation strategies would supplant the other, i.e. by investing in a particular country exports towards this country should diminish. If this would be true, focussing on one mode of internationalisation only would be sufficient to assess competitiveness. Albeit, empirical research suggests quite the opposite. FDI and trade streams can go hand in hand. This does also hold when specifically applied to the automotive industry. Based on panel data from the Japanese automobile industry Head and Ries (2001) find net complementarity between trade and FDI. Trade in intermediate inputs as well as exports from supplying firms facilitate this connection. Beyond this argument of an internationally embedded value chain, different stages in the individual product life cycle might also require different internationalisation strategies. This concept put forward initially by Vernon (1966) states that the uncertainty associated with new products requires closer customer interaction in production which could best be accomplished by on-site operations and hence foreign direct investment. Once the product becomes more ripe and standardised cost considerations become the central driver of production decisions and therefore markets will best be served through exports from the most cost effective production sites. In conclusion, an analysis that confines the performance on international markets to trade aspects would be incomplete. Thus, the subsequent sections feature both trade and FDI to gain maximum insight on the performance of the European automotive industry on international markets.

3.2.1   International Trade

Imports and exports have always been a major driver for the competitive positioning of countries. Not surprisingly the success in international trade is deeply connected to the post-war recoveries of Germany, Japan and South Korea. The exposure to the fierce competition in international markets forced domestic companies to enter a virtuous circle of demanding customer feedback, peer pressure from global competitors and growing domestic excellence in operations. Only the most efficient and responsive companies could survive this competition but those few remaining global champions would reap the benefits. Besides, from an economic perspective trade implies production at home which translates into jobs and tax revenues. Subsequently, trade performance is a cornerstone of any competitive analysis among nations.

Trade theory dates back to Ricardo who introduced import and export flows among countries as a result of differing comparative advantages. Heckscher and Ohlin deviated from that concept and explained trade as a consequence of varying factor endowments among countries. Krugman and the New Trade Theory finally stress the importance of economies of scale in imperfect markets. Still, tracing the roots of trade is not at the core of this analysis. Instead, the European position in trade in automotive products should be an important indicator for its competitiveness. Following the framework for competitiveness suggested by Buckley et al. (1988) the position in trade should give useful insight both with respect to competitive performance as well as competitive potential.[34] The former represents the past up to the present and can best be described by the world market shares of the European automotive industry. The latter, though, indicates whether this performance will be sustainable in the future. Concepts of comparative advantage should give valuable insights in this field. The subsequent sections will highlight both aspects: performance and potential.

The following presentation emphasises the main developments and sets some focal points. The interested reader might turn to the appendix for the full set of trade related data (exports, imports, trade surpluses, world market shares and RCAs).

A brief overview sets the stage and should help to put the following numbers into context. In 2001 all OECD countries combined exported automotive products (SITC 78) worth almost USD 523 bn to the world (total merchandise exports were almost 4 trillion USD). 58% of that value were exports of passenger cars (SITC 781), 10% trucks (SITC 782), 3% buses (SITC 783) and 25% parts (SITC 784).[35] EU-15 accounted for almost USD 270 bn of those exports while only USD 85 bn were exports outside EU-15. Since the comparison with non-European competitors was at the centre of this analysis internationally comparable data was required. The OECD provides this data. Unfortunately, not all new member states are covered by the OECD. Still, the major automotive producing countries, among them Poland, the Czech Republic, the Slovak Republic and Hungary, are included.

---

[34]   Buckley et al. (1988) find three levels of competitiveness: competitive performance, competitive potential and management process. Obviously, the contribution of the management process on turning competitive potential into performance is considerable. Albeit, it is a deeply firm specific factor and would hardly fit into the predominantly country comparison framework presented below. Therefore, this factor will only be included through selective mentioning while performance and potential can safely be presented on a country level.

[35]   All numbers based on data from OECD: ITCS – International Trade By Commodity Statistics, Rev. 3, 2001, 2002.

They exported a combined total of USD 13.6 bn to the world. The USA exported automotive products worth USD 56.7 bn, Japan USD 80.8 bn. The former is only the third largest export country in that field, the latter the second largest. Germany tops the list with USD 105 bn exports. Canada is ranked fourth (USD 52.7 bn), France is fifth (USD 38.9 bn). In terms of export growth total merchandise exports from OECD countries grew by 11% between 1998 and 2001 as did automotive products as a whole; cars increased by 16%, trucks by 12% and parts by 7%, only exports of buses to the world market fell by 20%.

With an eye on imports in 2001, OECD countries combined imported automotive products worth almost USD 486 bn (total merchandise imports were almost 4 trillion USD) from the world. The division among the automotive segments is almost identical to the export segmentation mentioned above. EU-15 imported roughly USD 231 bn in automotive products, while only USD 46 bn stemmed from outside EU-15. Poland, the Czech Republic, the Slovak Republic and Hungary imported almost USD 11 bn in automotive products. Automotive product imports to the USA accounted for almost USD 159 bn whereas Japan imported only USD 9.6 bn. This makes the USA by far the largest import country for automotive products followed by Germany (USD 44.5 bn), the United Kingdom (USD 38.8 bn), Canada (USD 37.3 bn) and France (USD 30.7 bn).

Trade in absolute numbers gives a good idea of the importance and the size of the sector for the global economy. The performance of a particular country, though, is best assessed in comparison with major competitors on the global markets. Figure 25 shows the world market shares for major exporting countries.

From a European perspective, the most eye-catching fact from this figure is the strong performance of Germany across all market segments. It commands world market shares well above 20% for cars and buses, with a significant lead in each segment. For trucks and parts Germany finishes second. What is more, Germany's world market shares differ hardly from what they were in 1991. Obviously, Germany has performed well as the prime location for car manufacturing in the world.

A closer look at the car segment reveals Japan in second place. Although 17.6% of the large world trade market for cars in 2001 is quite an accomplishment it pales compared to the 27% Japan enjoyed in 1991. Canada follows in third place. Both Canada and Mexico increased their world market shares over the last ten years which should be due to NAFTA and the consequent easier access to the large US market. The USA itself accounts for only 6% of world car exports which is lower than France and Belgium/Luxembourg, the European forces in car exports behind Germany. On the downside, the weak performance of Italy in world car exports should be mentioned. Being among the major car producing countries in Europe its share in the world trade markets declined from 3.5% in 1991 to a weak 2.3% in 2001. It is now also below the South Korean world market share of 4% which is South Korea's only significant showing in international markets apart from the bus segment. Against common belief South Korea's car export share is only expanding slowly from 3.2% in 1995.

Fig. 25. World market shares 2001 in percent for major exporting countries (share of export value among OECD countries)

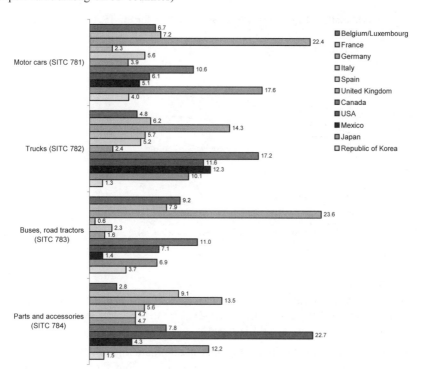

Source: NIW calculation using data from OECD: ITCS – International Trade By Commodity Statistics, Rev. 3, 2001, 2002.

In the truck segment the strength of the NAFTA countries becomes apparent. Canada holds the largest world market share, Mexico is third and the USA fourth. Only Germany squeezes between them in second place. Still, a fair amount of trade in trucks should happen among the NAFTA countries. Canada and Mexico are the most important trading partners for US truck exports. While US and Canadian world market shares are virtually unchanged compared to 1991, Mexico remarkably leveraged its share from half a percentage point in 1991 to more than 12% in 2001. This trend indicates that new truck assembly opportunities in the NAFTA region were largely realised in Mexico to supply the whole market. The most troubling signs in the truck segment come from Japan which lost more than half of its world market share between 1991 (24%) and 2001 (10%). From a European perspective the major truck producing countries defended their world market during this ten year time span. This fact is especially encouraging for Germany which maintained its world market share at an already high level. Another positive sign for the European truck producing industry is Spain which was able to gain ground in the international markets. It roughly doubled its share in world exports from 2.2% in 1991 to 5.2% in 2001. Apparently, Spain increased its competitiveness as an operation site for truck assembly with the goal of supplying foreign markets.

Fig. 26.   World market shares 1991, 1995, 1998 and 2001 for EU-15, USA and Japan

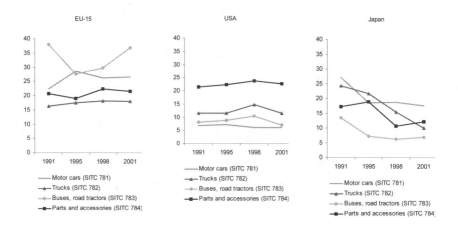

Source: NIW calculation using data from OECD: ITCS – International Trade By Commodity Statistics, Rev. 3, 2001, 2002; EU-15 excludes intra EU-15 trade; World market shares calculated as share of exports on OECD exports.

In bus exports, too, Germany exhibits a dominant market position. Almost every fourth bus exported in the world 2001 stems from there. What is more, Germany expanded its world market share from an already high level of 20.8% in 1991. Canada and Belgium/Luxembourg follow as the distant second and third. While the former has increased its world market share significantly since 1991, the latter fell during that time from 13.4% to 9.2%. The loss of world market shares is more extreme for Japan the 2001 value of which (6.9%) is almost half of what it was in 1991 (13.5%). This slide might be due to strongly increased bus production in other Asian markets that traditionally relied on imports from Japan but benefit now from lower labour costs at home. While Japan suffers significant losses in world market shares, South Korea was able to expand its share in bus exports from 2.3% in 1995 to 3.7% in 2001. With an eye on the European situation Italy again shows some worrying signs. It held a bus world market share of 4.6% in 1991 which almost completely evaporated and is at 0.6% in 2001.

As automotive value chains become more internationally dispersed exports of intermediate automotive products, part and accessories gain more importance. In this segment the USA is the undisputed world market leader. It defends its world market share which has been well above 20% since 1991. Some of this remarkable lead might be due to the strategy of major American car producers to invest abroad and supply local markets from American production sites, e.g. General Motors operates in the European market largely through their Opel and Vauxhall operations. This would necessarily result in weaker export shares for cars from the

USA but would still open up export channels for intermediate products or parts from supplying firms. This argument should also hold for automotive value chains that span NAFTA. Accordingly, Mexico's world market share in the parts segment skyrocketed from 0.7% in 1991 to 4.4% in 2001, while Canada's share remained relatively stable during that time at 7.8%. Nevertheless, even in light of these value chain effects the continued lead of US parts exporting firms in direct competition with local competitors at the transplant assembly sites underscores the extraordinary performance of the USA in this field. The global number two in world market shares for parts is Germany which largely defended its 13.5% share consistently from 1991 till 2001. Japan as the third largest player in international parts exports comes close with 12.2%. Still, compared with its share of 17.1% in 1991 the loss is significant. Unfortunately, from a European perspective the UK (1991: 8.1%; 2001: 4.7%) and France (1991: 12%; 2001: 9%) suffered significant setbacks.

As stated previously the world market shares give a good idea of the competitive performance of a country in the past. The concept is transparent and straightforward. Whether this performance is sustainable for the future, i.e. generates competitive potential, requires a slightly more elaborated construct. The revealed comparative advantage (RCA) appears better suited for that task. It treats imports and exports simultaneously and puts them into the context of the overall import-export relation of a particular country. The concept originates from Balassa (1965). Its formulation in logarithmic terms yields at the same time continuous, unbound and symmetric results (Wolter, 1977). Mathematically it is described as follows:

$$RCA_{ij} = 100 \ln \left[\frac{X_{ij} / M_{ij}}{\left(\sum_j X_{ij} \right) / \left(\sum_j M_{ij} \right)} \right]$$

with X: Exports; M: Imports; i: Country index; j: Product group index.

In essence, the strength of the RCA analysis stems from the opportunity to assess how successful a country was on foreign markets (exports) in comparison to the foothold foreign competitors were able to gain in the domestic market (imports). Additionally this ratio is compared to the overall export/import ratio of a particular country with the world. To be precise, this concept measures not only whether exports of a specific product have outweighed imports, but also whether the trade position for this particular product is stronger than the overall trade performance of this country. Hence, RCA is a comprehensive measurement of competitiveness in international markets that stresses specialisation for one particular product or product group. Therefore, positive RCA values indicate advantages in competitiveness while negative values imply disadvantages. Obviously, RCAs are vulnerable to any trade distorting measures, e.g. import duties, export subsidies. When interpreting the results this shortcoming should not be ignored. Still, following the purpose of this report, the concept was applied anyway under the explicit assumption that this trade distorting measures were non-existent or applied by all countries under consideration to more or less the same degree. Figure 27 summarises the 2001 RCAs for major automotive producing countries while Figure 28 puts those numbers for EU-15, Japan and the USA in a historic perspective.

Fig. 27.   Revealed comparative advantage (RCA) 2001 for major exporting countries

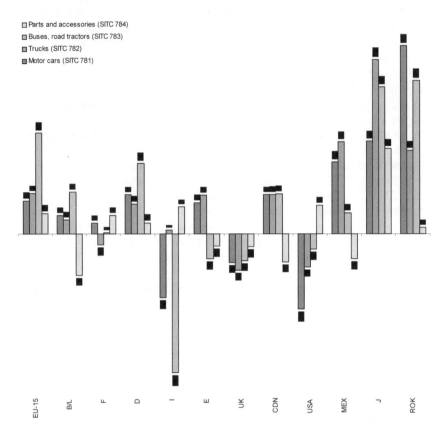

Source: NIW calculation using data from OECD: ITCS – International Trade By Commodity Statistics, Rev. 3, 2001, 2002; EU-15 excludes intra EU-15 trade.

Even at first glance it becomes clear, that the distinction between competitive performance (via world market shares) and competitive potential (via RCA) makes sense. Incorporating automotive imports and the overall trade position of a country allows significantly more insights.

Japan is a good example to illustrate how the RCA as an instrument of specialisation works. From the presentation on competitive performance one would expect, that Japan's diminishing world market shares would also have translated into lower competitive performance. In fact, this is not the case. What happened was a relatively strong increase in overall merchandise imports to Japan between 1991 and 2001 while overall exports grew more modestly. This translates into a diminishing denominator in the RCA formula above. Eyeing specifically the car segment now, the diminishing world market share shows that Japanese car exports expanded slower than the world market. Albeit, its car imports to the Japanese markets grew almost in unison with Japanese exports, which implies that the car export/import ratio (the numerator in the RCA formula) is 2001 close to what it was in 1991. Besides, this ratio is still strong: Japan exported 2001 roughly 8 times more cars (measured in value) than it imported, an export strength that is second only to South Korea. Accordingly, overall foreign companies became more successful in the Japanese market compared to the fate of Japanese firms overseas and their export performance; but this is not true for Japanese car manufacturers which defended their home market almost to the same extent as they were able to gain ground abroad. Therein lies the strength of the RCA as a specialisation measurement concept. Japan has superior competitive potential in the truck segment, while its RCAs are second best in cars and buses. Still, cars are the only segment where its RCAs significantly increased compared to what they were in 1991, trucks developed relatively flat, while current RCAs in buses and parts are 25% and 14% respectively below 1991 values.

Fig. 28.   Revealed comparative advantage (RCA) 1991, 1995, 1998 and 2001 for EU-15, USA and Japan

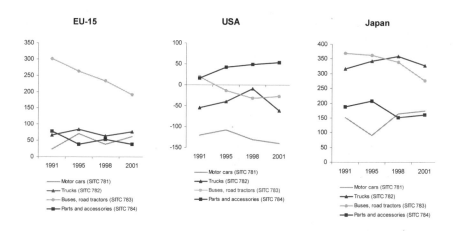

Source: NIW calculation using data from OECD: ITCS – International Trade By Commodity Statistics, Rev. 3, 2001, 2002; EU-15 excludes intra EU-15 trade.

The other Asian country under consideration, South Korea, has also very strong RCAs in the cars, trucks and buses segments. As mentioned before, South Korea benefits from superior performance in car exports compared to imports. In 2001 it exported roughly 48 times the value in cars that it imported. Not surprisingly, its RCA is high. Compared to 1995, South Korea even improved on its RCA position both cars and trucks, while the trend for buses is negative. Remarkable is the South Korean performance in the parts segment where they turned a negative RCA in 1995 (-76) into a positive one in 2001. This is mostly due to the fact that

South Korea reversed its position in trade in parts from being a net importer in 1995 towards being a net exporter in 2001. However, the strong South Korean numbers should be interpreted carefully. They rest on weak automotive imports to South Korea. Since those absent import streams are partly the result of an environment that posts obstacles to free trade, they should be interpreted carefully and do not adequately represent the competitive potential of South Korea.

The NAFTA countries show an interesting picture. While in cars, trucks and buses the USA show a negative RCA, Canada and Mexico post strong numbers. In sharp contrast, the parts segment turns this impression upside down. The import and export streams among those countries are highly intertwined in the value chain. As imports from Canada and Mexico lower the US RCAs in assembled vehicles, they rely heavily on parts and intermediate automotive products from the USA. Therefore, the competitive potential for the USA in cars, trucks and buses might be small, but it is strong when it comes to the parts segment. In the case of Mexico its current car RCA (136) looks impressive but the 1991 counterpart was well above 300. The Mexican trend is more impressive in trucks (+145% between 1991 and 2001) and in buses where they turned a highly negative RCA in the mid and early 90s into a positive one in 2001.

From a European perspective the majority of automotive trade happens within the European Union. Therefore, export advantages of a particular country necessarily translate into import induced disadvantages for partner countries. EU-15 without its intra trade has the strongest RCA's and hence competitive potential in the bus segment. While these numbers tend to decline over time the RCA's for cars, trucks and parts are fluctuating but consistently positive. Exploring the competitive potential for major automotive exporting member states gives some additional insights.

In the cars segment the competitiveness potential for Germany, France, Belgium/Luxembourg and Spain is strong while it is bleak for Italy and the UK which post negative RCAs since 1991. Germany boosted its RCAs most compared to 1991 which is mostly due to the fact the German export/import ratio in cars shifted from 1.5 in 1991 towards 2.8 in 2001. In trucks, the most troubling signs come from the UK with a negative turnaround in RCA since 1991. The UK used to export trucks worth 1.6 of what it imported in 1991, a value that shifted towards 0.4 in 2001. Besides, the revealed comparative disadvantages for France in this segment has hardly changed since 1991. All other European countries under consideration here show positive competitive potential for trucks with the strongest improvements compared to 1991 for Spain and Germany. In the buses segment, the downturn in British competitive potential since 1991 is almost a mirror image of the truck situation. France achieved a notable positive RCA in 2001 while it exhibited negative values in this area previously. Still, the highest potential lies in Germany and Belgium/Luxembourg which are also the countries that improved their RCA position most since 1991. The competitive potential for Italy lies in the parts segment where its exports consistently outpace imports. Accordingly, the optimal positioning for Italy in a European automotive value chain lies in the parts segment. Germany and France exhibit advantages in that field, too, but their RCAs are declining compared to 1991. Spain, the UK and Belgium/Luxembourg are on a consistent negative RCA trend.

3.2.1.1   Special Focus on the New Member States

Foreign trade plays a very important role in the NMS automotive sector on the export as well as on the import side. In 2002, the largest exporters of road vehicles were the Czech Republic, exporting road vehicles and parts (SITC 78) worth USD 8 bn, Poland (USD 3.8 bn), Hungary (USD 3 bn) and Slovakia (USD 2.9 bn), followed with a certain distance by Slovenia (USD 1.3 bn); see Table 78.

The most important import market for road vehicles and parts was Poland, absorbing USD 4.9 bn, followed by the Czech Republic (USD 4.2 bn), Hungary (USD 3 bn), Slovakia (USD 1.9 bn) and Slovenia (USD 1.2 bn). The Baltic countries, Cyprus and Malta were rather small players due to their small size and lacking specialisation in this field (Table 78).

Typically, the sectoral trade balance is positive or balanced for those NMS specialising in the automotive industry (Czech Republic, Hungary, Slovakia and Slovenia) and negative for the rest, including Poland, which has the second largest automotive production of the region but the share of this industry in total manufacturing being relatively small (see Figure 29 and Table 78).

Fig. 29.   NMS trade in road vehicles (SITC 78), 2002

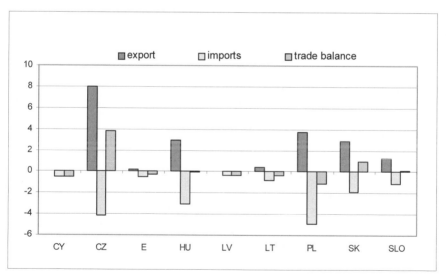

Source: UN trade database.

Moreover, in the NMS with a relative big automotive industry, the export quotas are extremely high, particularly in the foreign invested enterprises (FIEs). According to the wiiw FIE database in the year 2001, export sales made up 81% of total sales of FIEs in the Czech automotive industry, 92% in Hungary, 64% in Poland and 82% in Slovenia. The export shares of domestic enterprises were significantly lower, between 50% and 60% and only 14% in Poland (see Table 79). The export share in the automotive industry was rising over time. The disproportionate growth of automotive exports is also reflected in their shares in total manufacturing exports rising significantly. In the Czech Republic, for instance, road vehicle exports (including bodies and parts, SITC 78) came up to 8% of total manufacturing exports in 1995 but reached 19% in 2002. In the Slovak Republic the rise was from 5% to 22%. In Hungary, the relative increase was somewhat less spectacular but the shares still doubled (from about 5% to 10%). Only in Slovenia the already high share (12%) did not increase (see Table 80). Passenger cars (SITC 781) are the backbone of NMS exports, also rising fastest, with some important exceptions as parts and bodies (SITC 784) in Poland and trucks and special purpose vehicles (SITC 782) in Slovenia.

3.2.1.2   The Increasing Role of the NMS in Automotive Trade Worldwide and in the EU

As a consequence of this dynamic development, the world market shares of those NMS specialising in automotive production have risen as well, although from very low levels – and they are still small. The rise was most significant in the Czech Republic, increasing from 0.4% in 1995 to 1.4%, followed by Slovakia (0.09% to 0.51%), Hungary (0.17% to 0.53%) and Poland (0.27% to 0.67%) – the world market share of Slovenia remained constant at 0.23% (see Table 81).

However, the bulk of NMS trade in automotive products is with the European Union and with Germany in particular. In 2002, the share of the EU-15 in total road vehicle exports (SITC 78) was around 80% in most countries (see Table 12). Only in the Baltic states, where automotive exports are small any way and comprise parts and bodies for vehicles (SITC 784) mainly, EU trade is less dominant due to their traditional trade links with the former Soviet Union. Also, in the case of the Czech Republic, a significant share of automotive exports went to the neighbouring NMS, in particular to Slovakia, but to Poland and Hungary as well with the three countries reaching a combined share of more than 13% in total exports and outpacing individual trading partners in the EU, except, of course, Germany (35%). In general, the exports of the major product group which are passenger cars (SITC 781) were most heavily geared to the OMS, while vehicle parts and bodies (SITC 784) are being increasingly sold in the neighbouring NMS as well. This underpins the emergence of an automotive cluster in the region, comprising the Czech and the Slovak Republic, the south of Poland and western Hungary – forming a kind of 'oval' (Lepape and Boillot, 2004). In some cases, where prominent foreign investors come from countries outside the European Union, such as GM (USA) and Suzuki (Japan) in Hungary, exports of vehicle parts to the mother country of the foreign investors play a certain role as well.

Table 12. EU-15-shares in vehicle trade of the NMS, in % (2002)

	Exports[1]					Imports[2]				
	78	781	782	782	784	78	781	782	782	784
Cyprus	100.0				100.0	49.9	54.2	36.8	83.6	57.1
Czech Rep.	74.1	71.5	25.3	68.2	80.6	85.1	81.0	91.6	86.0	87.5
Estonia	34.8	20.0	39.8	14.2	54.2	70.6	62.3	83.1	89.4	83.0
Hungary	84.4	97.2	53.2	10.6	73.8	77.1	74.0	75.8	72.3	81.8
Latvia	41.1	39.0	10.7	54.8	52.7	73.4	74.0	81.2	63.3	73.4
Lithuania	5.3	3.5	7.1	17.3	29.2	80.5	77.5	94.5	96.9	68.7
Malta	93.5				93.5	76.8	80.5	58.5	72.7	70.7
Poland	86.5	90.3	91.3	61.0	83.9	82.8	79.8	97.3	95.2	77.9
Slovak Rep.	80.2	81.4	10.3	52.0	79.6	72.9	50.0	81.5	74.5	83.0
Slovenia	86.6	87.9	71.1	34.0	87.9	88.2	84.1	97.6	85.7	89.9

[1]) Exports to the EU-15 divided by total exports of the respective product group.
[2]) Imports from EU-15 divided by total imports of the respective product group.
Source: UN Trade database, wiiw calculations.

The European Union is a dominant source for automotive imports of the NMS as well, including the Baltic states. However, except in the Baltics, the EU-15 sometimes played a lesser role in imports than in exports, because of overseas suppliers penetrating the growing NMS automotive market – especially in the passenger car segment where the EU-15 share was typically around 75%. However, their share in the NMS market is still small.[36] Intra-regional exports of parts and accessories find their expression in imports as well – this is particularly true for the Slovak Republic where imports (of cars and parts) from the Czech Republic play an important role.

3.2.1.3   Revealed Comparative Advantage (RCA) of Different Product Groups

RCAs as defined in Table 81 compare the relative shares of exports and imports of a particular industry with the share of the country's total manufacturing exports and imports. A positive value indicates a relative competitive *advantage*, while a negative value points to a competitive *disadvantage* in this field. Our results show a large competitive advantage in the automotive industry as a whole (SITC 78) for the Czech Republic and Slovakia, but only a small competitive advantage for Hungary and Slovenia, and a competitive disadvantage for Poland, the Baltic states and the two Mediterranean NMS. At the level of subgroups, the revealed comparative advantage was typically largest for passenger cars (SITC 781), fol-

---

[36]   A notable exception is Cyprus, where Japanese vehicle imports reached 42% but also Estonia, where vehicle imports from Japan ran up to 14% and those from Russia had a share of 6% in 2002 (UN trade data base).

lowed by parts & bodies for motor vehicles (SITC 784). Regarding the other sub-groups SITC 782 and 783), only Poland shows a slight comparative advantage in trucks etc. (goods, special transport vehicles (SITC 782).

3.2.1.4 Conclusion

In conclusion, the European automotive industry shows mixed signs: First of all, the performance of the German and French industry is strong. Their success in international markets is substantial and sustained. Furthermore, they show positive competitive potential (RCAs) for the future which indicates that the management processes applied in German and French automotive companies succeed in turning the performance of the past into sustainable potential for the future. Spanish firms appear also to be moving towards growing success in international markets. Still, the signals coming out of Italy and the UK are less promising. Both countries have not only lost shares in the automotive world market but their RCAs have significantly declined. As a result, their automotive competitive potential for the future is in danger. Albeit, this is notably not true for the Italian parts segment. Still, the vast majority of trade of European automotive companies takes place within the European Union. The single market facilitates production concentration on few sites from which subsequently the whole European market is supplied. This necessarily translates into more import and export activities. A current study by ECG (2004) shows that automotive manufacturers are moving towards plants that produce a single model or two at maximum. Moreover, they show that 75% of all vehicles produced in EU-15 are destined for another country, 58% for another member state.

The same rationale appears to apply to the NAFTA areas where stable or diminishing trends in Canada and the USA respectively are offset by the growing performance and potential of Mexico. Apparently, the automotive value chain configurations in the NAFTA region place vehicle assembly in Canada and increasingly Mexico while the parts stem predominantly from the USA. The Asian competitors Japan and South Korea show differing signals. South Korea expands its presence on international markets as Japan's world market shares decline. Both countries post strong RCA numbers indicating competitive potential but this is largely due to low imports from the rest of the world. This deficit in imports can only partly be explained by superior competitive performance. Substantial parts of it are due to measures that hamper free trade. These must not necessarily take the form of tariffs but can also imply a lack of harmonisation in regulations, standards and certifications. Therefore, those RCA values can very well be compared among segments (giving Japan the most competitive potential in trucks, and South Korea in cars) but cannot be applied in direct comparisons among countries.

Trade indicators give some important insight into a country's performance in international competition. Still, as indicated before the times when only finished products or vehicles could cross borders are long gone. Increasing mobility, international integration and diminishing transaction costs facilitate value chain configurations that span across different countries leveraging performance reservoirs that can only be fully exploited by operating locally. The following section analyses these trends as the second major pillar of internationalisation: foreign direct investment.

3.2.2   Foreign Direct Investment

Investments abroad have become a significant factor in corporate internationalisation strategies. Dunning (1981) describes three major reasons why multinational companies should invest in a particular country: (1) The ownership advantage stems from the multinational corporation itself and may lie in size or better resource capability and usage. (2) The location advantage implies certain immobile factors that can only be fully utilised in the area where they exist. (3) Finally, the internalisation advantage originates in market imperfections that might be of structural (e.g. imperfect competition) or cognitive nature (e.g. costly or scarce information on the marketed products).

Fig. 30.   Global leverage points

Source: Lessard (2003).

In the same context, Bartlett and Goshal (1989) find three "leverage points" that can be augmented through different forms of internationalisation: Efficiency (global economies of scale, comparative advantage of location), knowledge (use people and ideas globally), responsiveness (adapt to local customer demands) leverage. The European automotive industry could potentially benefit from all those leverage points. The question remains whether it prefers to use the market mechanism to utilise them, i.e. trade, or invest directly abroad. The latter appears especially appropriate since production expertise and customer preferences are sticky, i.e. they can hardly be extracted and formalised to be transferred from one country to another without substantial losses or at high costs. Investing in especially influential regions be it for R&D, production or distribution reasons opens up a more efficient channel for companies to harness these forms of tacit knowledge from abroad. On a side note it should be mentioned that extensive trade distorting measures may also pressure foreign companies into investing directly in a particular country. From an economic perspective this result is far from efficient. Still, it is a reality on international markets and should be borne in mind when interpreting the results.

With an eye on outgoing FDI the German automotive industry is the most active in Europe among major producing countries followed by France, Italy and the UK; but all are significantly below the outgoing US-FDI. Summed up over the last five available years FDI from the automotive sector has the most importance in Germany (5% of all outgoing FDI). For Italy this key figure is at 3.7%, France 3.3%, the UK 1.4% and the USA shows 3.2%.

Fig. 31. Outgoing FDI from major automotive producing countries in EUR mn (NACE 34)

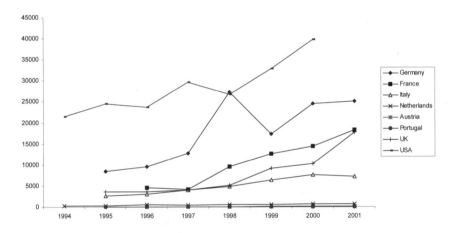

Source: Eurostat (2003), by definition of reporting country.

The strong outgoing FDI numbers for Germany might be due to the decelerating growth trends in the home market as well as the importance of foreign markets for German brands (Figure 23). This could point towards a possible responsiveness leverage abroad which German manufacturers try to gain through FDI by opening up new growth potentials outside their home market. The USA as the prime target of German outgoing FDI (Figure 32) supports that argument. The high involvement of the French automotive sector in Japan indicates a knowledge leverage FDI strategy. The example of Renault and Nissan shows that these transfers of knowledge are no one way street. As industry experts indicate, Renault gained access to Nissan's excellence in production while Nissan benefited from Renault's abilities in streamlining the value chain. Additionally, the importance of FDI in other EU member states becomes obvious. Considering the single European market those engagements should primarily be driven by efficiency and comparative advantages since minuscule border barriers among member states make it easy to supply the EU as a whole from few production or distribution sites.

Fig. 32. Top 5 sum of outgoing FDI 1997-2001 from selected European automotive producing countries by country of destination in EUR bn (NACE 34)

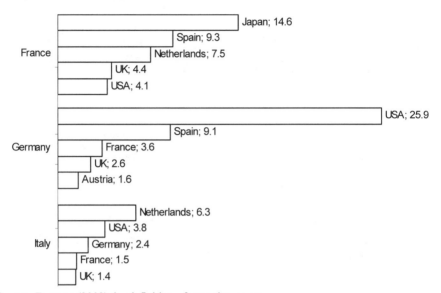

Source: Eurostat (2003), by definition of reporting country.

Assessing ingoing FDI streams the performance of major European countries is far behind FDI flows towards the USA. Especially the increase of ingoing FDI for the US automotive industry is remarkable, whereas the development in Europe is relatively flat. This does not hold for the UK where FDI inflows are the strongest among European countries under consideration both in absolute level and in relative growth terms. Considering the importance of the FDI inflows for the automotive sector as a fraction of all FDI inflows (combined over the last five available years), Italy shows the highest ratio (4.1%) followed by the UK with (2.8%). In France and Germany this factor is of less importance with percentage rates of 1.6% and 1.2% respectively. The corresponding value for the USA is 3.7%.

Closer inspection on the sources of those foreign direct investments in major automotive producing countries in the EU (Figure 34) shows that the USA is a major player in that field especially in Germany. Additionally, the strong engagement of other EU member states becomes obvious, pointing towards the utilisation of resources that are only available on a regional level but can be leveraged later on for the European Union as a whole.

Fig. 33.   Ingoing FDI for major automotive producing countries in EUR mn (NACE 34)

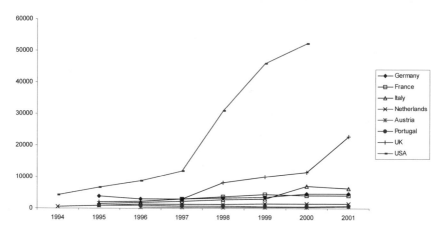

Source: Eurostat (2003), by definition of reporting country.

Fig. 34.   Sum of ingoing FDI from 1997 till 2001 for selected European automotive producing countries by country of origin in EUR bn (NACE 34)

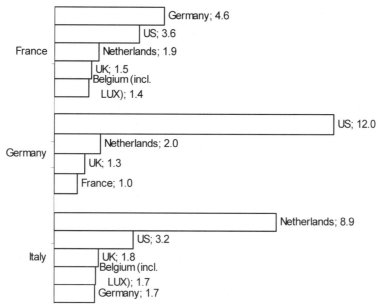

Source: Eurostat (2003), by definition of reporting country; numbers for Belgium include
Luxembourg.

Equal evidence for corporate strategies towards internationalisation beyond exports can be found on the company level. Figure 35 shows how strict export

driven strategies from a home market have lost importance in the automotive sector. Not only do motor vehicle producers realise sizeable if not dominant (Volvo) shares of their sales abroad, but they also hold significant assets there.[37] This trend is especially strong for Honda, BMW and Volvo. In terms of employment Toyota, Volvo and Ford show the strongest tendency for operating outside the home market. To the contrary, DaimlerChrysler, BMW, Nissan and Renault rely mostly on employees in their home market. However, DaimlerChrysler should be interpreted carefully here since it is considered the only company with multiple home economies (Germany and the USA).

Fig. 35. Share of foreign assets, sales and employment for major motor vehicle producing companies 2001 (home economies in brackets)

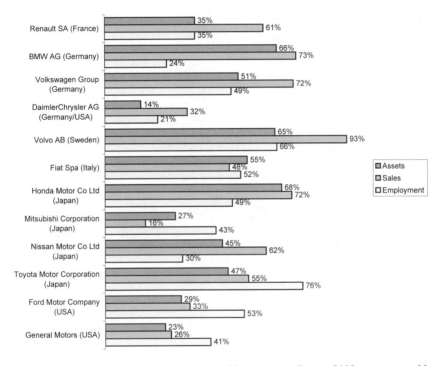

Source: ZEW calculation using UNCTAD World Investment Report 2003; no comparable data available for PSA Citroen.

Figure 36 puts these figures into a strategic context. Large portions of sales abroad appear to require also a strategic shift in assets towards foreign countries. Those investments abroad should generate the crucial sticky information from the

---

[37]   All data provided by UNCTAD relies on company annual reports or revised data based on company survey. The numbers should be interpreted as proxies since precise asset classification and valuation (e.g. financial assets, depreciation) can hardly be achieved at a cross-country comparison level.

target markets for the multinational company as a whole both in terms of a knowl-edge (e.g. R&D infrastructure, access to clusters of expertise) and a responsive-ness (e.g. market trends, customer needs) leverage. Especially, in the case of BMW this must not necessarily imply a massive shift of employment out of the domestic country. The diagram in Figure 35 indicates that the kind of information mentioned before can be channelled through the company without moving the more labour intensive production out of the home market. Still, most manufactur-ers (Volvo, Toyota, Honda, Volkswagen, Fiat) accompany their international market orientation in sales not only with the investment in assets abroad, but they also transfer employment out of the home market. Those companies most likely utilise all leverage points (efficiency, knowledge and responsiveness) in their internationalisation strategies. On the other hand, those enterprises with relatively low shares of sales abroad (General Motors, Ford, Mitsubishi) and high shares of employment abroad appear to be following primarily an efficiency leverage inter-nationalisation strategy by utilising comparative advantages especially in labour costs in foreign countries.

Fig. 36.   Strategic perspective on foreign assets, sales and employment for major motor vehicle producing companies 2001

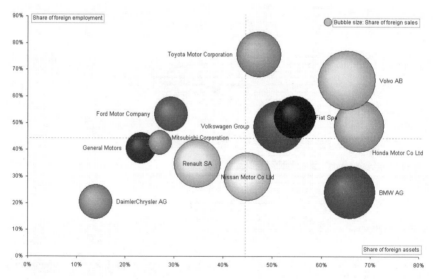

Source: ZEW calculation using UNCTAD World Investment Report 2003; no comparable data available for PSA Citroen.

3.2.2.1   Special Focus on the New Member States

Inward foreign direct investment plays a far bigger role for the automotive sector in the NMS than in the OMS[38]. Many global vehicle producers and suppliers have put up establishments in the region and the development of the automotive industry in the individual countries is closely linked to the location decisions of these global players. The countries which have attracted most FDI in the automotive sector are the same which show a strong specialisation in this industry, namely the Czech Republic, Hungary, Poland and more recently Slovakia as well. Slovenia is the only country with a significant automotive industry, but relatively little foreign direct investment. At the end of 2002, the Hungarian automotive industry showed the biggest stock of foreign direct investment, followed by the Czech Republic and Poland (see Table 77).[39] Taking into account the different absolute size of the economies, the FDI stock *per employee* is probably a better indicator for the relative attractiveness of individual countries as a target for FDI in the automotive industry. As demonstrated in Figure 37, Hungary is top again, but Poland looks less impressive than measured in absolute figures. Notably, the FDI stock per employee is above manufacturing average in virtually all countries. The high attractiveness of the automotive industry for foreign direct investment is confirmed by our data from the wiiw FIE database, showing the distribution of foreign invested enterprises (FIEs) across individual industries.

Fig. 37.   Inward FDI stock per employee 2002/2001

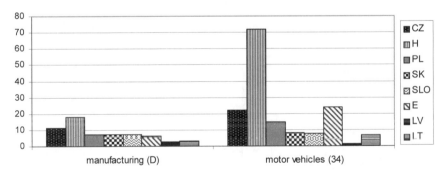

Source: wiiw FDI database.

---

[38]   Outward direct investment on the other hand does not play any role in these countries.
[39]   For Hungary and Poland FDI data were available at the level of the transport equipment industry (DM) only, including motor vehicles (34) and other transport equipment (45). But as this industry is a minor target for FDI in the NMS, the data are fairly comparable.

3.2.2.2 Foreign Penetration

The dominant role of foreign investors in the automotive industry is best demonstrated by the extremely high penetration rate which can be measured by the share of foreign invested enterprises in various performance indicators of the industry.

Table 13. Foreign penetration of the NMS automotive industry (NACE 34) 1995-2001, in %

Equity	1995	1996	1997	1998	1999	2000	2001
CZ 1)	61.4	64.3	71.2	71.1	83.9	82.3	83.1
H 2)	73.7	76.1	92.7	96.1	94.9	97.9	99.6
PL	62.5	82.1	81.4	85.6	84.5	80.0	83.3
SK 3)	36.8	48.5	54.0	47.1	72.6	73.0	78.6
SLO	74.3	120.2	136.9	133.0	69.7	75.8	76.7
Sales							
CZ	61.3	66.9	76.5	81.5	90.4	87.7	91.0
H	88.1	84.8	95.4	96.8	96.0	93.9	93.9
PL	55.4	82.5	86.8	89.9	90.7	91.4	93.2
SK 3)	56.6	61.4	n/a	92.1	n/a	93.3	95.1
SLO	72.3	82.3	81.8	83.1	82.0	78.8	82.7
Export sales							
CZ	n/a	n/a	82.3	88.0	94.8	90.9	94.0
H	94.1	90.4	98.5	99.1	98.7	96.7	96.6
PL	88.4	93.3	94.2	95.7	96.1	97.4	98.4
SK	n/a	n/a	n/a	n/a	n/a	n/a	n/a
SLO	80.8	86.3	86.5	87.1	84.0	80.1	86.2
Investment							
CZ	70.0	80.2	83.2	85.4	93.8	91.8	94.0
H	94.4	96.1	84.9	98.4	98.5	96.4	97.5
PL	52.9	88.1	79.2	80.0	96.0	94.8	95.3
SK	85.0	33.8	92.6	86.9	94.4	92.6	97.8
SLO	n/a	n/a	n/a	n/a	n/a	n/a	n/a

Notes: 1) 1995, 1996 own capital. 2) 1995-1999 nominal capital. 3) 1995, 1996 DM (=NACE 34+35). 4) Output.
Source: wiiw FIE database.

In 2001 (the last year available), foreign invested enterprises owned 83% of the *equity capital* in the Czech automotive industry, made 94% of all *investments,* sold 91% of all vehicles and had a share of 94% in the industry's exports. These shares were even higher in Hungary and lowest in Slovenia (equity: 76.7%, sales 82.7%, exports: 86.2% see Table 13). In all countries, foreign penetration has increased over time. Notably, foreign invested enterprises are more export oriented, as reflected in their higher share in export sales than in total sales. As will be shown in our trade analysis below, production sites in the NMS are used as an export platform to the OMS mainly.

Table 14. Assembly plants in Central and Eastern Europe

Manufacturer	Country (country of mother company)	Plant site / Name	Products
Andoria-Mot Sp. z.o.o.	Poland	Andrychow	Honker Suv, Lublin
Audi Hungaria Motor Kft.	Hungary (VW Germany)	Györ	Audi TTCoupé/Roadster
Automobile Dacia S.A.	Romania (Renault France)	Potesti	Dacia Berlina/Break, pick up, Supernova
Daewoo Automobile Romania, S.A.	Romania (Rep. Korea)	Rodae, Craiova	Daewoo Cielo, Matiz, Nubiera, Lanos, Takuma (CKD)
Daewoo Avia	Czech Republic (Rep. Korea)	Prague	Avia small trucks
Daewoo-FSO Motor	Poland (Rep. Korea)	Warsaw	Daewoo Matiz, Nubria, Lanos, Fiat Polonez
Fiat Auto	Poland (Italy)	Tychny	Fiat Palio Weekend, Seicento, Nuova Panda
GM Poland	Poland (USA)	Warsaw	Astra Classic
Magyar Suzuki	Hungary (Japan)	Esztergom	Suzuki: Wagon R+, Ignis
MAN	Poland (DaimlerChrysler Germany)	Poznan/Tarnovo Podgorne	Buses
NABI	Hungary	Kaposvar	Compobus vehs.
Opel Polska Sp.z.o.o.	Poland (GM USA)	Gliwice	Opel Agila
Revoz	Slovenia (Renault France)	Novo Mesto	Renault Clio
Skoda Auto a.s.	Czech Republic (Germany)	Kvasiny Mlada Boleslav Vrchlabi	Superb Fabia, Octavia Octavia
Volkswagen Poznan Sp.z.o.o.	Poland (VW Germany)	Poznan	Skoda, Fabia, VW: T5
Volkswagen/Skoda	Czech Republic (Germany)	Vrchlabi	Skoda: Felicia, Octavia
Volkswagen Slovakia	Slovakia (Germany)	Bratislava	VW: Bora, Polo A04, Golf R32, Golf A4, Touareg, Porsche Cayenne bodies, SEAT Ibiza
Volvo Trucks	Poland (Sweden, Scania)	Wroclaw	Volvo trucks

Source: Ward's Automotive Yearbook 2003, p. 18 f.

Table 15. Planned investments in assembly plants in Central and Eastern Europe

Manufacturer	Country (country of mother company)	Plant site/ Name	Products
Hyundai	Slovakia (Rep. Korea)	Zilina	Investment: EUR 700 mn; production starting 2006; employment 3,000-4,000, annual output planned: 200,000-300,000; Kia
PSA Peugeot Citroen	Slovakia (France)	Trnava	Investment: EUR 700 mn, production starting 2006; output planned: 300,000
Toyota /PSA Peugeot Citroen	Czech Republic (Japan / France)	Kolin	Investment: EUR 1.5 bn, starting 2005, output planned: 300,000

Source: Kurier, 6 March 2003.

As mentioned in the overview already, the bulk of foreign direct investment in the NMS comes from manufacturers with European origin[40]. But with the enlargement at the doorsteps, overseas investors have become more interested in the region recently, attracted by growing markets but using the NMS as a location for their all-European exports as well. This has been stated, for instance, by the Hyundai company, which decided in March 2004 to put up its first European assembly plant in Slovakia, with a capacity of 200,000 to 300,000 cars per year, see Table 14. If the investment plans of the other two big ventures become true, namely PSA Peugeot Citroen (Slovakia) and a consortium of Toyota and PSA Peugeot (Czech Republic), the production capacity in the NMS will rise to over 2 million passenger cars in 2006, roughly double the production of 2002, which will definitely be more than can be sold in the region.

3.2.2.3 Conclusion

From a strategic point of view American vehicle manufacturers appear to be the ones who rely the most on their home market. This could certainly be explained by the size of their domestic market. European and Japanese manufacturers are much more multinational not only in sales but also assets and employment. There is neither a unique European nor a unique Japanese pattern when it comes to internalisation.

European automotive companies have been very active in investing abroad. They have mostly adjusted to particular country disadvantages in their home market and chosen sites that allow them to optimise their value chain within the European Union. A second strong flow of foreign direct investment went into the USA in order to tap the large market. Still, both ingoing and outgoing FDI in the auto-

---

[40]   However, with the formation of automotive groups and all kinds of cooperations between individual companies also across groups, the term 'county of origin' becomes increasingly blurred in the automotive industry.

motive sector has played only a minor role in total FDI streams to and from Europe. European automotive manufacturers appear to have positioned themselves well to fully utilise all strategic leverage points in international competition.

3.2.3   Emerging Markets

The focus of this analysis on cross country comparisons makes it sometimes difficult to cover the unique aspects of a particular country especially if they do not show off in the date or cannot be adequately covered yet. Hence, two promising automotive markets were singled out to give a more in-depth look: China and Russia.

3.2.3.1   China

Table 16. Important data on the Chinese economy

GDP (billions USD, 2002 est.)	5989	Passenger cars in use (1000 units, 2002)	5570
GDP growth (2002 est.)	8%	Passenger cars new registrations (1000 units, 2002)	1,126
GDP per capita (2002 est.)	4,700	Passenger cars per 1,000 inhabitants (2002)	4.34
Population (billions, 2003 est.)	1,287	Commercial vehicles in use (1000 units, 2002)	14,960
Area in sqkm	9,596,960	Commercial vehicles new registrations (1000 units, 2002)	2,122
Population density (inhabitants per sqkm, 2003 est.)	134	Car production (1000 units, 2002)	1,091
Urban unemployment rate* (2002 est.)	10%	Truck production (1000 units, 2002)	2,160

Source: CIA World Factbook 2003, VDA International Auto Statistics 2003, Wards Automotive Yearbook 2003; *Urban unemployment roughly 10%; substantial unemployment and underemployment in rural areas (2002 est.).

The Chinese Automotive Market

Especially since China joined the Word Trade Organisation (WTO) in December 2001, it is easier for Western companies to set up businesses. The Chinese government welcomes foreign direct investment, which has been flowing into China at a rate of 60 billion USD a year (Wong, 2003). Hence, as Figure 38 shows, Chinese automotive market is growing very rapidly, so there is much opportunity within the country. In the first nine months of 2003 unit sales even increased by 69% reaching 1.45 million cars (Automotive Resources Asia, 2003). Sales of commercial vehicles increased by about 30% from 1999 until 2002 and buses even doubled in the same time. According to forecasts, China will be the third largest market for automobiles by the end of the decade (VDA International Auto Statistics, 2003). Against the backdrop of a highly saturated market in the triad, the enormous potential of the Chinese market has the effect of a magnet on the international automobile industry (Zhang and Taylor, 2001).

Due to China's persistent economic growth, decreasing prices boosted up private demand for automobiles. While in the 1990s the major part was sold to firms for commercial fleets (e.g. taxis) and to the government, the focus moved towards private customers, who will also be the crucial market segment in the future (Weidner, 2004). The increase of private demand will speed up in the next years. Besides, sinking prices due to increased competition and the intent of the Chinese government for making cars more affordable by decreasing charges and taxes propel this development (Hein, 2004).

Fig. 38.   Index of new registrations or sales of passenger cars 1999-2002

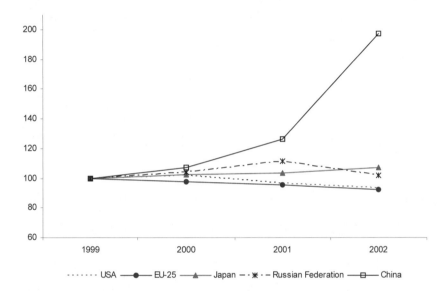

Source: ZEW calculation using VDA data; base year 1999 = 100.

Although the automotive market is growing, most of the Chinese cannot afford automobiles in the next decades. The growing middle class in Eastern Chinese cities will take the advantage from the increasing prosperity. In the year 2002 only 6 million Chinese citizens had an income of more than USD 6,000 while this population class will rise to 15 million in 2007. Furthermore, car purchases are not inexpensive in China. High import tolls and government determined prices for imports and cars produced in China by foreign companies like VW make automobiles up to 40% more expensive than in Europe. In addition, luxury license number plates and street taxes as well as expensive parking lots (up to EUR 7,500 per year) and street tolls make up keeping a car costly. Nevertheless, automotive demand is increasing. For the Chinese middle class owning a car signals independence, individuality and, above all, wealth and advancement (Weidner, 2004).

This status symbol value is only partly reflected in horse power or cubic capacity, but in design and equipment. For Chinese customers, a car has to look like a dragon: It needs a head and a tail; otherwise it is not a fully-fledged car. The biggest cars are driven with the smallest motors. VW managers in Beijing explain this by the fact that Chinese do not gear up because they drive cars like a bicycle. Accordingly, traffic congestion is not a large problem yet. Besides, two out of ten cars sold in China belong to the upper class limousine segment, which shows that Chinese customers are all the more aware of status and equipment (Weidner, 2004).

Production Conditions for the Chinese Automotive Industry

In 1995 there were 122 automotive manufacturers in China, which produced in low scale for isolated regional markets. Every manufacturer has its own supplier chain on hand. Furthermore, the local automotive industry is protected and supported by the local government. Inland barriers to trade, small economically not survivable automotive manufacturers and component suppliers, inefficient production conditions and technologies put a large burden on the international competitiveness of the Chinese automotive industry until today (Huang, 2002).

Since 1994 Chinese government has followed up an explicit industrial policy for the automotive sector. The objective is to set up an own and independent automotive industry. To ensure international competitiveness the Chinese government follows the strategy of involving international automobile corporations through minority joint ventures with local firms. By doing so China not only retrieves capital and technologies from other countries, but also valuable know-how for the domestic automotive industry. It also dictates the rules for international companies: Imports are constricted, earnings have to be reinvested and component suppliers and their prices are predetermined, too (Hoon-Halbauer, 1999).

Chinese automotive manufacturers are learning very quickly. They profit from the technology transfer by establishing joint ventures with more than only one international manufacturer (Zhang and Taylor, 2001).

Beside, China aims to restructure its own automotive industry, to propel competitiveness through economies of scale. For that purpose, the number of manufacturers should be reduced or combined to manufacturer groups. The same should happen to the component suppliers with a target of 5 to 10 companies. The update of the Chinese automotive policy issued by the National Development and Reform Commission (NDRC) in Spring 2004 addressed some of these issues (Yu, 2004): Minimum investment thresholds for new auto projects (2 bn yuan) and production permit withdrawal mechanisms were enacted to prevent a further dissipation of the market. Then again, multinational automotive producers can still own not more than 50% in a joint venture with Chinese partners. The stated goal of the new policy is to satisfy Chinese demand through domestically produced vehicles before 2010 and enter international markets significantly. While the policy also encourages private car ownership and auto loans it primarily appears to focus on facilitating a sustainable pace in a highly dynamic market. The positive effect of the new policy on automotive exports from China remains doubtful. The combination of the need to source from local less efficient and hence more costly suppliers with the capital intensive production methods of foreign producers that do not fully leverage China's advantage of affordable labour puts Chinese automotive products in a difficult position on international markets (Farrel, 2004).

Fig. 39.   Joint ventures of international and Chinese automotive manufacturers for passenger cars production in China

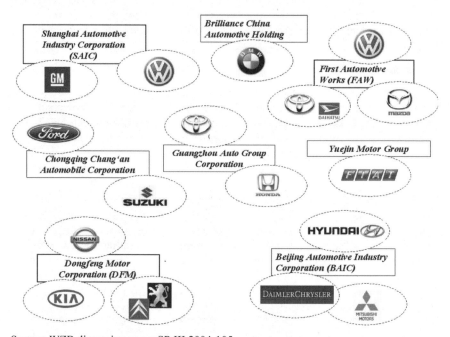

Source: WZB discussion paper SP III 2004-105.

Since China joined the World Trade Organisation the automotive industry has been subject to more deregulation. Import quotas for foreign automotive manufacturers were increased by 20% per year until 2006, starting from 30,000 units. The quota will be eliminated by 2006. Furthermore, import duties will decrease from 80-100% to 25% following 2006 (10% on components). Companies are allowed to finance car purchases by foreign non-banks (Weidner, 2004; Zhang and Taylor, 2001).

As Table 17 shows all major car manufacturers are moving aggressively into the Chinese market. This is mostly realised through the buildup of new production capacities. This fact in combination with the elimination of import barriers described above points towards increased rivalry and hence diminishing profit margins. Although labour costs in China are low, it remains to be seen whether Chinese plants will be able to produce efficiently enough to turn domestic overcapacities into exports. Table 17 highlights the risk exposure that foreign producers incur by investing in China. Volkswagen still benefits from its first mover advantage in the market. Accordingly, it is most vulnerable to the risks of the Chinese market but not to a troubling degree. Besides, there is no special pattern in the way European companies enter the market compared to major international rivals. Some manufacturers in the premium segment (BMW, DaimlerChrysler) are moving cautiously which might be due to the fact that the protection of intellectual property rights (e.g. technology, design) is still difficult in China and there are obstacles for the manufacturers in controlling the quality of their value chain in services and repair which in turn could tarnish their reputation.

Table 17. Rated auto manufacturers exposure to mainland China market

Company	Exposure to China market (2002)	Units
Heavy existing or planned exposure		
Hyundai Motor Co./Kia Motors Corp.	3% of total unit sales	Current: 100,000; by 2007: 650,000 (incl. Kia)
Nissan Motor Co. Ltd.	Some import activity	Current: 0; by 2010: 900,000 (passenger cars and commercial vehicles)
Volkswagen AG	10.3% of total unit sales	Current: 600,000; by 2006: 1.6 million
Medium existing or planned exposure		
Fiat SpA	1.5% of total unit sales	Current: 70,000; by 2007: 150,000
General Motors Corp.	3.3% of total unit sales	Current: 380,000; by 2006: 766,000
Mitsubishi Motors Corp.	5.8% of total unit sales	Current: 120,000; by 2010: 300,000
Peugeot S.A.	3.0% of total unit sales	Current: 150,000; by 2006: 300,000
Toyota Motor Corp.	3.8% of unit sales (total Asia excl. Japan)	Current: 180,000; by 2010: 650,000 (incl. Daihatsu)
Limited existing or planned exposure		
BMW AG	1.7% of total unit sales	Current: 0; by 2005: 30,000
DaimlerChrysler AG	4.4% of revenues (total Asia)	Production capacity expansion from 80,000 to 100,000 units
Ford Motor Co.	3.3% of revenues (total Asia-Pacific)	Current: 20,000; future: 150,000
Honda Motor Co. Ltd.	1.2% of total unit sales	Current: 150,000; by 2004: 290,000
Renault S.A.	0	0
Suzuki Motor Corp.	n/a	Current: 250,000; expansion plans: 0

Source: ACEA and Standard & Poor's (2004).

In conclusion, the deregulation leads to a stronger competitive pressure for Chinese as well as foreign manufacturers. Earning margins as a result of officially predetermined prices will considerably decrease. But Volkswagen Group CEO Bernd Pischetsrieder and rating agency Standard & Poor's warned to be aware of increasing competition, price decline and overcapacities. Considering the still existing legal uncertainty on the Chinese market and its intensifying competition on the one hand as well as the estimated increase of the automotive market by 25 to 30% in 2004 on the other, aggressive engagement holds risks while growth prospects are undeniably strong (SPIEGEL-ONLINE, 2004).

3.2.3.2 The Russian Federation

Automotive Industry in the Russian Federation

The Russian automotive fleet has more than doubled over the last ten years from 10 million cars in 1992 to 22 million at the end of 2002 with an average annual growth rate of 8%, reaching 152 cars per 1,000 inhabitants (Figure 40). This rate of growth is stronger than in the European Union and this trend is likely to continue. The Russian government estimates that car ownership in Russia will reach 230 cars per 1,000 inhabitants within the next ten years which means an additional growth by 12 million cars (Ashrafian and Richet, 2001; PricewaterhouseCoopers, 2002a).

About 70% of the market demand in 2000 is for passenger cars priced below USD 5,000. In the near future demand is expected to shift to passenger cars in the USD 5,000-10,000 price range and to a lesser degree to USD 10,000-15,000 priced cars. The segment for more expensive cars is expected to remain stable. These changes will be the result of price increases for locally produced cars and the introduction of import tariffs on used foreign cars in the segment below USD 5,000 (Ashrafian and Richet, 2001).

Table 18. Important data on the Russian economy

GDP (USD bn 2002 est.)	1,409	Passenger cars in use (1,000 units, 2002)	22,100
GDP growth (2002 est.)	4.3%	Passenger cars new registrations (1,000 units, 2002)	941,908
GDP per capita (2002 est.)	9,700	Passenger cars per 1,000 inhabitants (2002)	152.22
Population (millions, 2003 est.)	145	Commercial vehicles in use (1,000 units, 2002)	4,540
Area in sqkm	17,075,200	Commercial vehicles new registrations (1,000 units, 2002)	178,954
Population density (inhabitants per sqkm, 2003 est.)	8.5	Car production (1,000 units, 2002)	980
Urban unemployment rate* (2002 est.)	7.9%	Truck production (1,000 units, 2002)	239

Source: CIA World Factbook 2003, VDA International Auto Statistics 2003, Wards Automotive Yearbook 2003.

Fig. 40.   Index of car ownership per 1,000 inhabitants for selected markets

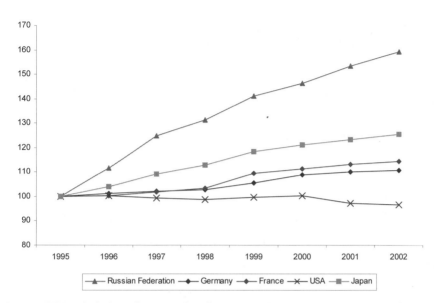

Source: ZEW calculation using VDA data; base year 1995 = 100.

Replacement sales are a big factor. Only one third of the passenger cars in Russia today are less than five years old. Nearly 47% are between five and ten years old and the rest of the fleet is more than ten years old. The average age of cars is 10.8 years. The main reason for this is the low purchasing power (OSEC, 2003). Older vehicles will become more expensive to operate as auto insurance becomes compulsory by about mid-2004. Ernst & Young expect these factors to push many people into newer vehicles, including imported used vehicles. Nevertheless, demand for new cars has been growing at an overall rate of more than 10% annually. There is great potential for stronger growth, especially for foreign brands because usually they offer better quality and reliability (Ernst & Young, 2003).

In Russia sedans are much more popular than coupes. Among the wealthy class sports utility vehicles are popular. In used cars, German and Japanese models are in high demand. Volkswagen is by far the most popular used-car brand with more than 215,000 passenger cars currently rolling on Russian roads, although the biggest new-car import brands in Russia are Toyota, Daewoo, Mitsubishi and Renault (Ernst & Young, 2003).

Like in China, Russian automotive manufacturers are still organised as huge industrial complexes that include auxiliary and component-producing facilities. They supply 80% of the market demand in Russia. The biggest companies are AvtoVAZ, GAZ, IzhMash-Auto and UAZ. The large manufacturers still produce up to 70% of their components on their own, thus preventing Russian manufacturers from operating efficiently (Kansky, 2000). Furthermore most of them use outdated and inefficient technologies which hamper improvements in product quality and labour productivity. The models the plants produce are 15 to 20 years out of date by world standards. Still, this is the main reason why high production volumes have been possible. There has been a lack of investment to develop new models, although the situation has changed with new Russian strategic investors (Ashrafian and Richet, 2001).

Russian car manufacturers have to cope with the new competitive environment like the presence of foreign car makers in the country, the lowering of tariffs and the new constraints coming from the WTO regulation when Russia will join the WTO. Recently some companies began implementing restructuring programmes, which include shifting component production to independent companies. It seems likely that efficiency will increase. But this also means that some companies vanish from the market. Moskvic, the fifth biggest manufacturer in 1999, is an example for this dynamic in negative terms, while other producers like IzhMash Auto increased production significantly (VDA International Auto Statistics, 2003).

In order to survive the relentless increase in competition in the industry, Russian manufacturers have begun exploring ways of cooperating with Western car and component makers mainly through joint ventures (PwC, 2002a). Peugeot delivers engines for other models of Russia's largest carmaker AvtoVAZ. BMW and Kia assemble their cars (BMW 2,200, Kia 3,500 cars in 2002) at the Avtotor facility in Kalingrad based on imported assembly kits. Ford has chosen a different way on a green field site near St. Petersburg. The Focus models are produced there with about 1,700 vehicles in its first year of production 2002. The current capacity is 25,000 cars a year but could be boosted up to 100,000 if demand continuous increasing (WardsAuto.com, 2003). Volkswagen, the most successful foreign brand in Russia, has not announced any intentions to produce in Russia, while Toyota recently signalled plans to produce their Landcruiser model there in 2006 (PwC, 2002a).

In contrast with most other emerging automotive markets Russia and the EU are direct neighbours with a shared land border. Hence, the potential trade channels are broader and more flexible. Not surprisingly, car exports from EU-15 to Russia have sharply increased since 1993 (Figure 41). Interestingly, used car exports have paved the way for the entrance of European cars in the Russian market. Apparently, Russian customers cannot yet afford new cars but show strong interest in European brands anyway. Right now this interest is covered through used cars but these exports should give European producers an edge in brand recognition once incomes in Russia will increase and customers begin shifting their attention to new cars.

Russia is facing an increase in the automotive industry and may soon follow China as next big new market in this sector (Ernst & Young, 2003). Demand for vehicles is rising quickly, but manufacturers and suppliers face unique challenges. The forthcoming entry of the WTO could be the necessary spark that ignites the coming out of the emerging Russian market. Albeit, recent developments in Russian trade regulation behaviour (35% tariffs on imported cars) cast serious doubts on Russia's readiness to be a responsible partner in free trade.

Fig. 41.   Index of new and used car exports from EU-15 to Russia 1993-2002, value

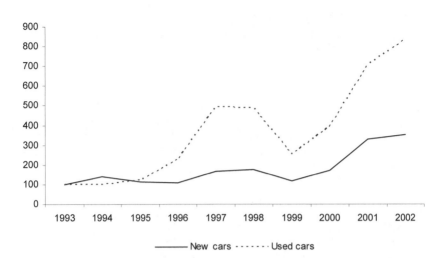

Source: ZEW calculations using Eurostat intra- and extra-EU trade 2003 data. Base year 1993 = 100.

3.2.4   Conclusion

The position of the European automotive industry in international markets is strong. Major European producing countries control considerable shares of the world market. Still, as developments in trade and FDI streams show European producers rely on streamlining their operations within Europe. Besides, they have managed to tap valuable resources outside of Europe both in terms of knowledge and customer responsiveness.

3.3   The Home Market

3.3.1   Market Size

A large home market enables domestic firms to utilise economies of scale and scope. Hence, they benefit early in the product life cycle from learning curve effects and an increasing expertise in production. This in turn leads to diminishing unit costs and consequently prices which make the domestic products more competitive on foreign markets. Besides, a large domestic customer base provides the invaluable feedback for innovative products and features that shape their future design. A significant home market for primary products also opens up new opportunities for secondary products and services that might not reach the necessary critical mass to evolve elsewhere. Therefore, a comprehensive assessment of home market size as a possible source of competitiveness includes both the market in total numbers and its segmentation.

3.3.1.1 Passenger Cars

With 209 million passenger cars in use in 2002 the European Union (EU-25) is by far the largest single market for cars in the world. It accounts for roughly 38% of all cars on major international markets, followed by the USA and Japan. Table 38 in the appendix gives the total numbers for all countries under consideration.

Size becomes more important in relative terms. Car ownership in Europe varies widely indicating the relative importance of cars for citizens of different countries. On average four out of ten EU inhabitants own a car which is fairly in line with data from Japan and the USA. Luxembourg, Italy and Germany post the highest values here among member states. For countries with high ownership ratios we expect cars to have the highest importance not only in terms of use but also as a status symbol.

Explaining the differences in car density should yield some interesting insights on market segmentation. Assessing this segmentation in demand on an aggregated country comparison level requires the identification of meaningful drivers in demand for passenger cars that are also available internationally in comparable format. Thus, those factors are necessarily broad.

Building on the reasonable assumption that there is an internationally equally optimal level of car density national deviations from this level become the centre of interest. Or to put it more simply: Why would some countries buy more cars than others?

Obviously, the mere need of passenger transportation comes to mind. This factor should be especially important in countries with low population densities, since the citizens of those countries need to travel longer distances on average for every aspect of social interaction. Still, this factor may be not totally comparable among countries since those distances could also be overcome through bus, rail or air transportation. Availability, affordability and flexibility of those alternative modes of transport influence their relative attractiveness. Those connections should not be ignored when analysing the results but incorporating every aspect of a particular national transportation system would clearly not serve the purpose of this analysis. Additionally, cars are by far the dominant mode of transportation in the European Union while the combined contribution of all other modes of transportation is slightly below 20%.[41] Transport by car has some unique advantages over all other forms of traffic. It is essentially the only mode of transportation that enables the users to choose their travel time and exact destination individually. Besides, it is the only option in a customer's transportation portfolio that allows direct door to door trips. Hence, the benefits from owning a car as the dominant mode of passenger transportation should be directly connected to the customer's need for

---

[41]   Passenger cars accounted for 80.4% of all passenger kilometres in EU-15 2001; European Commission (2003).

transportation which in turn is related to population density. Accordingly, people per square kilometre was utilised as a proxy for the necessity to own a car for citizens to get from point A to point B.

Fig. 42.   Passenger cars in use in major international markets 2002

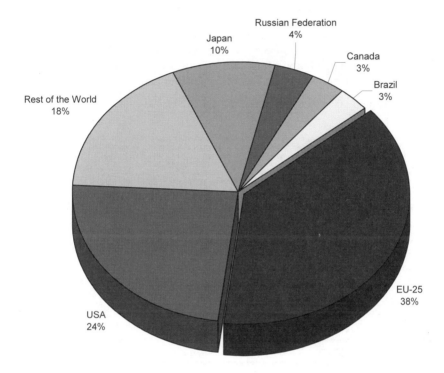

Source: ZEW calculation using ACEA, VDA, EUROSTAT data; for Cyprus, Estonia, Latvia, Lithuania and Malta 2001 data was used.

On the other hand, cars and the attitude of owners towards them appear to run much deeper than their practical value in use. Although this argument might have been dominant in the early days of motorisation, the days of a "one size fits all" black Ford T model are long gone. Today's car manufacturers offer a startling variety of different models to facilitate their customer's needs. Those needs include rational deliberations like the wish for spacious family vans. Then again, the Volkswagen New Beetle or the Chrysler PT Cruiser hardly fit that category. The success of cross utility vehicles and sports utility vehicles, not to mention the established convertible segment, clearly indicates that through the eyes of the customer cars are more than just four wheels and an engine. Today even the small and medium sized car segments have a luxury segment that finds its customers as exemplified by BMW's new Mini. Cars have become an element of style and empower their drivers to express themselves and their individuality. The choice in car models reflects this clearly as does the wide variety of supplementary interior and exterior car equipment. Cars have a social signalling function, proofing that one can afford a special car or even more than one. This trend certainly reflects a country's wealth but also its general tendency to treat cars as a status symbol. As a proxy variable for this impact factor GDP per capita was used. Other possible income related variables might have some advantages over GDP per capita but its availability and comparability across countries outweighs its deficiencies. Figure 44 shows the relationship between the proxy variables and car density.

Fig. 43.   Cars per 1,000 inhabitants 2002

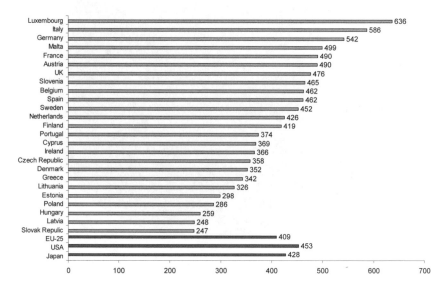

Source: ZEW calculation using ACEA, VDA, EUROSTAT data; for Cyprus, Estonia, Latvia, Lithuania and Malta 2001 data was used.

An accompanying multivariate regression analysis shows that GDP per capita has a highly significant positive impact on car density whereas population density shows only a positive influence at an 80% significance level. In major European markets (Netherlands, Belgium, Germany, Italy, UK) high car density ratios can hardly be explained by the need for transportation among sparsely populated areas. Instead, these countries appear relatively affluent and invest in cars, which points towards the previously mentioned argument of an affinity for cars beyond mere practical use. The same is true for Japan. For the USA, Australia, Canada, Spain, Sweden and France affordability as well as the transportation motive appear in more congruence. Especially in the new member states high car densities appear to be mostly motivated by the requirement to own a car as the primary source of mobility and less as a status symbol.

Fig. 44.   Population density, GDP per capita and cars per 1,000 inhabitants 2001 for major markets

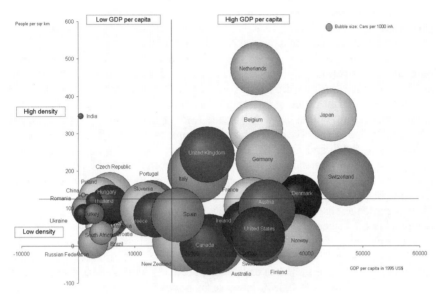

Source: ZEW calculation using ACEA, VDA, Worldbank World Development Indicators data; covering 38 major car markets.

Consequently, the member states of the European Union cover all customer segments in this relatively broad classification which appears reasonable for country comparisons. The mix of states with a primary interest in affordable passenger transportation and better-off car-enthusiast member states should prevent the industry from myopic, idiosyncratic product designs.

Excursus: For What It Is Worth – The Preferences of German New Car Consumers

From the description above one might easily argue that there is no uniform European car buyer and market segmentation should go much deeper. To get a clearer picture of the typical new car customer and its preferences it makes sense to focus on a single national market in more detail. The largest national European market, Germany, is an obvious choice.

Modern cars are complex products. They bring various functions to their owners: speed, safety, security, entertainment, individuality, to name a few. Still, they can only buy the whole bundle when purchasing a car. Disentangling those value drivers through the eyes of the customer should give some valuable insight into what exactly people cherish in their cars. The best setting to observe such preferences is not in hypothetical survey situations but when customers actually buy a car on the market. The idea is to treat the individual car purchase not as a black box product but instead as a bundle of functional components that in combination generate enough value for the individual customer to justify the price. Therefore, through econometric analysis it becomes possible to estimate a relationship between prices and corresponding quality features. This so-called hedonic method is widely used for the quality adjustment of price indices. The presentation here focuses on the results. The interested reader might turn to the appendix for the full set of the applied hedonic functions and econometric details.[42]

In essence, the hedonic approach uses a large number of price and corresponding quality information and infers how and to what degree these price differentials can be explained through differences in quality. For this analysis we used the information on 1,160 different passenger car models that where available on the German market in 2000 as provided by the leading market intelligence company Schwacke.[43] The sample covered car models from 28 different brands with prices between EUR 7,000 and EUR 121,000 and engines from 42 hp to 420 hp. Additionally, we had information on major quality characteristics like the type of engine or the availability of an anti-lock braking system. Figure 45 shows the available variables and the coefficients of the regression results. These numbers are mostly denoted as shadow prices since they put a price tag on a quality component that could not have been priced individually before.

Not surprisingly, German customers are willing to accept price increases in exchange for stronger motor performance. Both engine performance and cylinder capacity should be interpreted as elasticities, i.e. a 1% increase in kW engine performance would justify a 0,48% increase in price through the eyes of the customer. All other quality features can be interpreted more easily since they were introduced as so-called dummy variables indicating whether a quality component was included or not. For example, German customers would accept a mark-up of 17% in price if the car was a convertible or coupe. From a broader perspective, German customers are willing to pay for features that make their car more unique (e.g. convertible, wide base tires, real leather). This fits nicely with the status symbol argument presented previously. Most likely the accepted price increase of 8% for a diesel car is justified through lower fuel costs during the time of ownership. The willingness to spend on safety features (ABS, ASR) is significantly smaller while the picture is unclear for convenience elements. German customers prefer driving convenience (automatic) over day-to-day comfort (power windows).

---

[42]   For a full description of the hedonic analysis see Berndt (1991). In accordance with most contributions to the field and as a result of the Box Cox procedure the hedonic function containing price and quality information was estimated in the double log functional form.

[43]   All models were treated equally as one observation. Weights for sales volumes would have been preferable but were not available for most models. Besides, the pricing information reflects list prices which do not incorporate any rebates, trade-ins or throw-ins. These arrangements are quite common in car purchasing. Albeit, in the absence of more detailed price information, list prices should be a reliable proxy.

Fig. 45.   Price mark-ups due to quality improvements on the German new car market 2000

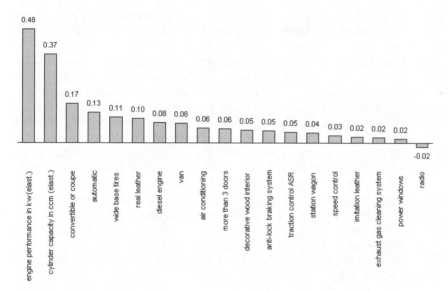

Source: ZEW calculation using Schwacke data, where indicated values should be inter-preted as elasticities.

Still, customers would also assign a lower shadow price to a particular compo-nent if they consider it granted that this item should be included or they prefer replacing it anyway which might explain the radio coefficient. This set of quality features explains roughly 90% of the price differentiation among car models on the German markets. While this overall high number indicates that German cus-tomers make a rather rational decision on what car to buy there may still be some unobserved characteristic that allows some car manufacturers to charge higher prices than others. Those elements might include the value of the car in resale or the assumed reliability of the car translating into lower repair costs. Additionally, some quality characteristics might be more accentuated in different car models than in others. It is possible that the quality characteristics in use do not address these particularities comprehensively. Nevertheless, all these aspects are usually not attributed to a specific car but to the car brand as a whole. To capture these brand effects a second hedonic equation was estimated taking into account the car brand. Figure 46 gives the results.

Accurately defined, Figure 46 gives the relative price mark-up a customer is willing to accept for the brand of his/her new car compared to what (s)he would be willing to pay for an equally equipped reference car (Kia was chosen as reference here). Apparently, Porsche is the most valuable brand here. Customers would pay twice the price of the reference car with equal features, a unique position among the brands in the German market. Obviously, this fact indicates an enormous ex-cellence in operations at every stage of the value chain. It not only ends in design and production but notably includes customer communication. Porsche makes its customers realise the premium quality of the product and those in turn are willing to pay superior prices. The 40%+ premium segment in Germany is dominated by European brands. Notably, half of the brands in this category (Jaguar, Saab and Volvo) are non-German brands. Volkswagen is an interesting case in this analysis. Its branches Audi, Volkswagen, Seat and Skoda are well positioned along the brand scale: Audi in the high mark-up segment, Volkswagen in the upper middle-class, Seat in the lower middle class and Skoda in the more price sensitive section at the bottom of the scale. It becomes apparent that the Volkswagen company as a group with different brands targets all price segments with an individual brand.

The different brands make it easier for the customers to assign themselves to a particular market segment and find an individual brand as a counterpart instead of a one size fits all Volkswagen brand. Still, this differentiation materialises in the cognition of the customer and leaves room for integrated procurement and production systems across different Volkswagen brands, hence realising economies of scale and scope. Honda is the non-European brand with the best brand value. Ford and Opel as the branches of major US car manufacturers in Europe can't enter the segment with high brand esteem. Among European players, Fiat, Rover and Skoda don't get much brand-based price mark-up from German customers.

In conclusion, in the largest European car market Germany, higher price margins can best be achieved through features that improve driving performance and convenience or make the vehicle more exclusive or individual. Besides, German customers recognise quality through the car brand and are willing to pay for it accordingly. Porsche exhibits the best performance in leveraging its assigned quality perception while Volkswagen executes a matching multi-brand strategy for each segment.

To be precise, at this point of the analysis this demand advantage is an attribute of the market not the industry. This strategic resource turns only for those producers into a defendable competitive advantage that have complete access to the relevant market and customer information. The question remains whether European car manufacturers benefit predominantly from the size of their home market.

It becomes reasonable here to switch to a brand perspective since the brands are the primary channels through which the customers recognise the manufacturers. Figure 47 shows the market shares of major brands in selected markets. It suggests a strong affiliation of French and German car buyers towards brands that originated in their respective home market. This implies an atmosphere of trust into cars that were domestically built and designed. For Italian, Swedish and British brands this link is weaker. Customers there appear to be less focused on domestic brands but keep a strong interest in other European brands. Combined European brand shares command more than 80% of the market in the five selected European markets. Korean and Japanese brands exhibit significantly smaller shares but are slightly better positioned in European countries without a strong home market brand affiliation.

Fig. 46. Price mark-ups due to brand esteem on the German new car market 2000 in relative positioning to an equally equipped Kia car

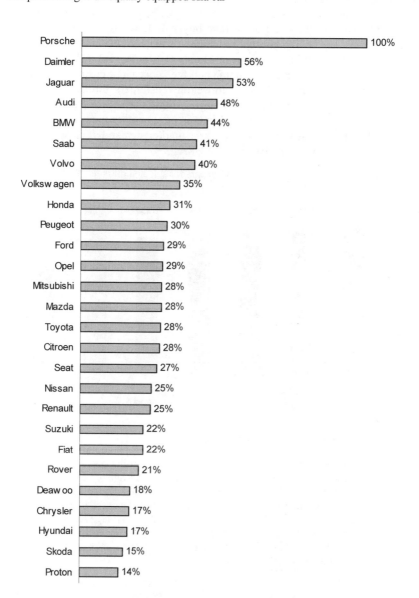

Source: ZEW calculation using Schwacke data; to control for equal quality among brands the quality characteristics from Figure 46 were introduced to the hedonic function again, but will only be reported in the appendix.

In contrast Japanese brands enjoy an enormous popularity in their home market where all other brands are of minor importance. In sharp contrast, American brands command only about 60% of first car registrations. At least in terms of units sold Japanese brands control a large portion of the US market for new cars.

There is evidence that this demand advantage in the home market has already translated into success abroad. The average buyer of European brand cars in the USA has a far higher median household income (USD 115,492) than the customers of Asian (USD 70,353) or American brands (USD 58,154).[44] This indicates that the demand for premium cars at home and the subsequent customer feedback help to shape products that are attractive to wealthy customers abroad.

In essence, the European Union is the largest single market for passenger cars. European car buyers prefer their national brands or substitute them to a large degree with other European brands. This home market demand leverage is even more accentuated in Japan but weaker in the USA.

Fig. 47.   Brand segmentation in first registration cars for selected markets 2002

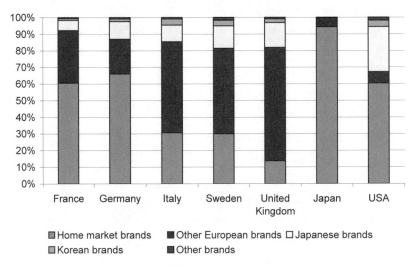

Note: German brands (Audi, BMW, Ford, Mercedes, Opel, Porsche, Smart, Volkswagen), French brands (Citroen, Peugeot, Renault), Italian brands (Alfa Romeo, Ferrari, Fiat, Lamborghini, Lancia, Maserati), British brands (Ford, Jaguar, Land Rover, Lotus, Morgan, Rolls Royce, Rover, Vauxhall), Swedish brands (Saab, Volvo), Japanese brands (Daihatsu, Honda, Isuzu, Mazda, Mitsubishi, Nissan, Subaru, Suzuki, Toyota), American brands (Chrysler, Ford, General Motors), Korean brands (Asia, Daewoo, Hyundai, Hyundai Prec., Kia, Ssangyong), also European brands (Seat, Skoda).
Source: ZEW calculation using ACEA, VDA data.

3.3.1.2 Commercial Vehicles

The European Union is the second largest market in the world for commercial vehicles with slightly more than 30 mn vehicles in use in 2002 followed by Japan

---

[44]   See Ward's Automotive Yearbook 2003.

and China. Still, the USA's 92 mn commercial vehicles make it a distant second. Significant pieces of that gap might be due to the fact that light trucks have made remarkable inroads in the US market for passenger cars. In 2002, 8.1 million passenger cars were newly registered in the US compared to 8.7 million light trucks.[45] There is currently no meaningful distinction between light trucks that supplant passenger cars in the private use segment and those that go into traditional commercial use. Accordingly, this gap should be interpreted carefully. Table 39 in the appendix gives the relevant information on use and sales for all countries under consideration.

Fig. 48.   Commercial vehicles in use in major international markets 2002

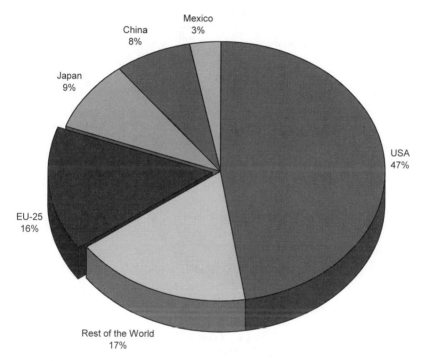

Source: ZEW calculation using ACEA, VDA, EUROSTAT data; for Cyprus, Estonia, Latvia, Lithuania and Malta only 2001 data was used.

From the intra-perspective on the European Union France holds the largest share (19.8%) of commercial vehicles in use in 2002 followed by Spain (14.1%), Italy (12.8%) and Germany (11.5).

Demand for commercial vehicles is certainly a derivative of the importance of freight transportation on the road. This degree of reliance on commercial vehicles is highly influenced by an adequate infrastructure and the opportunity costs of alternative modes of transportation which include not only price differences but

---

[45]   See VDA: International Auto Statistics 2003.

also availability and flexibility in use. In Greece and Ireland road transportation appears to be the almost indisputable dominant form of transportation. This trend is also strong in Italy, Portugal, Spain and the UK. To the contrary, only 40% or less of goods transport ton-kilometres in Lithuania, the Slovak Republic, Estonia and Latvia are performed on the road. Although the intermodal split of goods transportation is not unanimous among EU member states road transportation is a strong if not dominant pillar in most EU countries' transportation backbone. Accordingly, demand for commercial vehicles should remain substantial.

Fig. 49.   Commercial vehicles in use in the European Union 2002

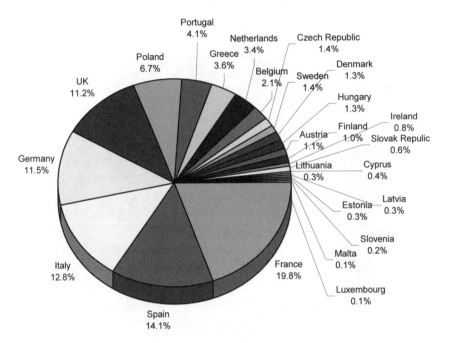

Source: ZEW calculation using ACEA, VDA, EUROSTAT data; for Cyprus, Estonia, Latvia, Lithuania and Malta only 2001 data was used.

By combining transported goods and kilometres travelled, the diagram above disguises the primary fields of use for commercial vehicles in the EU. Figure 51 draws a clearer picture in this regard. Most goods in the European Union (as indicated by their weight in tons) are transported over rather short distances. Especially in Ireland, Germany, Finland and Austria the vast majority of transport happens over distances below 150 kilometres. In other member countries this relationship is weaker (Belgium, Italy, Luxembourg) but the share of short distance transportation volume is still above 60%. Consequently, the emphasis on shorter distance road transportation in the European Union should give rise to commercial vehicle concepts that address their specific needs. These could include intelligent and flexible transport solutions with sophisticated but cost effective command and control infrastructures instead of maximum distance transport units. Those longer distance commercial vehicles would primarily transport lower weight products in the EU.

Fig. 50.   Percentage share of goods transport ton-kilometres on the road in total goods transport 2001

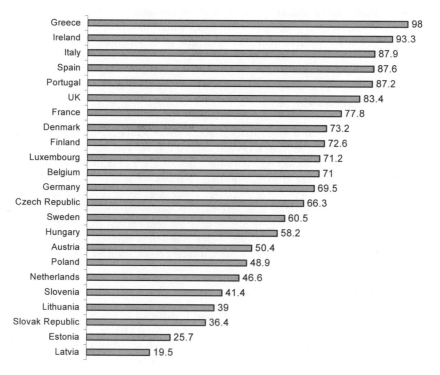

Source: EU Energy and Transport in Figures 2003; for new member states 2000 data was used; no data available for Cyprus and Malta.

Fig. 51.   Share of million tons transported on the road by distance 2001

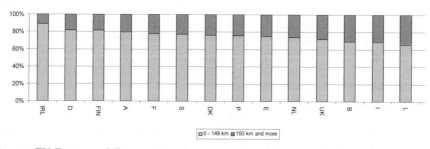

Source: EU Energy and Transport in Figures 2003; no data available for Greece and the new member states.

The special impact of light trucks for private use in the USA should not be overemphasised. The European Union is still an attractive volume market for commercial vehicles. Most European countries rely heavily on road transportation. This fact reflects heavy investments in a suitable infrastructure both from the private (e.g. value chain configurations) and the public sector. These sunk costs provide significant obstacles for alternative modes of transportation and ensure a stable demand for commercial vehicles in the foreseeable future. Most road freight in the EU is transported over shorter distances which should open up opportunities in this segment for vehicle manufacturers, due to experienced and sophisticated customers.

3.3.2   Market Growth

It has been shown that a large market size can generate significant sources of competitive advantage. Still, to a certain degree this reflects a market dynamic of the past. At this point the second important determinant of demand attractiveness enters the picture: market growth. Naturally, already large markets can still generate strong volume growth but it becomes more and more difficult for them to provide relative growth. It is this sort of new sales opportunities, though, that helps automotive companies to continue to grow and benefit from the up-to-date input of dynamic markets. As a result, market growth is as much a prerequisite for home market demand advantages in international competition as market size.

3.3.2.1 Passenger Cars

Some measurement concepts of growth find it difficult to cover cyclical fluctuations of demand or are highly sensitive to the base year choice. Furthermore, simple relative percentage growth rates usually promise stellar market expansion while they are mostly due to small base numbers and growth in unit terms remains rather limited. To avoid those pitfalls an alternative concept was utilised. By estimating the slope of an assumed linear trend in demand over several years, market growth can be safely represented. This concept incorporates both the market dynamic and the volume increase factor. Figure 87 illustrates this concept distinguishing between a long and a short-term trend. It should be mentioned that this procedure is primarily designed to cover trends from the past and should not be misinterpreted as a precise prediction for the future. Such forecasting techniques would certainly need to take into account demographic trends as well as the cyclical (an obviously non-linear) nature of automotive demand. The concept applied here aims at covering basic multi-year market trends that can easily be compared among countries. It was designed for that specific purpose and should be treated as a supplement, not substitute, for traditional market prognosis.

The separation between long-term and short-term trends allows more insight into general trends but also more recent developments. Both trends are obviously intertwined but the factors that drive them can be quite different. The long-term trend in car sales is driven by more fundamental elements. Among the most time persistent ones are customer preferences towards cars or alternative modes of transportation respectively. The same is true for factors like availability, quality and affordability of the infrastructure. For car passenger transportation as well as all other modes of transportation the infrastructure upgrades (e.g. railway tracks, motorways) take years to be planned and implemented. On the other hand, short-term trends might be more influenced by the overall economic situation or the customer confidence in the future economic developments that influence their present consumption behaviour. Those trends might include unemployment or the fear thereof, as well as fluctuations in interest rates. Since most new car sales today substitute only the buyers' previous car the majority of owners can easily postpone the replacement purchase and stick with what they have for a longer period of time. Differences in the average age of the car fleets across major European countries reflect this mechanism. In 2002 the average car in Belgium was 7.6 years old while its counterpart in Greece was 11.3 years of age.[46] Hence, customers can easily control their time of purchase which could severely influence the short-term trend while the long-term trend should be hardly affected.

Besides, the combined information from the short- and the long-term development of the market in unit terms gives valuable insight into a country's potential for the future. Using Figure 87 as an example, the long-term trend would suggest a splendid future for this car market while the short-term trend indicates that this impression is mostly due to the more distant past while more recent observations point towards a levelling off. Presenting this information as well as setting this into context is the rationale for the following passages.

Table 34 shows the trend numbers for all member states. In the long run the UK, Spain and Italy show the strongest increase in demand. Austria, Poland and Europe's largest market, Germany, follow a negative trend. All other member states show a slightly upwards trend. In the short run, again the UK shows a remarkable growth trend. If this trend continues new registrations could go up there by 133,000 cars annually. Additionally, Hungary and France are on a strongly increasing trend, although significantly below the UK. Still, the majority of member states (16 out of 25) shows a negative trend, with the Netherlands, Poland and Germany at the end of the scale. If this negative short-term trend in the EU would continue, new registrations in the EU-25 would go down by more than 300,000 cars per year. While this number is troubling, it should be emphasised that it reflects only the four year short-term trend and given the cyclical nature of demand in cars, the linear trend assumption could easily overstate the actual development. The long-term trend is more revealing and it indicates continuing growth for the EU-15 (unfortunately there is no comparable time series data available for the new member states) of roughly 190,000 units a year. Albeit, the short-term trend for EU-15 points downwards in almost the same order of magnitude. In essence, growth in the European car market is decelerating.

A look outside the boundaries of the EU helps to put these numbers into perspective (Table 35). The countries under consideration with the strongest long-

---

[46]   Information specifically compiled by ANFAC.

term growth trend are Brazil, India, Mexico, South Korea and Australia. On a long-term shrinking trend are Romania, Turkey, USA and Japan.

The numbers for passenger cars in the USA might be somewhat misleading since demand for light trucks in private use has significantly picked up there and this form of substitution might put additional pressure on the sales of traditional passenger cars. For US environmental requirements (CAFE) it is preferable to register especially the popular SUVs as light trucks instead of passenger cars. Put simply, in the traditional international segmentation this inflates the US numbers in commercial vehicles and lowers the equivalents in passenger cars. To account for this special effect, some studies combine cars and light trucks to a segment usually called light vehicles. Using the available information, 16.8 million light vehicles were sold in the USA in 2002, 8.1 passenger cars and 8.7 light trucks. The distinction in the truck segment is rather new. Therefore only a short-term growth trend for light vehicles in the USA could be estimated. As expected, the trend differs from the passenger car trend. Still, the short-term direction of the market for light vehicles is the same. Judging from the last four available years the linear trend suggests that sales diminish by roughly 73,000 light vehicles annually. While this trend is certainly of interest when analysing the USA the lack in comparable data makes it hardly applicable in cross country comparisons. Since this is the central aspect of this analysis the traditional segmentation appears better suited while the interpretation of the US results has to be conducted carefully and with the special trend in mind.

Over the most recent four year observation period the massive increase in demand for cars in China jumps to mind, followed by South Korea, Japan, Mexico and Brazil, making these countries the most intriguing markets for growth in passenger cars. From a European perspective only the UK would also fall into this category. For Japan this short-term upward trend indicates that the negative long-term trend has been overcome. On the downside are Argentina, Turkey and the USA where large parts of the decrease can be attributed to the popularity of light trucks. To facilitate a conclusion the long-term and short-term growth trends have been combined into the following matrix (Figure 52).

There is no uniform development in long-term and short-term growth trends for Europe. The most troubling signs come from Europe's largest car market. Germany suffers from downward pressures. Most European countries are on a positive upward trend while there are strong indications that they might have reached a growth plateau. Still, a couple of member states posts promising growth trends both from a long and a short-term perspective. The UK clearly stands out in the EU car market with growth trends that make it one of the most attractive car markets in the world. On an international level, besides China optimistic long-term and even stronger short-term trends make Brazil, Mexico and South Korea excellent growth markets.

Fig. 52.   Algebraic signs of short-term and long-term growth trends for passenger cars

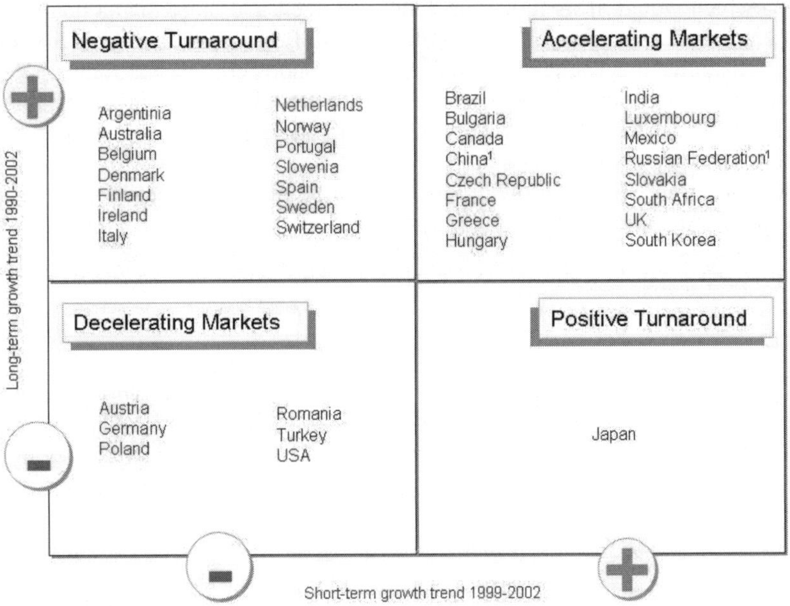

Negative Turnaround		Accelerating Markets	
Argentinia	Netherlands	Brazil	India
Australia	Norway	Bulgaria	Luxembourg
Belgium	Portugal	Canada	Mexico
Denmark	Slovenia	China[1]	Russian Federation[1]
Finland	Spain	Czech Republic	Slovakia
Ireland	Sweden	France	South Africa
Italy	Switzerland	Greece	UK
		Hungary	South Korea
Decelerating Markets		**Positive Turnaround**	
Austria	Romania		
Germany	Turkey	Japan	
Poland	USA		

Long-term growth trend 1990-2002 (vertical axis)

Short-term growth trend 1999-2002 (horizontal axis)

[1] Due to data availability long-term trend was only estimated for 1995-2002.
Source: ZEW.

3.3.2.2 Commercial Vehicles

The same technique was applied to commercial vehicles new registrations or sales figures. Table 36 shows the results. The long-term trend here is positive for almost all EU member states with the large markets Italy, Spain, France and the UK in lead. A notable downward trend is only recognisable in Poland. Over the shorter four year observation period Italy, the UK and France perform best. Most member states find themselves on a sidewards track. Germany, Spain and Portugal exhibit the strongest downward slope which indicates that their positive long-term trends might come to an end. EU-25 as a whole would loose 24,000 new registrations annually if the short-term trend continues. EU-15, for which a long-term trend is available, adds more than 50,000 new registrations in commercial vehicles a year according to the long-term trend while the short-term trend is negative with almost -10,000 new registrations annually.

Major markets outside should be considered to put the EU numbers into perspective (Table 37). In the USA long-term and short-term growth trends are strong which, again, should be interpreted carefully since a significant number of light trucks in that segment supplants passenger cars instead of going into traditional commercial use. Besides, Canada, Australia, Brazil and Mexico show the best long-term growth trends. On the downside, South Korea and notably Japan are on a highly negative trend. Over the last four years a number of countries has entered a significant positive demand trend for commercial vehicles. On top of the list is China which would, if its four year trend continues, add more than a quarter million commercial vehicles new registrations to its fleet. Excluding the USA, Indonesia, Australia and Thailand are also on strong short-term growth trends. Declining demand for commercial vehicles becomes visible in Turkey and Argentina but foremost Japan where the long-term downward trend appears to have been accelerating in recent years.

As before, the market growth potential can be evaluated best by putting long and short-term trends together.

Fig. 53.   Algebraic signs of short-term and long-term growth trends for commercial vehicles

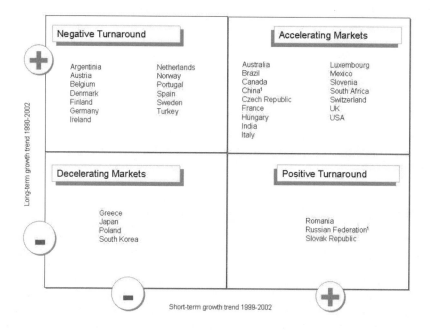

[1] Due to data availability long-term trend was only estimated for 1995-2002.
Source: ZEW.

Demand for commercial vehicles in the EU is on a relatively stable long-term growth trend in most member states. However, some negative short-term country trends indicate that the climax of this growth has been surmounted. Then again, the trend development looks especially promising in the large markets Italy, France and the UK. Outside the EU China exhibits remarkable growth trends, which spearheads other growth markets in the Asian region.

3.3.3   Special Focus on the New Member States

Income levels, the most important indicator for vehicle demand, are relatively low in all NMS. In 2003, GDP/capita (at purchasing power parities) varied from around 40% (the Baltic states and Slovakia) to 75% (Malta, Slovenia) of EU-15 average. Only Cyprus reached 86% and the two South European candidate countries had a GDP/capita of less than 30% of EU-15 average only (see Table 19). But the NMS economies have been growing faster than the OMS for the last couple of years and the catch-up process is expected to continue in the future. Between 1995 and 2003, the Baltic countries showed average annual growth rates of about 5% and in most of the other NMS GDP rose faster than 3% annually.

Table 19. GDP per capita at current PPPs (EUR), from 2004 at constant PPPs

	1990	1995	1999	2000	2001	2002	2003	2004	2005 [1]	2006 [1]	2010 [1]	2015 [1]
Czech Rep.	10,319	11,137	12,701	12,491	13,248	14,063	14,599	15,081	15,684	16,312	19,082	23,216
Hungary	7,797	7,844	10,200	11,032	12,018	12,845	13,404	13,846	14,386	14,962	17,503	21,295
Poland	4,974	6,177	8,405	8,955	9,546	9,901	10,355	10,769	11,200	11,648	13,627	16,579
Slovak Rep.	6,553	7,114	9,161	9,914	10,479	11,329	11,714	12,241	12,853	13,367	15,638	19,026
Slovenia	9,793	10,240	13,494	15,044	15,843	16,597	16,535	17,097	17,696	18,403	21,529	26,194
Estonia	.	5,500	7,515	8,492	9,015	9,661	10,322	10,900	11,456	11,915	13,938	16,958
Latvia	7,815	4,636	6,434	7,138	7,791	8,382	9,325	9,810	10,370	10,784	12,616	15,350
Lithuania	8,059	5,454	7,312	7,959	8,690	9,413	10,287	10,873	11,526	11,987	14,023	17,061
Cyprus	10,173	13,185	15,815	17,192	18,189	18,299	18,749	19,499	20,279	21,090	24,673	30,018
Malta	.	11,134	14,052	15,062	15,123	15,479	15,620	16,244	16,894	17,570	20,554	25,008

European Union (25) average = 100

	1990	1995	1999	2000	2001	2002	2003	2004	2005	2006	2010	2015
Czech Rep.	.	68	66	61	62	64	66	66	68	69	75	82
Hungary	.	48	53	54	57	58	60	61	62	63	69	76
Poland	.	38	43	44	45	45	47	47	48	49	53	59
Slovak Rep.	.	43	47	48	49	52	53	54	56	57	61	67
Slovenia	.	62	70	73	75	76	74	75	76	78	84	93
Estonia	.	33	39	41	42	44	46	48	50	50	55	60
Latvia	.	28	33	35	37	38	42	43	45	46	49	54
Lithuania	.	33	38	39	41	43	46	48	50	51	55	61
Cyprus	.	80	82	84	86	83	84	86	88	89	97	106
Malta	.	68	73	73	71	70	70	72	73	74	80	89

[1] Projection assuming 4% p.a. GDP growth and zero population growth p.a.
Sources: National statistics, Eurostat, wiiw estimates.

For 2004 and 2005, the Vienna Institute for International Economic Studies (wiiw) has forecast annual growth rates between 4%-5% for most of the NMS and even higher rates for the Baltic states (see Table 73). In a longer term perspective until the year 2015, wiiw thus expects some of the NMS to approach EU-average incomes (Cyprus, Malta, Slovenia, Czech Republic) and the others to have reached more than 60% of the average level. Industrial production, as an important determinant for transport services and thus commercial vehicles, is expected to grow even faster than GDP in many countries (see Table 74).

Looking more specific at the development and status quo of vehicle use and motorisation in the NMS, the picture is as follows:

3.3.3.1 Vehicles in Use

As in other countries, passenger cars take the lion's share of all vehicles used in the NMS. Accordingly, in absolute figures, the highest increase of vehicles used in the major NMS[47] between 1995 and 2002 was in this category, rising from 14 million to 19 million, at an average annual rate of about 4%, much faster than in the OMS on average. Although the number of trucks increased from 2.6 million to 4 million only, the relative increase was even faster, reaching nearly 6% p.a., reflecting the higher growth of industrial output than GDP mentioned above. The number of buses stayed nearly constant as an indicator of the poor and deteriorating public transport systems in most NMS, handicapped by the curtailment of public expenditure (see Table 75 and Figure 54).

Fig. 54.   Vehicles in use 1995-2002 (CZ, HU, PL, SK, SL)

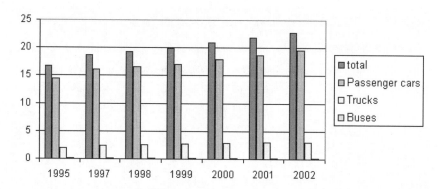

Source; VDA, International Auto Statistics.

Despite the rapid increase of trucks in use, transport in the NMS is still much more relying on railways than in the OMS, pointing to a large potential for further growth in road transport. This is particularly true for the economically less advanced countries, such as the Baltic states but Poland as well. Apart from lower

---

[47]   No comparable data were available for the Baltic states, Malta and Cyprus.

income levels than in the OMS, the low motorway density in the NMS plays a certain role as well. Motorway density is particularly poor in Poland as for instance compared to the Czech Republic and Hungary, but all countries (except Cyprus and Slovenia) compared badly with the EU-15 in 2001[48]. The improvement of the road infra-structure will thus be a great challenge for the future and an important determinant for the development of car use in the NMS.

3.3.3.2 Motorisation Rate

Over the period 1995-2002, the number of passenger cars per 1,000 inhabitants in the NMS increased much faster than in the OMS, but was still significantly below EU-15 average at the end of the period in all countries, except in Slovenia and Malta. This points to a considerable growth potential for passenger cars in the long run. The motorisation rate was between 250 and 350 cars per 1,000 inhabitants in most NMS, compared to about 450 in the EU-15 on average (see Figure 55 and Table 76).

Fig. 55. Passenger cars per 1,000 inhabitants

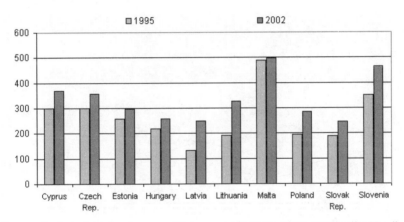

Source: Statistical yearbook on candidate countries, 2000, 2002, 2003; wiiw Handbook of Statistics 2003; VDA.

3.3.3.3 First Registration of Cars

From a longer term point of view, under-motorisation and catching-up of the NMS in terms of per capita GDP suggests a faster growth of car sales in these countries than in the OMS. However, in the shorter run, satisfaction of pent-up demand, business cycle fluctuations and consumer confidence play a significant role as well.

---

[48]   See Eurostat, Statistical Yearbook on Candidate Countries 2003.

As depicted in Figure 56, the number of first registrations does not show a smooth upward trend but relatively strong fluctuations and an explicit downward trend after a certain peak, typically around 1997, in various countries.

Fig. 56.   First registrations of cars

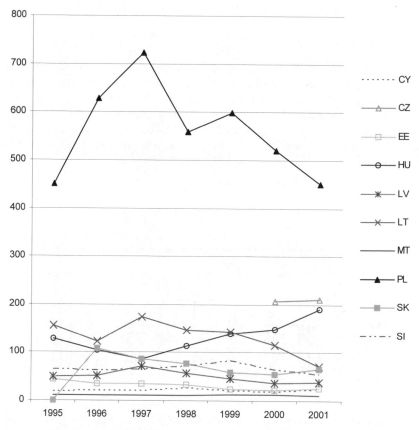

Source: Statistical yearbook on candidate and south-east European countries, yearbook 2000, p.168; Statistical yearbook on candidate countries, 2002 and 2003 edition; pp. 142 and 154.

3.3.4   Conclusion

3.3.4.1 Passenger Cars

The European Union is the major market for passenger cars in the world. The car fondness of its citizens seems to go beyond simple practical value in use. This turns into an important home market advantage since European customers are loyal to their home brands or alternative European brands. This fact ensures that

European producers primarily benefit from the leverage of the huge market in terms of economies of scale and scope. Besides, it allows European manufacturers to gain the necessary critical mass audience for the new products early and benefit from the feedback of a large sophisticated customer base.

In terms of market growth, though, Europe has apparently reached a growth plateau in unit terms. New car registrations increase much stronger in other world regions. This should not come as a surprise on a relatively established and ripe European market.

The feedback from sophisticated users in their home market in combination with the easy access to customer and market information through superior customer loyalty has given European brands already an edge in the premium segment of the important US market. This advantage is stable and can hardly be copied by competitors from abroad. Therefore, it should open up more sales opportunities abroad.

European customers are attracted to new cars if the environment is right. Short-term trends indicate that the economic downturn translates into declining markets. Still, the example of the remarkable growth of the British market – where according to industry experts a backlog in demand in combination with promising macroeconomic trends triggered the current car boom – shows that customers are ready and willing to invest into new cars under more promising economic conditions.

3.3.4.2 Commercial Vehicles

In the commercial vehicle segment Europe also has a strong position when it comes to market size. The tonnage bulk of Europe's road transportation is conducted over shorter distances, which indicates that feedback for vehicle producers from this market segment should be especially accentuated and hence valuable. Growth trends of new registrations of commercial vehicles in Europe have been modest. However, in terms of growth EU markets can hardly compete with the dynamics on major Asian markets.

The European transport system relies heavily on the road as its backbone and therefore ensures stable demand for commercial vehicles. The reliance on road transportation is deeply entrenched in the European transport configuration and only massive interventions could disturb this relationship in the foreseeable future. Hence, alternative modes of transportation that would supplant road freight transportation and consequently the demand for commercial vehicles face enormous barriers to entry.

The commercial vehicles segment, too, has felt the fallout from the economic downturn in major European markets. Therefore, short-term growth trends are negative. A continuing weakness in economic development in Europe would certainly shrink the market even further.

4 Innovation and Competitiveness

Thomas Cleff, Georg Licht, Alfred Spielkamp, and Waltraud Urban

The ability of firms to compete in foreign and home markets crucially depends on innovative products which can be produced and sold at attractive prices. In the short run productivity and labour costs are important drivers of competitiveness. In the long run the ability of firms to innovate and invest in R&D and innovation are crucial determinants of competitiveness. Hence, this section looks at these factors driving competitiveness more closely. The analysis looks at the position of EU member states relative to the most important car producing countries. Hence, our approach focuses on countries and not firms. So, data and interpretations might differ from a company based view which looks at the company or brand no matter where the production takes place. The approach rests on the international comparison of both, levels (e.g. the labour cost comparison) and trends of different factors fostering competitiveness.

(EU)

4.1 Labour Costs, Labour Productivity and Unit Labour Costs

J24 J31 L22
L62 O32 O34

4.1.1 Data

Data presented in this section mainly rests on the Groningen Industry Labour Productivity Database (ILPD) described in detail in O'Mahony and van Ark (Eds.) (2003). This database is updated – where necessary – for the years 2000-2001 using the most recent version of the OECD/STAN database (web-version March 2004) from which the main parts of ILPD are derived. Data for Japan and Korea are directly taken from STAN. In addition, the database is augmented with estimates for average working hours per person employed for Japan and Korea from national sources. Also, value added deflators – not contained in STAN – are updated for some countries (e.g. Portugal) for the period 1996-2001 using a mixture of national sources and aggregated sector level information (e.g. transport equipment). When possible the database is enlarged by data on the value of shipments and intermediate products in order to allow unit labour cost comparisons.

International comparisons of productivity levels crucially rest on an appropriate conversion of national currencies into a common currency. The preferable option is to use industry-specific conversion factors (industry PPPs) which take into account international differences in product specific taxes, specific production levies, and more importantly differences in the prices in the countries at hand. Price differences mainly rest on car quality differences, international differences in brand reputation but also pricing strategies.

However, we do not follow van Ark/O'Mahony in two important dimensions. We develop different conversion factors for the conversion of national currencies into USD. In addition, we use these conversion factors to derive EU-15 aggregates instead of using a national currency per euro conversion based on exchange rates.

Industry PPPs have been developed for the automotive industry by Baily and Gersbach (1995) for Japan, the US and Germany (see also MGI, 1993, for details). Their analyses point towards an industry PPP for the German automotive sector of 2.22 DM/USD (~1.13 EUR/USD) and for the Japanese car production of around 150 Yen/USD for the year 1990.[49] In a study of productivity of the automotive sector of France and Germany MGI (McKinsey Global Institute, 2002) report an industry PPP for final car production of 0.962 EUR/USD for cars produced in Germany for 1999. More recently, O'Mahony and van Ark (Eds.) (2003) published sectoral industry PPPs for the EU vs. the US. Referring to the study of van Mulligen (2003) they use a value for the EUR/USD relation of 1.47 for German and US cars for 1997. Van Mulligen derive industry PPPs based on hedonic regressions in various EU countries, the US and Japan. A closer inspection of the estimates and comparison with other studies using hedonic techniques for quality-adjusted car prices[50] makes us suppose that these estimates are severely upward biased with respect to the quality of US cars leading to quite unreliable industry PPPs.[51]

---

[49]   Estimates of industry PPP are especially troublesome for industries with heterogeneous products. In addition, the automotive industry not only consists of heterogeneous final products but also includes a wide variety of intermediate products making international price comparisons in this industry much more burdensome and imprecise than price comparisons for manufacturing as a whole. See van Ark and Timmer (2002) for more details involved in the calculation of industry PPPs.

[50]   For an explanation of hedonic techniques see e.g. Triplett (1987, 2002). References for hedonic prices for car industries can be found in van Mulligan (2003).

[51]   This assessment is based on the following arguments: Reliable hedonic prices crucially depend on detailed information on quality characteristics of goods at hand and on a correct specification of the functional form of the underlying regression. Van Mulligen's estimates only rely on engine power and car size. Moch et al. (2002) show for the car market in Germany that engine power and engine size should enter the regression model in a non-linear form when car quality is controlled for by these variables only. The non-linearity implies decreasing elasticities for these two quality characteristics. Neglecting this non-linearity as it is done by van Mulligen leads to an overestimation of quality adjusted prices for cars with high-powered engines and large-sized cars. As US produced cars are typically larger (about 10% compared to Germany) and have more horse power (about 50%) resulting industry PPPs for the EU/US comparison are severely overestimated (as also shown by e.g. Moch et al. (2002) for Germany, Bode and van Dalen (2001) for the Netherlands (see also section 4.3.3). Van Mulligen's results suffer from omitted variable biases and a wrong specification of the functional form. Adding more quality characteristics (like ABS, engine type) to the hedonic regression model typically leads to a significant drop in the estimated impact of engine power and car size on quality adjusted prices. In addition, new car quality characteristics are often introduced earlier in Japanese and EU cars.

In addition, although these studies refer to different years it's not clear how to reconcile traditional industry PPPs estimates and hedonic estimates. Comparing price differentials of some selected cars (e.g. Mercedes Benz S-Class, BMW 5 series) in US and Germany we find a 50% difference of car quality in Germany and US quite unrealistic and hence base our estimates on MGI type of industry PPPs.[52] This also enables us to use comparable estimates for industry PPPs for the Japanese and Korean automotive sector derived also by MGI in another study (MGI, 1998).

To derive industry PPPs for all EU-15 member states we follow O'Mahony and van Ark (2003)[53] and use their benchmark values for the year 1997 to determine industry PPPs for European countries relative to Germany. Then we take the industry PPP for the German-US comparison to derive industry PPPs for conversion of national currency values to USD dollar for EU member states. An industry PPP for 1997 for DM/USD is gained by interpolation of the values found in the 1993 MGI study (referring to the year 1990) and the 2002 study (referring to 1999).

In addition, taking a closer look at productivity levels over time calls for the extension of PPP values of the benchmark year 1997 to other years. Such an extension becomes all the more problematic the longer the time period between the benchmarking year and the year for which the extension is performed because consumers will adjust the demanded bundle of goods due to the changes of relative prices. As a consequence the bundle of goods sold/produced in the base year may no longer be valid in other years. Hence, the industry PPP will change not only due to the changes in the relative prices but also because of shifts in the bundle of goods used for weighting. Despite this caveat we adjust industry PPPs derived for benchmark years by multiplying industry PPPs by the relation of indices of the value added deflators between the country at hand and the US (after rebasing the value added deflator in 1997 to 1).

For testing the robustness of results we use three different conversion factors in our analyses. Here we follow van Ark (2002) who suggests to use both expenditure PPPs and industry PPPs to test for the sensitivity of results. Hence, we present two approaches:
1. Automotive industry PPPs as described above. We also use here the term automotive unit values in the Table 57.
2. Expenditure PPPs for GDP as published by the OECD and Eurostat. When referring to this concept we use the abbreviation PPP.

These new characteristics often become cheaper in later phases (see Moch et al., 2002). Thus, EU and Japanese cars might even have an "unmeasured quality" surplus against US cars (weighted by production shares). In conclusion, an EUR /USD industry PPP for Germany/US car production of 1.47 EUR /USD rests on a mis-specified regression model. An industry PPP of around 1 EUR /USD seems much more realistic.

[52]   This corresponds to a matched-model approach traditionally used in official statistics including an ad-hoc, expert based correction on quality differences.

[53]   Industry PPPs between EU countries and Germany are based on a matched-model type of approach (see Inklar et al., 2003).

Consequently, international productivity level comparisons should be interpreted with care. Indicators derived from the described database sometimes still show problems in international comparisons of productivity and labour cost levels for some years. These cases are marked in the tables where appropriate.

Data for the new member states differ due to data availability from the concepts described above. Three important differences should be kept in mind: (1) Value added in constant prices is not available for the new member states. Hence, we have to rely on production (value added + intermediate inputs) as an indicator of automotive industry output when calculating labour productivity. (2) Average annual working hours per employee at the level of NACE 34 (automotive industry) is also not available for the majority of new member states. (3) No estimates for unit values (or industry PPPs) are available for the automotive production and automotive value added. To overcome this lack of data we use as a proxy for automotive industry unit values the expenditure PPP for the capital goods. In addition, expenditure PPPs at the GDP level and capital goods expenditure PPPs are available for new member states for the year 1999 only. We use the 1999 values for the time period 1997-2001 and omit adjusting these values because of the short time period involved. Because such types of currency conversion factors change only gradually from year to year this will involve only a minor problem. The data for automotive industry in new member states stems from the WIIW sectoral database.

4.1.2   Labour Costs

Low production costs are one of the main sources of international competitiveness of an industry. High-cost countries can only compete against low-cost countries if their products are of superior quality. Given the increased openness and the increasing global presence of suppliers standardised intermediate products will be increasingly similar in price. Likewise, the international presence of major manufacturers and large scale suppliers will tend to equalise the costs of capital. Hence, international differences in labour costs are a major source of differences in production costs. In order to compare the level of labour costs one has to convert all data into the same currency. Exchange rates will do the job. But given the large fluctuations of currency exchange rates international labour cost comparison might give a misleading picture on structural differences when looking at a certain year. Hence, we used the purchasing power parity rates calculated by the OECD to convert national currency to dollar. Said simply, the PPP values are based on a bundle of goods contained in the GDP indicating the costs to the consumers of buying these bundles in different countries using the national currency. So, the following comparison of labour costs should be viewed from the perspective of the worker who earns the wages. However, instead of looking simply at wages our comparison also includes other elements of labour costs besides wages and salaries (e.g. employer's contribution to social security).

The following table gives the total labour compensation per hour in USD. In the short run, swings in exchange rates might also affect the ability of a country to sell products on the international markets. Hence, we also give information for the dollar values of labour compensation based on exchange rates.[54] The data refer to the year 2001 which is the most recent year available. In addition, to highlight the development of labour costs we include the years 1995 and 1990 in the table. The comparison over time also allows inferring the trend in labour costs in the EU-15 countries and the most important competitors in international car markets. It also highlights the differential impact of exchange rate fluctuations on international competitiveness in labour costs.

Table 20. International comparison of hourly labour costs in automotive industry

	Conversion to USD based on PPPs			Conversion to USD based on exchange rates		
	1990	1995	2001	1990	1995	2001
Korea	5.4	8.4	12.9	4.3	8.0	7.3
Japan	17.8	24.1	29.0	24.0	43.5	35.7
USA	25.4	34.3	33.8	25.4	34.3	33.8
EU-15	19.1	26.3	32.7	23.1	31.6	25.7
Austria	13.4	21.0	23.8	16.6	28.6	19.7
Belgium	20.7	27.9	31.5	24.4	34.7	25.2
Denmark	12.8	17.0	21.4	26.4	40.8	31.5
Finland	12.5	18.3	21.0	19.4	25.5	21.7
France	17.4	22.2	25.6	19.2	19.0	15.8
Germany	20.5	29.0	36.8	20.8	24.5	18.6
Greece	7.4	10.6	12.2	21.1	28.7	21.1
Ireland	9.5	13.1	17.5	6.5	9.3	8.0
Italy	17.0	21.4	23.9	10.9	13.3	15.6
Luxembourg	13.0	14.8	19.2	20.2	20.4	17.2
Netherlands	13.2	17.2	24.1	15.5	19.5	17.2
Portugal	8.1	14.7	18.3	15.7	21.8	19.7
Spain	17.9	19.4	23.3	5.9	11.7	11.1
Sweden	15.8	18.5	19.4	24.9	25.3	18.3
UK	17.9	22.3	26.2	19.2	23.0	24.2

Source: see text.

The most impressive result of this comparison is that EU-15 automotive indus-try has caught up with the US in terms of hourly labour compensation (based on PPP values). Now, the three most important production regions for automotive products (Japan, US, EU) are more similar with regard to labour cost than ever. One also should note that labour costs per hour in the US even in current values have stagnated in the last ten years. Hence, a positive impact on price competi-tiveness results from this development. When we convert currencies by relying on the exchange rate we arrive at a somewhat different picture. Due to the high valua-

---

[54]   Average yearly exchange rates and PPP values are based on OECD data and are taken directly from MSTI 2003-2.

tion of the USD in 2001 we see declining nominal labour costs in the EU and also Japan. This also makes clear the price competitiveness of the automotive industry is crucially influenced by exchange rate. In addition, we can conclude that in the current situation with a high valuation of the euro the labour cost position of the EU as location for automotive production is under stress. Having said this it is also quite obvious that automotive producers try to absorb the impact of exchange rate fluctuations also by the international distribution of production locations and internationalisation of the supply chain.

However, there are striking differences within Europe.[55] Germany is the most expensive country for automotive labour with labour costs per hour worked in the German automotive industry that are 8% above the US level in 2001. On the other hand, labour compensation per hour worked is below US and Japan in all other member states. E.g. labour costs in Portugal amount to only 54% of the US level. The high labour costs in Germany endanger the competitiveness at least if high labour costs are not matched with an above average labour productivity. In addition, given the currently low value of the USD labour costs in the EU are above US labour costs in a short run perspective. This currently puts the EU at a severe cost disadvantage against the US putting the cost competitiveness of EU produced cars against the US locations under pressure.[56]

Looking at the changes in labour cost in the 1990s Table 20 also makes clear that a significant cost advantage of Europe against the US diminished in the last decade. The catch-up in labour cost not only occurred in the high wage EU countries but even more in the low wage countries. As a rule hourly labour costs in low-cost countries show even a steeper increase there, than in the high cost countries (see e.g. Portugal or Greece). In the last decade differences in labour cost decreased within EU-15 and the wage increases become more and more uniform more recently.

Seen from the perspective of price competitiveness the change in labour costs relative to the increase in the product price is the more relevant indicator because it allows some conclusion whether – ceteris paribus – the industry is able to pass increased labour costs on to the customers. The growth of real product labour costs per hour is shown in Table 21. Ceteris paribus increasing price competitiveness is associated with negative values of this indicator. In addition, the table shows the difference between average annual compound growth rates of hourly labour productivity and hourly labour costs. Here, a positive value indicates that the increase in labour costs is overcompensated by the growth of labour productivity.

---

[55]   Labour cost differences also reflect differences in skill composition of the labour force and also the composition of the automotive industry. Typically, labour costs per hour worked is lower in the automotive parts (suppliers) industry than in car assembly.

[56]   Using the average EUR/USD exchange rate for 2001 labour costs in EU-15 amount to 76% of the US level. The average EUR /USD exchange rate in 2001 was about 1.12, the PPP value 0.88 EUR /USD.

Table 21. Average annual compound growth rates of real product hourly labour costs (%) and growth rate differentials between labour productivity per hour and hourly labour cost (%) in automotive industry

	Growth of real product hourly labour costs			Difference between growth rates of value added per hour and hourly labour costs		
	1981-1990	1991-1995	1996-2001	1981-1990	1991-1995	1996-2001
Korea	13.6	12.1	3.2	-1.4	-2.4	1.6
Japan	4.5	5.0	1.4	-1.0	-2.9	1.3
USA	-0.5	-0.6	-1.5	1.3	4.4	2.8
EU-15	2.8	2.8	1.7	1.7	0.5	-1.3
Austria	1.2	6.6	-2.1	-2.0	2.8	3.4
Belgium	2.5	2.0	4.8	2.7	1.7	-0.7
Denmark	-0.3	1.5	3.0	3.0	-4.9	2.0
Finland	1.9	4.8	3.8	1.5	-3.3	0.0
France	0.2	4.2	3.4	4.5	-0.4	5.7
Germany	1.4	3.1	0.1	0.8	-0.1	-1.0
Greece	0.2	7.5	5.8	-5.8	-1.5	2.9
Ireland	0.3	1.7	3.3	4.3	0.5	-5.4
Italy	5.2	2.2	0.0	1.5	-0.9	1.0
Luxembourg	3.1	-2.6	2.6	2.5	-4.4	-2.9
Netherlands	1.5	5.6	5.3	1.9	0.2	0.0
Portugal	0.8	3.3	1.9	0.9	5.3	6.6
Spain	4.5	-3.3	2.0	2.2	7.0	-2.1
Sweden	0.1	4.9	3.1	1.3	4.4	0.6
UK	3.1	4.0	2.4	3.1	-0.6	-0.8

Source: see text.

A look at the real product labour costs growth rates[57] reveals that the international ranking of countries in terms of average hourly earnings is only partly influenced by the labour cost increases in the country itself. E.g. in the German case the rate of increase of real product labour costs was quite low compared to other countries in the second half of the 1990s. However, due to an increasing purchasing power of the national currency German's labour cost disadvantage even increased further. Moreover, labour cost growth in Germany was larger in the last period than labour productivity increase. Both implies that Germany's price competitiveness in the automotive industry is under pressure. On the other hand French automotive industry significantly improved price competitiveness since 1996. This increase also overcompensates with regard to price competitiveness the increase in labour costs.

---

[57] Real product labour costs are defined as hourly labour compensation deflated by the country specific value added price index. The change in real product labour costs is equal to the change of value added based unit labour costs which refers to total labour costs divided by value added.

In EU-15 countries the growth of hourly labour costs regularly exceeds the growth of value added deflator whereas in the US the reverse is true. Taken together, labour cost development in the US strengthened the price competitiveness of the USA against Japan as well as against the EU. The position of the EU-15 with regard to price competitiveness strongly increased in the 1980s against the major other car producing countries. The first half of the 1990s shows a further positive development compared to Japan and Korea. In the last period (since 1996) EU is loosing against all other countries. The development within the EU was quite heterogeneous. Some countries improved their price competitiveness even further whereas others show a significant decline. As a consequence automotive industries in the latter countries are forced to reduce labour costs by increased international outsourcing of part of the value chain to other EU countries and in the last year to the new member states.

Unit labour costs relate labour costs to the value of production. Unit labour costs crucially depend on the composition of automotive industry. Usually, unit labour costs are larger in the supplier industry than in car assembly. Unit labour costs are also affected by the degree of outsourcing. So, labour costs are only one determinant of unit labour costs. In addition, unit labour costs also mirror the reaction of an industry to high wages e.g. via outsourcing. The table below show a wide variation of unit labour costs between countries. Unit labour cost is traditionally low in France. Low unit labour costs are also present in Korea, Ireland, Netherlands, Belgium and Spain. However, the reason behind these values is quite different. In the Belgium case unit labour costs are low despite high labour cost per hour because of a high labour productivity and an above average use of intermediate inputs from outside automotive industry. In the Netherlands, France, and Spain relatively high labour productivity helps to keep unit labour costs below average. Germany faces a strong decline in unit labour costs. This decline is mainly caused by increased outsourcing. This interpretation rests on the fact that the share of labour costs in value added has increased and intermediate inputs increase as well.

Unit labour costs strongly depend on the sectoral composition of the automotive industry. As a rule unit labour costs (based on gross production) are lower in car assembly than in manufacturing of car parts. Hence, the numbers given in Table 22 crucially depend on the share of assembly plants in total output of the automotive sector in a country. This notion is based on the different importance of intermediate inputs in different sub-sectors of the automotive industry. The decreasing trend in unit labour costs based on gross production is mainly due to increased outsourcing in automotive industry.

Hence, one can look at the ratio of total labour costs to value added. This ratio gives an impression about the relation of labour costs on the one hand and capital costs and capital enumeration on the other. Table 22 shows no clear trend. One can observe quite different developments within EU countries. In some countries the share of labour costs is increasing whereas in others it is decreasing. However,

Table 22. Unit labour costs in the automotive industry

	Total labour costs per gross production (%)			Total labour costs per value added (%)		
	1990	1995	2001	1990	1995	2001
Korea	14.4	16.7	12.2**	41.0	46.2	42.1
Japan	12.9	15.2	15.1*	52.0	60.2	55.6
USA	19.0	21.1	18.7	88.1	70.7	59.7
EU-15	n/a	n/a	n/a	75.0	73.2	78.9
Austria	20.8	18.1	15.9	74.6	64.9	53.1
Belgium	n/a	13.4	12.5*	76.3	70.1	73.2
Denmark	21.2	28.3	26.5	56.2	71.9	63.7
Finland	21.6	28.0	28.6	64.5	76.2	76.2
France	14.9	14.2	10.0	63.8	65.2	46.4
Germany	26.3	25.6	21.7	74.8	75.3	79.7
Greece	n/a	27.5	25.8	94.6	102.1	86.0
Ireland	19.6	17.5	14.1	98.0	95.3	n/a
Italy	n/a	n/a	n/a	70.9	74.1	69.6
Luxembourg	n/a	n/a	n/a	58.3	72.8	86.5
Netherlands	14.8	14.7	13.7*	74.9	74.0	73.9
Portugal	n/a	n/a	n/a	98.5	75.5	50.8
Spain	22.9	14.9	13.5*	88.9	62.6	70.9
Sweden	21.1	15.9	n/a	73.7	59.2	56.9
UK	24.0	21.8	20.1*	75.2	77.6	81.5

* 2000; ** based on employees only.
Source: OECD/STAN Database, Internet Version March 2004.

there are some remarkable international differences between the EU, Japan, USA and Korea. In the US automotive industry value added based unit labour costs are declining in the 1990s and are now significantly smaller than in the EU. Also, Japan and even more so Korea has much smaller shares of total labour costs in value added than the EU-15 average. While some EU-15 countries are on the same level as the US and Japan some others are far above. This again confirms that the EU position on labour cost competitiveness is under stress. [58] One of the most important factors causing high labour costs per hour in the EU is the low range of effective working hours per employee in automotive industry.

Different trends prevail in the last decade in the major automotive producing regions. Most remarkably, average yearly working hours in the USA increased by about 1% p.a. in the last 15 years. In Japan, Korea and EU-15 we can observe a downward trend in annual working hours in the last two decades amounting to about -0.5% per year. As a result we see large differences in the average yearly working time in automotive industry. As shown in Table 22, Japan and the US

[58]   Unit labour costs not only depend on labour enumeration. Also, production technology plays a crucial role here. Firms can react to high wages by substituting labour inputs by capital inputs and hence reducing unit labour costs.

Table 23. Average yearly working hours in the automotive industry by country

	Hours worked per employee per year relative to US US = 100					Average working hours per year per employee
	1981	1985	1991	1995	2001	2001
Korea	140.8	130.0	129.8	121.7	121.1	2,460
Japan	114.8	112.3	115.6	98.4	99.6	2,023
USA	100.0	100.0	100.0	100.0	100.0	2,032
EU-15	90.9	84.0	84.6	79.7	77.9	1,583
Austria	97.6	91.1	92.9	81.5	80.0	1,626
Belgium	92.5	86.1	87.7	80.2	77.2	1,569
Germany	82.5	78.5	78.0	73.8	71.2	1,447
Denmark	92.1	85.0	84.8	80.7	79.2	1,609
Spain	102.8	92.3	94.2	88.6	89.3	1,815
Finland	90.0	86.3	84.4	76.9	80.8	1,641
France	101.1	87.3	84.6	79.1	77.4	1,572
Greece	104.4	96.8	98.7	93.9	94.9	1,929
Ireland	103.7	94.8	99.2	89.6	82.8	1,682
Italy	87.4	80.7	84.2	77.8	80.3	1,631
Luxembourg	89.6	82.1	84.6	76.5	76.8	1,560
Netherlands	92.1	84.3	93.9	77.9	76.4	1,552
Portugal	100.1	93.1	97.2	89.0	84.4	1,714
Sweden	77.6	75.0	79.1	83.1	83.5	1,697
UK	96.7	94.3	98.0	91.5	88.9	1,806

Source: US and EU-15 based on Groningen Growth Centre Industry Data Base (van Ark/Mahony CD ROM) which is derived from OECD/STAN. (For some countries van Ark and Mahony use hours worked per employee in the transport sector as an approximation for automotive sector. The levels were checked with national sources available for some countries. It turns out that the approximation of hours worked in the automotive sector by hours worked per employee in the transport sector is fairly reliable).
Korea: OECD/STAN + Employment Outlook (cross-checked with ILO data): The trend development is based on STAN; however the level in 2001 (and hence for the rest of the period) is adjusted based on employment outlook data. (STAN data contains information on manufacturing only. No separated data on hours worked per employee are available for the automotive industry.)
Japan: OECD/STAN. In this case STAN gives data at the level of the transport sector (automotive and other transport equipment). Therefore, data are crosschecked and some minor adjustments are made based on data from the Japanese ministry of health, labour and welfare which refers to the automotive sector only.

show a quite similar yearly working time amounting to around 2,000 hours per employee. Despite some recent shortening of working time, Korean automotive industry still shows the longest working time. The EU-15 reaches only about 75% of the US labour time. Again, there are significant differences within the EU.

German workers face the lowest working hours amounting to only 70% of the US level. The strongest decline in working time in the last two decades can be observed in France where the annual working time declines by about 1.1% annually. However, in some EU-15 member states the downward trend to shorter working time stopped in the last 10 years. Some countries like Spain, Finland, Italy and Greece even follow the US trend of increased working time.

4.1.3   Labour Productivity[59]

Labour costs are only one side of the coin. If high labour costs are met by high labour productivity no negative impact may occur. Hence, we look more closely at labour productivity as an factor determining competitiveness. According to O'Mahony and van Ark (2003),[60] European productivity growth in manufacturing has fallen behind growth rates in the United States in the second half of the 1990s. However, the authors argue that an in-depth analysis should be carried out for individual industries. They also report significant differences with regard to individual industries. Similar to O'Mahony/van Ark, we find that labour productivity measured as current value added per employee in the EU-15 currently lags behind the USA and Japan.

The EU-15 automotive industry shows a significant labour productivity[61] gap compared to the US and Japan. However, the EU-15 automotive industry exhibited higher cumulative growth rates in labour productivity during the 1990s than both the USA and Japan when we look at labour productivity in USD converted via automotive unit values. But — as shown by the following table — the catching-up process proceeds only gradually. Looking at the case where automotive unit value ratios (UVR) are used to convert national currencies to USD we find that the Japanese automotive industry is losing its competitive edge compared to the US. Not surprisingly, we find a steep increase in the labour productivity in Korea. However, there is still a considerable productivity gap between Korea and the other leading automotive producing regions.

The table shows that the picture of international productivity trends strongly depends on the way we convert national currencies to USD taking into account the trends in automotive prices. For example based on automotive unit values Japan is losing its leading position in labour productivity in the automotive industry. When we convert Yen to USD using purchasing power parities we find a lower labour productivity level in Japan in the 1980s and a catching-up process with the US later. These different trends in the Japanese-US comparison rest on an increasing

---

[59]   We omit multi-factor productivity for two reasons: Data are only available for some EU countries. International productivity differences as well as productivity growth differentials in the automotive sector result mainly from the labour productivity part (see e.g. MGI, 2002, 2003).

[60]   See O'Mahony and van Ark (Eds.) (2003).

[61]   Labour productivity is defined here as value added per hour worked.

trend in the Yen/USD relation in the automotive unit value ratio and a decreasing trend in the Yen/USD relation in PPP conversion factors.

Table 24. Labour productivity in automotive industry relative to the US level (US=100)

| | Based on automotive unit values | | | Based on PPPs | | |
	1990	1995	2001	1990	1995	2001
EU-15	59.6	65.9	75.2	71.7	69.0	75.3
Korea	19.4	32.3	33.7	36.4	37.6	46.0
Japan	131.8	110.8	108.8	78.4	82.4	101.7
USA	100.0	100.0	100.0	100.0	100.0	100.0

Source: See text.

Fig. 57.   Labour productivity of EU-15 member states relative to EU-15 average 2001

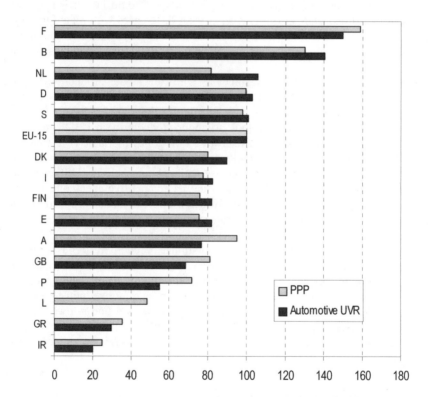

Source: See text.

Within Europe, the picture is mixed with France showing high productivity growth rates, while Germany had a disappointing negative performance, albeit coming from a high level. Recently, France is leading in labour productivity not only in Europe but even with regard to Japan and US. This position is based on a variety of reasons. Leading French manufacturers produce more standardised cars than the German industry which increasingly pins its hope on product differentiation and offers a highly diverse set of cars. The French strategy makes it easier to exploit economies of scale. Also, French industry seems to have some strategic advantage with regard to the implementation of the outsourcing process with a more efficient way of managing outsourcing processes at the level of final producers (see MGI 2002). In addition, privatisation of Renault seems to stimulate productivity development in the French automotive industry. However, we should also note that German automotive industry invests heavily in R&D in the late 1990s whereas the R&D investment of the French automotive industry is comparably more modest. In the short run R&D investment hampers labour productivity growth because the returns to R&D lag R&D investment. In order to economise on the huge R&D investment the German automotive industry has to realise a more rapid productivity growth in the near future. However, it is still unclear whether the R&D-prone strategy of the German automotive industry will be successful. A recent study of MGI (2002) argues that there is significant potential in German automotive industry to increase the efficiency of R&D investment.

Figure 57 shows the ranking of EU-15 countries with regard to labour productivity in the automotive industry in the year 2001. France and Belgium show a significant lead. Belgian, Dutch and German automotive sectors are slightly above EU-15 average. Greece and Ireland show the lowest labour productivity.

Some more insight can be gained when looking at the development of trend values of labour productivity as well as the trends in labour productivity growth. Here we employ a Hodrick-Prescott filter to eliminate cyclical, short-term variation. The results are depicted in Figures 58 and 59.

The basic messages of these figures are:

- The speed of the catching-up process of EU-15 against the US and Japan is slow. This is especially true against the US since 1995. More recently, the catching-up process of EU-15 against Japan nearly came to a standstill. It can be supposed that this slowdown in catching-up should be attributed to the sluggish European car market in the 1990s.
- The most remarkable development in labour productivity in EU-15 is the French productivity miracle which takes place in the 1990s. However, since the end of the 1990s the trend productivity growth in France is declining and the German trend productivity growth rates are revitalised.
- Similar to France, we can observe an extremely positive development of labour productivity in the Dutch, Belgian, Austrian and Swedish automotive industries. However, productivity advance has lost momentum in recent years in these countries.
- Labour productivity developments in smaller automotive producing countries are more volatile than in countries with a significant automotive industry.

Fig. 58.   Trend labour productivity by country 1981-2001 (USD; automotive UVR)

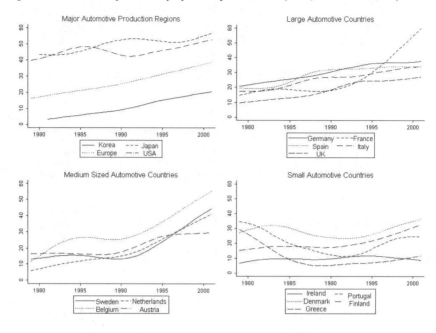

Fig. 59.   Trend labour productivity growth by country 1981-2001

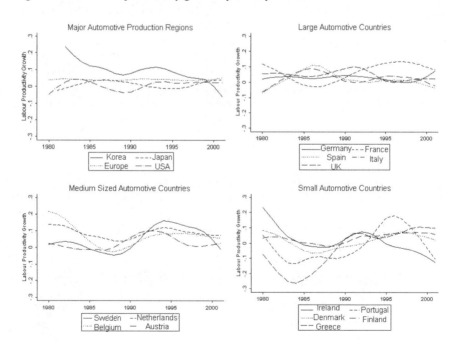

4.1.4   Special Focus on the New Member States

4.1.4.1 Employment

The role of the automotive industry as an employer is generally less prominent than as a producer, due to the capital-intensive character of the industry. However, in the NMS this difference is extreme. The difference is most prominent in Slovakia, with a production share of 17.2% and an employment share of 4.8%, pointing to a relatively high labour productivity (and capital intensity) in the Slovak automotive industry. This phenomenon is the consequence of a dramatic decline and labour shedding in the automotive industry during the first years of transition[62] and the emergence of a completely new industry, based on foreign direct investment thereafter. In most cases, the new owners either took over companies which had reached a low employment level already or set up new factories where they could make their employment decisions freely without bothering about existing staff and trade unions – at the same time having at their disposal a large skilled labour force, particularly in the field of engineering. Nevertheless, the automotive industry is one of the very few manufacturing industries in the NMS, where the number of employees has increased after 1995 (see Table 66), although limited to the countries with the fastest output growth (Czech Republic, Hungary and Slovak Republic) and to the production of bodies for motor vehicles (NACE 34.2) and parts and accessories (NACE 34.3).

4.1.4.2 Labour Productivity

Labour productivity, defined as gross output per employee (OUT/EMP) in the automotive industry,[63] is very high in the NMS compared to the manufacturing industry on average, due to the large amount of foreign direct investment and technology transfer as well as a relatively small number of persons employed. In Slovakia, the automotive industry reached 471% of the productivity level of the manufacturing industry on average. For the other big vehicle producers in the NMS, this ratio came up to 222% in the Czech Republic, 325% in Hungary and 187% in Poland in the year 2001 (see Table 67 and Table 68). Slovenia, which classifies as a small producer, but with a relatively high specialisation in the auto-

---

[62]   Firstly, the car industry was underdeveloped in all demand economies as the emphasis was placed on mass transportation. Secondly, existing products were not internationally competitive and faced a severe blow due to the economies' opening-up. Altogether, the transport equipment industry and vehicle production in particular were among the big losers of the transformational recession, with a worse development than average manufacturing in all transition countries (see Hanzl, 1999 and Urban, 1999).

[63]   Due to data availability we are forced to work with a different definition of labour productivity for the new member states. As mentioned above now data are available for value added at constant prices, working hours and automotive industry specific conversion rates for national currencies into euro.

motive industry, shows a very high productivity relative to total manufacturing, too (319%). In fact, the productivity lead of the automotive industry is far larger in the NMS than in the OMS where the industry reaches around 150% of manufacturing productivity on average only – although France and Spain, for instance, were showing a significantly higher margin of 195% in 2000.

Nevertheless, because of the much lower overall level of productivity in the NMS, productivity in the automotive industry is still lower than in the OMS in most countries – although to a far lesser extent than in most other industries.

Fig. 60.   Index of employment in the automotive industry (NACE 34) in the NMS (I)

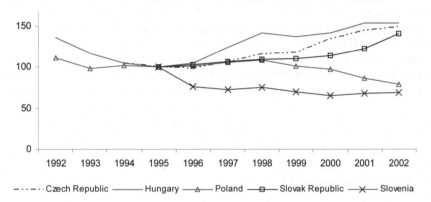

Source: wiiw Industrial Database; Panorama of Czech Industries, Eurostat, New Cronos, SBS; 1995=100.

Fig. 61.   Index of employment in the automotive industry (NACE 34) in the NMS (II)

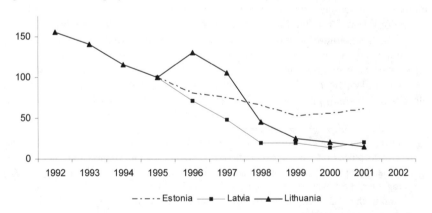

Source: wiiw Industrial Database; Panorama of Czech Industries, Eurostat, New Cronos, SBS; 1995=100.

However, the exact size of this productivity gap is difficult to measure, as for cross-country comparisons output data in national currency have to be converted to a common currency, the result of which should reflect the real value of production in the countries compared. The use of market exchange rates is not appropriate for this purpose, in particular not for the NMS with their currencies still undervalued and exchange rates fluctuating strongly. As an alternative, we may use purchasing power standards (PPS), taking account of the relative price levels in the countries. However, PPS are comparing prices for different 'baskets' of goods, such as consumer goods, investment goods or the GDP as a whole, but in order to compare (real) output levels in the automotive industry properly, information on relative prices in this specific industry is needed. Unfortunately, so-called (industry-specific) *unit value ratios* (UVRs), which compare prices of representative industrial products in different countries, are only available for a few NMS and for selected years in the past[64]. We therefore had to resort to the 'second best' method, using purchasing power standards. In order to allow for a broader range of prices, we have taken two different kinds of PPPs for conversion. Thus, our first data set for labour productivity in Table 67 results from national productivity figures converted with 1999 standard purchasing power parity factors for the *whole gross domestic product* (PPP99), and the second data set in Table 68 uses purchasing power standards (PPS) for *gross fixed capital formation* (PPPCAP99) instead. The latter estimates for productivity are lower, because prices for investment goods in the NMS are higher in relative terms (excluding services but comprising a higher share of imports). For the rare cases, where UVRs were available for comparison, they showed a closer correspondence to the latter measure and thus productivity levels expressed at PPPCAP99 are probably closer to reality. Hence, we use both measures here.[65]

According to our estimates, labour productivity in the automotive industry ranked highest in the Slovak Republic and Hungary, probably even surpassing the average productivity level of the automotive industry in the EU-15, followed by Slovenia, the Czech Republic and Poland, reaching between 58% and 97% (at PPP99 conversion rates) and 43%-83% (PPPCAP99) of the respective EU-15 level. Even when taking the lower measure, Slovakia and Hungary ranked among the top productivity performers in Western Europe, just behind France and Belgium, but before, for instance, Germany, Italy, the UK and Spain. In Slovenia, productivity (measured at PPPCAP99) is only slightly lower than in neighbouring Italy. However, the Czech Republic and Poland range more at the lower end of the Western car producers with respect to productivity (see Table 67 and Table 68).

The dramatic process of productivity catching-up in Slovakia, Hungary and the Czech Republic is clearly demonstrated in Figure 62, showing output growth and employment growth between 1995 and 2002. Productivity growth is indicated by the difference between the production and the employment line[66]. This figure also

---

[64]   UVR estimates for the year 1996 are available for the Czech Republic, Hungary and Poland relative to Germany from a joint research project by WIIW and the University of Groningen (Monnikhof and van Ark, 2000).

[65]   See, for instance, Dollar and Wolff, 1993.

[66]   Productivity = Output/Employment. For small changes we may thus assume: d Productivity = d Output − d Employment.

shows the relatively slow productivity growth in the automotive industry in Poland, Slovenia and particularly in Latvia.

Fig. 62.   Motor vehicles labour productivity 2002 (1995=100)

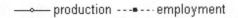

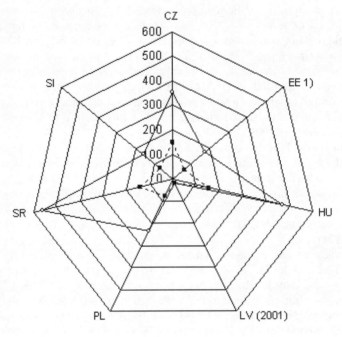

Source: wiiw.

4.1.4.3 Wages

Despite substantial wage increases in the past, wage levels in the NMS still stay
significantly below those of the OMS. Wages in the automotive industry are generally higher (due to higher labour productivity) than in the manufacturing industry on average and this is true for most NMS as well, with wages in this industry
varying between 145% and 115% of manufacturing average in the major vehicle
producing countries. However, if converted in euros (at market exchange rates), in
2001, wages in the automotive industry reached only between 6% (Lithuania) and
30% (Slovenia) of the average wage level in the EU-15 automotive industry (see
Table 69). Wages for Malta and Cyprus are available for some years only; they are
higher than in the Central and Eastern European countries, but are staying significantly below EU-average.

Table 25. Unit labour costs 1997-2002 for automotive industry (NACE 34)
(PPP99 conversion rates; calculated with gross wages)

	1997	1998	1999	2000	2001	2002	in % of total manufacturing 2001	in % of EU-15 2001 (EU 2000)
Czech Rep.	2.66	2.86	2.82	2.68	2.71	3.09	55.6	20.5
Estonia	5.74	6.54	5.19	5.42	4.79		68.7	36.3
Hungary	1.78	1.43	1.26	1.27	1.57	1.87	41.1	11.9
Latvia	8.75	4.75	15.28	5.58	8.61		116.4	65.3
Lithuania	27.27	8.99	10.58	6.55	2.47		46.6	18.7
Poland	3.98	3.66	3.78	3.78	4.46	3.97	61.6	33.8
Slovak Rep.	1.88	1.12	1.08	1.13	1.17	1.24	33.6	8.8
Slovenia	4.90	4.12	4.21	3.84	3.98	4.07	33.4	30.2
EU-15				13.19				

Source: wiiw Industrial Database; Panorama of Czech industries, Eurostat, New Cronos, SBS; unit labour cost, PPSGDP 99, 1997-2002; (calculated with gross wages) in %.

Table 26. Unit labour costs 1997-2002 for automotive industry (NACE 34)
(PPPCAP99 conversion rates; calculated with gross wages)

	1997	1998	1999	2000	2001	2002	in % of total manufacturing 2001	in % of EU-15 2001 (EU 2000)
Czech Rep.	3.83	4.12	4.07	3.87	3.90	4.46	55.6	29.6
Estonia	9.83	11.19	8.88	9.28	8.20		68.7	62.2
Hungary	2.65	2.13	1.87	1.90	2.35	2.79	41.1	17.8
Latvia	14.38	7.80	25.10	9.16	14.15		116.4	107.2
Lithuania	47.93	15.81	18.59	11.51	4.35		46.6	33.0
Poland	5.33	4.91	5.06	5.07	5.97	5.31	61.6	45.2
Slovak Rep.	3.21	1.90	1.84	1.93	1.99	2.11	33.6	15.1
Slovenia	5.77	4.85	4.95	4.52	4.68	4.79	33.4	35.5
EU-15				13.19				

Source: wiiw Industrial Database; Panorama of Czech industries, Eurostat, New Cronos, SBS; unit labour cost, PPSCAP 99, 1997-2002; (calculated with gross wages) in %.

In Table 70, total labour costs, including direct and indirect wage costs are given as well, which may be more relevant for international cost comparisons, but were not available for all countries. Compared to the EU-15, total labour costs seem to be relatively higher than wages, but not much.

High productivity in the automotive industry combined with low wages gives the NMS a clear competitive (cost-)advantage in this field, which can be measured by so-called unit labour costs.

4.1.4.4 Unit Labour Costs

Unit labour costs (ULC)[67], in the automotive industry are typically *much* lower in the NMS than in the OMS, indicating a very large competitive cost advantage of the NMS in this industry. According to the lower measure, using PPPs as a converter for output, ULCs ranged between 9% of EU-15 average in Slovakia and 65% in Latvia in 2001. When we base conversion on the price of fixed investment (PPPCAP99), the range was between 15% and 107% of EU-15 average. As can be seen from Table 25, apart from Slovakia, Hungary shows a particularly high relative cost-advantage, due to high levels of productivity combined with relatively low wages. It is followed by Lithuania, with very low wages compensating for low productivity and the Czech Republic with a relatively high productivity but higher wages than for instance Slovakia. Slovenia ranked 6th because of its high wages and Poland ranked 7th, showing a relatively lower productivity and relatively higher wages than the other NMS. (In the appendix in Table 71, ULCs based on total labour costs are given as well, however, the picture does not change much).

Given the existing very large cost-advantage of most NMS in the automotive industry, even substantial wage increases in these countries will not threaten their competitive advantage compared to the OMS in the foreseeable future. However, different wage developments in the individual NMS may – among other things – influence foreign investors' location decisions within the region.[68]

4.2   Human Resources in Science and Technology

Qualified people are vital for growth, innovation and international competitive strength. Well-trained workers and scientists are at the heart of the knowledge-driven economy and contribute to the generation, rapid dissemination and utilisa-

---

[67]   Unit labour costs are defined as labour costs (LC) per unit of output (OUT). ULC = LC/OUT. Labour costs were calculated as gross wages (W) multiplied by the number of employees (EMP; W: gross wages). As labour productivity (LP) is defined as output per employed person (LP =OUT/EMP), ULC may be rewritten as wages divided by productivity (W / LP): ULC = (W*EMP)/OUT = W/(OUT/EMP) = W/LP.

[68]   As ULCs are expressed in Euros for international comparison, exchange rate developments play a certain role as well.

tion of know-how. For this reason, qualified work and a high level of scientific research constitute the best conditions that highly developed economies have to offer in international competition.

In most European member states employees classified as Human Resource in Science and Technology (HRST)[69] count for about 25% of all employees, measured as the average share in services and manufacturing. And, it should be stressed that in almost every country the shares increase.[70]

Fig. 63. Human resources in science and technology (HRST) by country, 1995 and 2001 (in % of all employees)

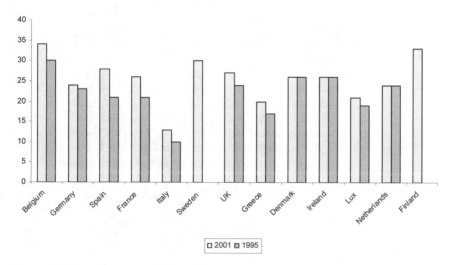

Source: EU labour force survey, Eurostat.

In the EU-15 medium high technology manufacturing sector – including the automotive industry – almost one quarter of all people employed (25-64 years old) have enjoyed tertiary education.[71] More precisely, in Germany, France, Spain,

---

[69]   HRST is defined as a person fulfilling one of the following conditions: successfully completed education at the third level in an S&T field of study; HRST comprise also persons which are not formally qualified as above, but employed in an S&T occupation where the above qualifications are normally required.

[70]   In EU-15 almost 1 million researchers were employed. Since 1996 the number has increased with an average annual growth rate of 3.9%. This is slightly under the growth rate in the US (4.3%) but distinctively higher than it is in Japan (1.8%). The absolute number of researchers is 1.3 million in the US and roughly 675,000 in Japan.

[71]   In 2001, about 2.2 million persons graduated from universities, nearly 600,000 in science and technology fields of study. In relation to the US and Japan EU-15 produces a higher share of graduates in science and technology: 14% earned their degree in engineering, 12% in science. The comparable figures for the US are 8% and 9%. In

Sweden, and the UK the share of HRST in the motor industry is at some 30%.[72] But, focusing on the motor industry it is obvious that in the motor vehicle industry HRST contribute to the overall figure of HRST in a country only to a minor extent. For example, roughly 3% of all HRST employees in Germany are from the motor vehicle industry, and this is the highest share of HRST compared with other European countries.

Fig. 64. Human resources in science and technology (HRST) in motor industry by country, 1995 and 2001 (in % of all HRST)

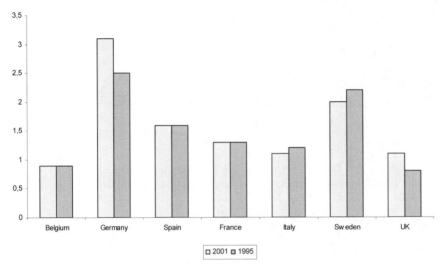

Source: EU labour force survey, Eurostat.

How does a relatively modest share of HRST employees fit in with the "technology leadership" claim of the motor industry that is supposed to be R&D-

---

Japan engineering played an important role with 19%, whereas science is on a very low level with 3%.

[72]   Compare HRST definition: HRST is defined as a person fulfilling one of the following conditions:
successfully completed education at the third level in an S&T field of study; not formally qualified as above, but employed in an S&T occupation where the above qualifications are normally required.
It should not be confused with the previous definition for Germany: Skill structure in the German automotive industry:
- 6% is only the intensity of scientists: "Share of engineers/natural scientists of all employees in %"
- the "skill-intensity in production – share of skilled (blue-collar) workers of blue-collar workers in %." or the "intensity of academics in services – share of academics (graduates) of white-collar workers in % " are more appropriate figures.

oriented and innovation-driven?[73] To answer this question a brief review of the developments and changes in the automotive industry during the early 1990s is quite helpful. Among other things the automotive industry was confronted with radical reorganisation processes of the value chain, the rise and diffusion of information and communication technologies, and international competition that became extremely fierce. These challenges caused enormous turbulence and adjustments at the company level both inside enterprises and between companies along the supply chain. New architectures of joint ventures, international networks with interlinked, cross-border supply chains were established. And, due to reduced vertical integration, new management and operation concepts such as lean production, just-in-time and total quality management were introduced.

Unsurprisingly, the structural and organisational changes had immense implications for human resource management and led to a split of the labour force. Trying to achieve an optimum price-performance ratio, companies developed concepts of human resource management that were economically feasible. The share of low skilled occupations was cut to the lowest possible minimum which resulted in a considerable decline in the number of jobs. Large numbers of employees were made redundant, low skilled labour in car factories was replaced, substituted by processes based on CAM, or outsourced to other companies. High skilled labour became more valuable and an asset for the enterprises. That is especially the case for R&D, engineering, industrial design and other knowledge-intensive tasks. A similar development took place on the supply side. Suppliers of high quality products and services – implying high skilled workers – stabilised their market position, and studies predict that their importance will increase by the year 2010.[74] Suppliers providing ubiquitous products and services lost their market position and were substituted using global-sourcing.

Driven by globalisation automotive companies seek opportunities to optimise performance along the value chain. European suppliers of standardised products, components and parts whose production could easily be moved to low cost countries are threatened most by this development. Simultaneously, an opportunity arises for those companies which provide "key technologies" or can compete with knowledge-intensive products and sophisticated services strengthening the market position.

The European automotive industry was able to recover from the slump at the beginning of the 1990s, and the number of people employed in the automotive industry has remained more or less constant recently. In the supply sector the workforce even expanded as a result of the sector taking on additional tasks in the value chain. But, the split of the workforce increased even more. The general labour qualification level is relatively low ("low skilled") in the EU motor vehicle industry, although a dynamic use of highly qualified people in R&D and knowledge-intensive occupations and of information technologies (IT) can be observed along with a high and growing IT-labour intensity (a greater intensity of use of IT

---

[73]   For the discussion of R&D and innovation see the part of the report "technological performance factors".

[74]   See Dudenhöffer (2003).

personnel) that is responsible for a relatively high percentage of high skilled labour.[75] Hence, a classification of the automotive sector as a "low skilled" sector (see e.g. Robinson et al.) is misleading because of the increasing split in qualifications.

Spotlight – Qualification Split in the German Motor Industry, 1999

A car is a highly complex product with a variety of features and components, and a number of tasks and processes have to be co-ordinated during the various stages of manufacturing. Inter and intra-industry linkages are the results of the disassembly of production and the division of labour. These factors are responsible for a heterogeneous pattern of employment in the German automotive industry with two extreme positions: In motor vehicles and engines (NACE 34.1) we find a relatively large number of academics or equally qualified employees in the field of

Table 27. Skill structure in the German automotive industry

	Manufacturing of				
	Motor vehicles NACE 34	Motor vehicles and engines NACE 34.1	Vehicle bodies, trailers, caravans NACE 34.2	Parts and accessories NACE 34.3	For comparison: Manufacturing
Production-intensity[1]	72.7	72.0	74.3	73.7	63.3
Skill-intensity in production[2]	43.7	46.6	63.0	32.5	46.1
Service-intensity[3]	27.3	28.0	25.7	26.3	36.7
Intensity of academics in services[4]	32.7	35.8	17.0	28.7	20.9
Intensity of academics[5]	8.9	10.0	4.4	7.5	7.7
Intensity of scientist[6]	6.0	6.9	2.2	4.8	4.4

1) Share of blue-collar workers of all employees in %.
2) Share of skilled (blue-collar) workers of blue-collar workers in %.
3) Share of white-collar workers of all employees in %.
4) Share of academics (graduates) of white-collar workers in %.
5) Share of academics (graduates) of all employees in %
6) Share of engineers/natural scientists of all employees in %.
Source: German Statistical Office.

business-oriented services – measured as the share of academics (graduates) in percent of white-collar workers, or as intensity of academics and scientists – as

---

[75]   See European Communities (2003).

well as a distinctive high number of low skilled jobs at the assembly line – measured as production-intensity. A split of the workforce is also visible in manufacturing of parts and accessories (NACE 34.3): a high share of employees with education and training as engineers for R&D or related work and at the same time a large number of jobs in production that do not require specific skills.[76]

4.3   R&D, Innovation, and Patents

4.3.1   Expenditures on R&D

Research and development is an investment in technological know-how which can be translated into new products, processes and services in subsequent years. In this regard, R&D activities also reflect a company's assessment of its future prospects, and its willingness to pursue market opportunities. Particularly in the industrial sector, technological R&D is crucial for innovation activity and an important factor in determining technological performance and competitive advantages.

In Japan, the US and the EU-15 high-tech industries account for 40% to 45% of manufacturing business enterprise R&D (BERD), medium-high-tech industries for about 45%, and medium-low-tech and low-tech industries for 10% to 15%. Japan (14.1%) dedicates a somewhat larger share of its business sector R&D to medium-low-tech and low-tech industries than either the EU-15 (11.0%) or the US (9.4%). On the other hand, the US (45.8%) spend a somewhat larger proportion of their business sector R&D in high-tech industries than either the EU-15 (41.4%) or Japan (39.3%). The differences are greater between EU member states than between Japan, the US and the EU-15.

Looking at R&D expenditures of the three major car producing regions – U.S., Japan and EU – there is a shift in R&D spending worth mentioning. Between 1995 and 2000 the EU enlarged its share with regard to overall R&D expenditures in the three regions from 34% to 38%. (see Figure 65).

Broken down by country we shed light on the R&D distribution within the EU as well as on the relative importance of automotive R&D for the R&D performance of the country as a whole. R&D expenditures by German car manufacturers account for more than 30% or roughly EUR 11 bn of total R&D expenditures in Germany in 2000. In Sweden the share is 18%, in France 16% and in Italy 16%. In these countries R&D activities undertaken by manufacturers of cars and other transport equipment have a significant impact on the national R&D investments. It is also obvious that automotive R&D is increasingly important in Germany. In addition, the expansion of the EU's worldwide R&D share is mainly due to the increased R&D intensity of the German automotive industry.

---

[76]   The above figure on skill structure in the German automotive industry rests on different definitions when compared to the HRST. HRST not only comprise academics and scientists but also third level education like the German vocational training "Masters" degree and technicians.

At the company level, relating the annual growth rate of R&D expenditure of the top 300 international companies to the absolute R&D expenditure levels, leads to interesting insights concerning the competitiveness of the automotive industry. This exercise shows that "IT hardware", "automobiles & parts" and "pharma & biotech" constitute the top three sectors in terms of absolute R&D expenditure levels in 2002. While "IT hardware" has grown hardly at all in recent years the two other sectors, especially "automobiles & parts" have experienced rapid growth.

Fig. 65.   R&D expenditures in the motor industry, 1995 and 2000 (in % of total expenditures in EU, Japan, U.S.)

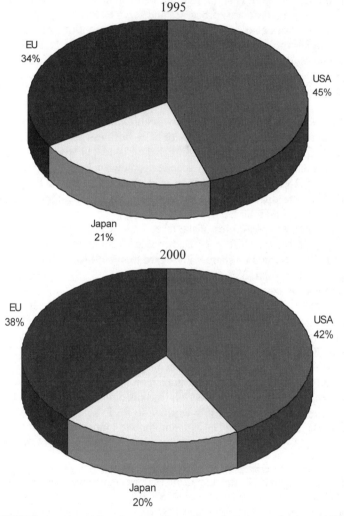

Source: OECD Research and Development Expenditure in Industry database, 1987-2001.

The increasing importance attached to R&D by European car manufacturers is also expressed by the share of the motor industry's R&D expenditures in R&D expenditures in total manufacturing. In the year 2000 the share of the European motor industry's R&D expenditures in the total manufacturing industry was close to 20%. That was a distinct increase between 1995 and the year 2000. The level exceeded comparable figures of the US (~15%) and Japan (~13%).

Fig. 66.   Share of R&D expenditures in the motor industry 1995 and 2000 (in % of total manufacturing)

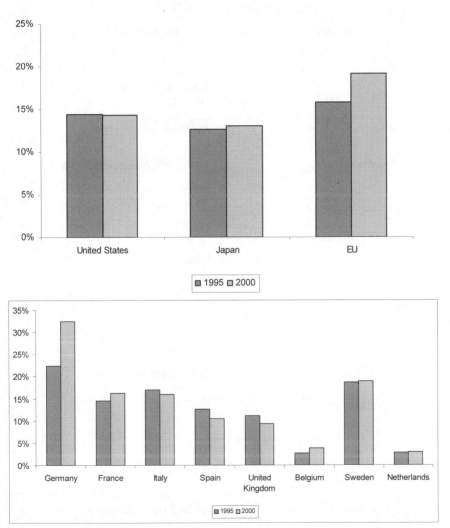

Source: OECD Research and Development Expenditure in Industry database, 1987-2001.

A sector-to-sector comparison of business R&D expenditure between EU-15 and US companies out of the top 300 international firms shows that EU-15 companies spend substantially less than their US counterparts in "pharma & biotech", "IT hardware" and "software & computer services", but maintain substantial leads in "automobiles & parts" and "electronics" (see Figure 67). In 2002 the top business R&D spenders in EU-15 invested more than EUR 24 bn, considering that Germany alone stands for about EUR 15 bn. That was nearly EUR 7 bn more than U.S. companies spent for R&D in the field of "automobiles and parts". The figure also suggests that the automotive sector is one of the few sectors where EU based multinationals have a competitive edge compared to the other triad regions.

Fig. 67.   R&D expenditure by top EU-15 and top US business R&D spenders in selected sectors, 2002

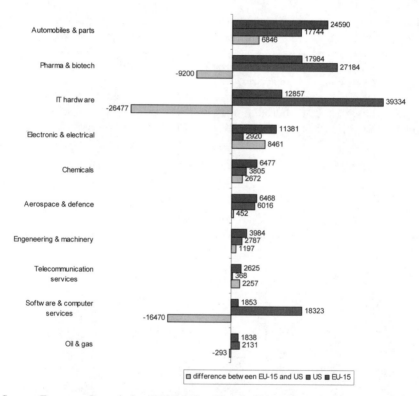

Source: European Commission (2004b). Key Figures 2003-2004.

4.3.2   Automotive Innovation as Mirrored in Patent Statistics

Looking at patent data will provide us with a more detailed picture. For international comparisons based on data from regional patent offices we have to bear in mind that the pure figures might be severely influenced by "home country advantages". The traditional approach to eliminate home market advantages is to look only at those inventions which are represented by patents at all relevant regional patent offices. Hence, this approach would suggest that for comparisons between US, Japan and EU one should focus on patents applied for at the USPTO, EPO and JPO. However, this approach involves severe time lags and is also burdensome to calculate at the level of sectors mainly due the availability of JPO data. Therefore, we look at EPO data only but account for differences between all patent classes and those patent classes which are most relevant for automotive innovation in the interpretation of the importance of the automotive sector. In addition, we are interested in Europe as the region where the R&D activity for which the patent is awarded has been performed. Hence, we look at the inventor's address (address where the inventor resides) to extract country information.[77]

The results confirm the conclusion drawn above. Europe (EU-25) is the leading region in automotive R&D. The EU's share in all EPO patent applications in automotive is around 60% and has increased since the mid-1990s. Japan, too, has increased its inventive capabilities in the light of patent statistics whereas the US and the "rest of the world" have lost "market share" in the patent domain. Comparing automotive patents with all patents we can further conclude that with regard to the ranking of regions the EU is clearly ahead of Japan which is ahead of the US. Inventive activity in the automotive sector is dominated by these three regions more than any other sphere of technological inventions.

Comparisons within the EU can also be performed using patent data. Here, the dominant position of Germany as leading country for automotive R&D is even more obvious. Germany accounts for nearly 60% of EPO applications in the automotive sector. This share has dramatically increased, especially in the 1990s. This corresponds nicely to the increasing share of automotive R&D performed in Germany as already shown. Other EU countries could hardly follow the momentum of the number of patent applications from Germany. Only Belgium, Austria and surprisingly the new member states could stand the momentum of patenting of the German automotive industry in the last ten years. However, the share of patent applications of the new member states is still very small. Compared to the significance of the new member states as production location, their share in automotive patenting is extremely small.

The increasing intensity of automotive patenting is predominantly driven by large companies. Not surprisingly, the leading vehicle manufacturers are among the leading patent applicants. However, patent data also reveal the importance of suppliers for automotive related inventions. For example the leading German company Bosch is among the leading patent applicants.

---

[77]   In those few cases were inventors from different countries are involved in the same patent application we randomly select (based on normal distribution) one inventor and assign the patent to the country where this inventor resides.

Fig. 68.   Share of EPO application in all patent classes and automotive related IPC classes

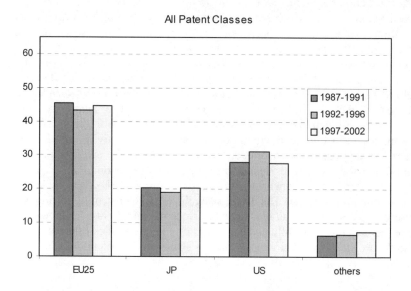

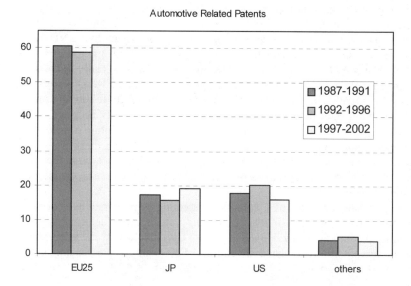

Automotive related patent classes are defined by the following IPC class numbers: B62D, B62J, B62K11, B62M7, B60B, B60C, B60D, B60F, B60G, B60H, B60J, B60K, B60L, B60N, B60P, B60Q, B60R, B60S, B60T, F01M, F02B, F02C, F02D, F02F, F02M, F02N, F02P, F16B, F16D, F16H, F16J, F16K, F16N, F21L, C08C, C10K.
Source: EPO-Espace, EPO-EPOline.

Fig. 69.   Distribution of Patent Application by country within the EU

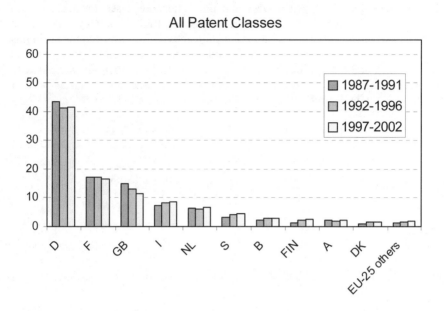

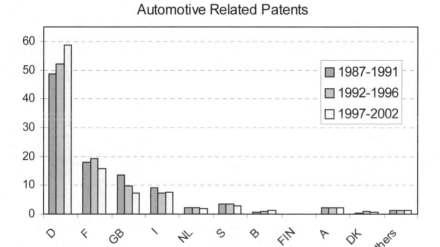

Source: EPA-Espace, EPO-EPOline.

4.3.3   Innovation Patterns

Technical progress, competitiveness and innovation are based on research and development. But even in R&D-intensive industries, R&D is only one aspect, but nevertheless the essential core of all innovation activities. Innovation means in this context the development and economic exploitation of new or improved products and services, and the optimisation of business processes. Innovation continuously redefines markets and opens up new sectors of economic and social activity. It concerns every industrial sector, especially the automotive industry.[78]

Table 28. Share of enterprises with innovation activity 1996 (in %) in NACE DM

Country	Innovation active enterprises	Process innovators	Product innovators	Innovators with products new to the market	Share of innovation active firms performing R&D
Belgium	41	30	30	12	65
Denmark	85	28	85	18	68
Germany	74	47	72	30	80
Spain	46	40	41	20	66
France	58	37	47	28	86
Ireland	88	71	76	21	88
Italy	49	43	38	29	62
Luxembourg	17	-	-	-	-
Netherlands	67	41	57	36	81
Austria	78	53	77	37	80
Portugal	26	18	12	3	24
Finland	45	26	35	21	92
Sweden	60	33	51	19	81
United Kingdom	65	47	57	19	54
EU-15	60	42	52	24	69
Benchmark: EU-15 manufacturing	54	39	44	21	68

NACE DM: Manufacture of transport equipment.
Source: Results of the second community innovation survey (CIS2) Eurostat.

---

[78]   The innovation activity conducted by individual firms is embedded in an extensive meshwork of incentives, rules, institutions and regulatory structures. Depending on their effect these factors have a significant influence on the intensity and direction of corporate innovation efforts. This includes technological means and human capital, mechanisms to protect revenue generated by innovation activities, know-how and its transfer. See for example Audretsch and Fritsch (2002); Porter (2000); Breschi (2000); Breschi and Malerba (1997); Tidd, Bessant and Pavitt (2001); Stoneman (1995); Dodgson and Rothwell (1994); Freeman (1994).

About 50% of the companies which belong to the EU-15 manufacturing sector introduced new or significantly improved products or processes, and are categorised as innovating enterprises. In the manufacturing of transport equipment[79] the share of innovators was slightly higher with nearly 60%. Germany accounted for the largest share of innovators where more than 70% of the car manufacturers introduced innovations, 72% developed product innovations, and 30% were innovators with new products also new to the market. Compared with the findings for Germany the other European car producing enterprises in France and Italy are less innovative. 52% of the EU-15 manufacturers of transport equipment are product innovators, and 24% are innovating companies with products also new to the market. In total, the weighted results for EU-15 are highly influenced by the performance of Germany – and to some extent by France, Sweden, and UK – based on the weight the countries have in the European automotive industry.

Comparing CIS II (1996) and CIS III (2000) results we find declining shares of innovative active firms in the leading car producing countries in the EU. Having the development of R&D in mind this indicates that the contribution to technological progress is more concentrated in recent years. However, the participation rate of technological innovation in the automotive industry is still above the average of the manufacturing sector. This shows that even second and – to a lesser extent – third tier suppliers have to perform innovation to stay in the market. On the other hand, the cost pressure in small supplier companies increased and some companies had to stop their innovating activities for financial reasons.

When it comes to R&D activities in innovating enterprises, the trends are even more pronounced than with innovation activity. R&D requires additional resources and organisational dimensions going beyond some sporadic or operative work related to innovation. Research activities are based on a strategic business decision with long-term perspectives. A company that established an R&D facility is determined to continuously reap benefits from this infrastructure. About 70% of the innovative firms in the manufacturing sector of transport equipment reported that they engaged continuously and/or occasionally in R&D, the same percentage was found for the entire manufacturing sector. R&D activities seem to be a necessary input factor for innovating enterprises in the automotive industry. Especially in Germany, France, and Sweden the propensity to R&D is very high. More than 80% of innovative enterprises engage in R&D. These countries are obviously more R&D-oriented than the other major European car competitors situated in Italy, Spain or U.K.

About 70% of the innovative firms in the manufacturing of transport equipment reported having engaged continuously and/or occasionally in R&D, the same

---

[79]   Data are only available at the level of transport equipment (NACE 34-35). Given the relative size of the automotive sector in terms of the number of enterprises (NACE 34) results presented mainly reflect the data of the automotive sector. In addition, data from CIS III referring to the year 2000 are not available at the two digit level. For selected countries we obtained some information of trends between 1996 and 2000 calculated in the IEEF project funded by the Commission. We will mention trends between 1996 and 2000 in the text where appropriate.

percentage reveals for the total manufacturing. R&D activities seem to be a necessary input factor for innovating enterprises in the automotive industry. Especially in Germany, France, and Sweden the propensity to R&D is very high. Over 80% of innovative enterprises engage in R&D. These countries are obviously stronger R&D-oriented than the other major European car competitors situated in Italy, Spain or U.K. Overall, only 30% of the innovating enterprises among EU-15 manufacturers of transport equipment are not R&D-related.

Table 29. Composition of total innovation expenditures (in % of total innovation expenditures) 1996, by NACE DM

Country	Industrial design (manufacturing sector) or preparations to introduce new services or methods (service sector)	Machinery and equipment acquisition	Market introduction of innovation	External technology acquisition	Extramural R&D	Intramural R&D	Training directly linked to technological innovation
Belgium	8	33	5	1	4	47	2
Denmark	3	11	1	11	2	72	-
Germany	6	11	3	1	24	53	1
Spain	10	19	2	2	7	60	1
France	4	12	17	-	11	53	3
Ireland	4	28	6	5	3	52	2
Italy	16	41	5	3	4	29	2
Netherlands	3	18	2	1	13	60	3
Austria	6	20	6	1	7	55	5
Portugal	10	32	1	28	1	28	-
Finland	2	14	3	6	15	58	2
Sweden	13	15	7	5	9	49	3
United Kingdom	2	33	5	4	-	53	3
EU-15	7	17	5	2	16	51	2
EU-15 manufacturing	6	22	4	4	9	53	2

NACE DM= Manufacture of transport equipment.
Source: Results of the second community innovation survey (CIS2) Eurostat.

In order to benefit from challenges due to innovation, companies have their own strategies and go different ways. One strategic concept places its focus on in-house R&D and combines in-house activities with additional R&D undertaken by external partners. The other strategic option tends more towards technology transfer by purchasing new equipment and machinery. For companies with less internal and/or external R&D the purchase of equipment, imitation and learning by doing seem to be valuable innovation strategies. Therefore, these firms invest in trial production, training and tooling-up in combination with industrial design and product design.

In general, EU-15 innovators spend most of their innovation expenditures for R&D, and invest the money in intramural and extramural research projects. Especially German companies are following this path of innovation. Here, 53% of the innovation budget goes into in-house R&D and 24% is dedicated towards joint projects with external R&D partners. The behaviour of companies in France and Sweden is comparable to companies in Germany. Italy and the U.K. prefer the other innovation process by using various channels of technology transfer and by innovating via R&D that is embodied in new equipment. Here, the companies purchase new machinery and equipment and integrate these installations into the in-house production and innovation processes. In Italy, for a change, industrial design is of some importance in the innovation process and an Italian strength.

The structure of innovation expenditure underlines the importance of suppliers and their specific contribution even during the R&D stage. The share of external R&D in the automotive sector is considerably larger than in manufacturing as a whole. And this is especially the case in those countries where automotive R&D is particularly strong (Finland seems to be an exception).

4.3.4   Innovation Networks

Empirical studies lead to the conclusion that countries and regions have different ways to disseminate knowledge and to carry out innovations in specific sectoral contexts. These specific features include in particular the type of market competition, the opportunities available for collaboration with other companies, the transfer of knowledge and know-how from universities and research institutes to businesses, and the criteria for the development of technological norms and standards. In many cases, it is not technologies or products that are transferred within the innovation networks, but knowledge, which enables companies to develop market-driven innovations in-house on their own, thus expanding their own innovative potential.

Some available sources of information for innovation are closer to the market, e.g. suppliers, customers or competitors. Other sources are more related to the scientific sector such as universities or private or government R&D labs. Market-related external information sources such as customers, suppliers or competitors are just as important as in-house sources. But suppliers of material and equipment or competitors are only valuable for a relatively small number of European vehicle manufacturers. Given that most firms are (1st, 2nd, or 3rd tier) suppliers the widespread use of customers as information source also underlines the vertical information flows in the sector.

Table 30. Share of innovation active enterprises maintaining collaboration with innovation project by type of partner chosen, 1996, by NACE DM (in %)

Country	Other enter-prises(s) within the group	Competitor(s)	Clients or cus-tomers	Consultancy enterprises	Suppliers [1]	Universities or other higher education insti-tutes	Government or private non-profit research institutes
Belgium	100	29	87	9	25	21	31
Denmark	81	12	43	6	43	37	37
Germany	60	41	34	29	68	44	41
Spain	65	8	40	19	50	35	27
France	69	19	48	17	72	28	20
Ireland	89	3	76	33	53	59	40
Italy	60	25	36	13	43	52	11
Luxembourg	-	-	-	-	-	-	-
Netherlands	58	33	53	31	70	31	46
Austria	88	38	75	12	57	43	19
Portugal	26	16	52	66	50	100	48
Finland	49	33	88	42	69	71	63
Sweden	46	25	84	28	39	54	9
United King-dom	54	14	34	31	51	53	18
EU-15	62	23	47	24	56	44	27
EU-15 manu-facturing	58	18	48	22	49	37	32

[1] Suppliers of equipment, materials and components of software.
Source: Results of the second community innovation survey (CIS2) Eurostat.

Cooperation in innovation projects and joint projects in innovating activities are increasingly important sources to achieve a competitive edge. But cooperative research projects are usually conditional on ongoing R&D activities in the companies involved. The cooperation partner can always contribute only complementary knowledge. In the car industry the average ratio of companies with R&D cooperation amounts to 34% and is higher than in total manufacturing (26%).

If companies decide to cooperate they consider every potential partner. Besides cooperation within the group manufacturers of transport equipment have strong ties with their suppliers. Around 50% of transport equipment manufacturers carry out collaborative innovation projects with suppliers and/or clients. Compared to the rest of manufacturing it is striking that competitors are often used as collaboration partners. This again reflects the intense links needed for the development of complex products. Thus, automotive innovation is not only characterised by vertical links but also by intense networking both between vehicle manufacturers and suppliers.

As we pointed out, any information provided by universities or institutions of higher education is not very important for the innovation activities of a firm. On the other hand, knowledge from the science sectors influences ongoing research in companies and is sometimes even the first step to an innovation.[80] We found that universities are an important cooperation partner for companies with cooperative relations in innovation. On average, 44% of innovating and cooperating enterprises cooperate closely with an university, and are searching for a technology push. In the manufacturing sector the share of science-business links, measures by cooperation between companies and universities, is somewhat lower with 37%.

Cooperation partners were mostly chosen at the national level. In addition, enterprises cooperate with other European companies. Innovation projects with U.S. partners rank third. The ranking is comparable with the manufacturing sector.

4.3.5 Summary

Against the background of the economic potential of mass production, combined with the complexity of specific goods such as cars and other transport equipment the risks of failure related to radical innovations are very high. Therefore, processes and products are developed incrementally on the basis of earlier experience coming from improvement of machinery as well as from the assembly line and operations management. In-house R&D activities and product engineering are the main strength for technical progress. Additionally, the work of specialised suppliers – sometimes research facilities – is integrated into the value chain. The important tasks of innovating companies consist in taking incremental steps forward, and to diffuse knowledge throughout the company or group. Therefore, information technologies now offer opportunities to save time and money.

Technological progress in the automotive industry is to a certain degree "path dependent." In other words, learning, experience curve effects and long-term factors lay the foundation for the respective innovation system and its development and have to be linked to opportunities arising due to information and communication technologies and human resources. As a result, the innovative strengths of the European automotive industry gradually improve, thus leading to standardised high-quality products that fulfil customers' needs and expectation. This development is based on production regimes that require sophisticated skills in handling

---

[80]   Particularly in the case of cooperative projects with public-sector research institutions, companies cannot outsource the competency to design market-driven product/process innovations. Universities and public-sector institutions, remote as they are from the marketplace, are only to a limited degree suited for developing finished products for the actual market. Cooperative projects both between the science sector and the industry and inter-company collaborations, are the most effective form of knowledge and technology transfer.

complex processes, maintenance service and close customer relations – namely, diversified high-quality production.

EU-15 firms have increased their investments in new products, new processes and new technologies considerably in the 1990s. Compared to the USA and Japan, EU has gained market share both in terms of investment in innovation (R&D) and with regard to results of R&D (as measured by patents). The technological competitiveness of the EU-15 rests not only on the presence of leading car makers but also on innovation activities wide-spread within the supplier part of the industry. Intense networking of the suppliers and assembly firms is present in Europe and also has contributed to a high technological competitiveness of EU automotive industry.

4.4   Innovation and Restructuring of the Value Chain

In recent years the demand for cars has increased only slowly in many developed countries, and the sale of new automobiles only covered the replacement demand. Apart from the US, a significant increase in sales is only observed in emerging markets. The maturity of the European market is characterised by the intensive use of marketing instruments such as price and product policy. The customers expect additional enhancements from vehicle manufacturers, but are not willing to pay higher prices. Therefore, product innovations have to be financed with an increased efficiency along the value chain which includes component suppliers as well as after-sales services.

In addition, future innovations in vehicle manufacturing will be closely intertwined with electronics and software control systems. These innovations have to be linked with the traditional mechanical automobile components. The traditional component supplier or other companies, which are new in the sector, will take over these new value added activities. Also, new entrants (specialised suppliers) are expected to appear on the scene. The result will be that the R&D and the value added activities will shift to the component suppliers. The vehicle manufacturers will try to ensure their added value share with cost pressure on the component supplier and cost optimisation on the side of their retail business. Changes in the legal framework like Block Exemption as well as new channels of distribution like internet sales will also influence the value chain of vehicle manufacturers in the future. The organisational and market strategic changes, which will arise from the physical innovations, will be described below.

4.4.1   Innovation in the Value Chain

It is no secret, that firms in modern management terms are rather regarded as network elements than as isolated entities. Therefore the organisation and optimisation of inter-organisational structures is a prerequisite for successful business. Only if the configuration of inter-company interfaces from the original supplier through end user succeeds in creating products, services, and information that add value for customers and stakeholders, can be offered (Lambert et al., 1997).

The vehicle manufacturers succeeded like no other industry in managing the organisation and strategic control of the whole value chain. Intermediate inputs from the chemical, steel, electric and textile industry are integrated in the value chain as well as downstream sectors like automobile retail, body shops, petrol station and other services.

Innovation in vehicle manufacturing will also in future affect the value chain. Suppliers own specific and unique knowledge concerning the functioning and integration of electronic parts in vehicle components. Those will play a larger role in the innovation and value added process in the future.

4.4.2   The Relation Between Supplier and Vehicle Manufacturer

In the 1980s the modern passenger car consisted of up to 10,000 different parts. The special knowledge of vehicle manufacturers concerns the management of the complexity of the production process, which required co-ordinating up to 2,500 suppliers, of course, depending on manufacturer and model (Womack and Jones, 1991). Contract periods for standard products in general were disposed with short notice and suppliers were regarded rather as specific suppliers than strategic partners in innovation (see Fieten, 1995).

In the scope of vehicle manufacturers' make-or-buy decisions, a very high integration of the production was an advantage in competition. Above all American manufacturers like General Motors purchase 70% of their parts from own production which in the end requires innovations and capital lockup respectively (Terporten, 1999).

At the beginning of the 1990s, new developments could barely be accomplished by manufacturers because of the high pressure to innovate. In addition cost pressures led to a reduction of the manufacturing task to the so-called "core manufacture" (Terporten, 1999). Hence, the development of the vertical range of manufacture in the sector "Manufacture and assembly of motor vehicles and engines" (which is the quotient of gross value added and the gross value added of the whole automotive industry, see NACE 34.1-34.3) shows a decreasing drift. The share of the value added of vehicle manufacturers in total automotive value added declined from 18% in 1995 to 12.8% in 2001 in the German case. Another decline can be registered likewise for the UK (about -5.9 percentage points), Italy (about -5.3 percentage points), Spain (-3.8 percentage points) and France (-2.1 percentage points). Only in Sweden the vehicle manufacturers' proportion of the value added increased compared to the other sectors of the automobile industry. Simultaneously the absolute number of employees declined, but the number of people employed in and the gross value added of the supplier industry increased in the respective period (NACE 34.3).[81]

---

[81]   That relation is also influenced by reconfigurations in the cross-border changes in the value added chain.

Fig. 70.   Share of gross value added of "manufacture and assembly of motor vehicles and engines" (NACE 34.1) and automotive industry (NACE 34.1-34.3)

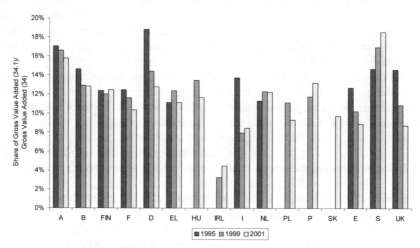

Source: Eurostat and German Association of the Automotive Industry VDA: International Auto Statistics Edition 2003, Frankfurt.

Because of the fact, that the decrease of the vertical range of manufacture does not reduce the complexity of the whole process of vehicle manufacturing, but rather relocates tasks on the value chain, several suppliers take responsibility for greater systems of vehicles (components/modules), for example the petrol injection. This responsibility of the first tier suppliers not only comprehends the construction of systems, the just-in-time delivery to vehicle manufacturers and the co-ordination of second and third tier suppliers but the corresponding R&D of the system, too. Thus half of the total R&D activity of the automobile industry has been allocated to the suppliers in the last few years. Merely in the areas engine and car body the vehicle manufacturers still retain the highest control (Larsson, 2002 and McKinsey&Company, 2003).

Due to this trend a pyramid of manufacturers emerged, with first tier supplier becoming a close partner in the innovation and production process of the vehicle manufacturers at the forefront leaving second and third tier suppliers with no direct contact to vehicle manufacturers (Terporten, 1999).

Therefore only suppliers with large knowledge with respect to the integration of their own products into the final automotive output, which have adequate capabilities to finance R&D and which can follow vehicle manufacturers in their ambition to become global players will be considered as first tier supplier in the future. Concerning globalisation not only following to the manufacturers' particular international locations is required, but also the realisation of cost reduction potential through using advantages of low-cost locations. With a view to increasing globalisation, the expectances of manufacturers and the resulting pressure for suppliers are accordingly high albeit there seems to be a larger demand for international players on the side of the vehicle manufacturers than on the suppliers' side (see Larsson, 2002 and Doran and Roome, 2003).

Fig. 71. Turnover, gross value added and persons employed in "manufacture of parts and accessories for motor vehicles" (NACE 34.3)

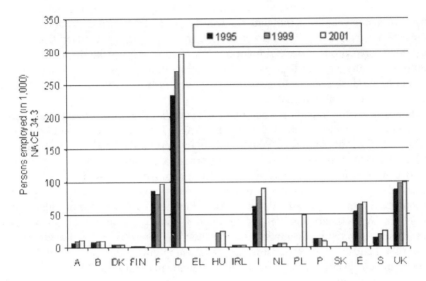

Source: Eurostat and German Association of the Automotive Industry VDA: International Auto Statistics Edition 2003, Frankfurt.

Fig. 72. Supplier market shares by degree of internationality

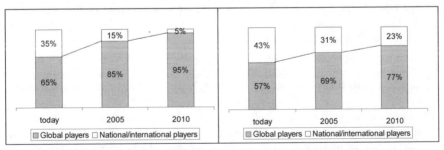

Source: Roland Berger & Partners (2000).

In the late 1990s only a small part of first tier suppliers succeeded in realising these tasks on their own. The worldwide number of first tier suppliers will continue to decrease as a result of M&A, joint ventures and "down-grading" to the second tier supplier level, even though this process has slowed down since 2001. This consolidation continues for a short time on the level of second tier suppliers. A PricewaterhouseCoopers study on M&A in 2002 comes to the conclusion, that the cost pressure forwarded by vehicle manufacturers to first tier suppliers is passed on to second tier suppliers. Increasing requirements regarding global sourcing and innovation thus demand from second tier suppliers an international business orientation, too. These rather small and medium-sized companies are often only capable of accomplishing these challenges by joint ventures or joint foundations (Burwell and Wylie, 2002).

Comparing developments in Europe, North America, and Japan, one realises, that European vehicle manufacturers led the trend of modular production and downstream integration. The European industry has a large specialised firm structure for shared product development and production tasks at its disposal. "If the future lies in the increased specialisation of actors in the value chain, the European automotive industry seems to be particularly well positioned in terms of structures and capabilities" (Jürgens, 2003).

The American companies – but also PSA and Fiat in Europe – reduce in-house production via spin-off activities (Jürgens, 2003). However, the proportion of the value added of the American vehicle manufacturers in the total American added value of the automobile industry still lies around 55% and hence way above the European production structure. Also Japanese companies follow this trend rather reserved. 15.4% of the value added of the automotive sector is allotted by vehicle manufacturers in Japan. This value is above the values of most car producing EU countries. A modularisation of the production took place in-house. Toyota and Honda see a strategic advantage rather in the total control of the value chain and avoid the hand-over of responsibilities to the supplying industry. Specific know-how in the electronic/IT area is to be built strategically (Jürgens, 2003).

There are different opinions with regard to the future development of the interface between suppliers and vehicle manufacturers:

- The management consultants Roland Berger & Partners expect a worldwide fall of the number of suppliers from 5,600 at present to 3,500 by the end of the decade. In this period the number of first tier suppliers per module/system is said to fall from today's 7-8 to 5-3, with a simultaneous decrease of the number of modules/systems per vehicle from 20-18 today to about 10 in the year 2010 (Berger & Partners, 2000).
- PricewaterhouseCoopers – using obviously another definition of tier 1 and tier 2 supplier – expect a decrease in the number of first tier suppliers from 800 to 35 and a reduction of second tier suppliers from 10,000 to 800 in the same time period.
- The associations of the automotive industry are questioning this degree of consolidation: If a continually decreasing number of first tier suppliers meets a continually increasing demand on behalf of the vehicle manufacturers, the result will be an adjournment in the power of negotiation to the disadvantage of the automobile manufacturers. The manufacturers try to abide a credible threat of an upstream integration and to apply a dual sourcing strategy for the different vehicle components.[82]

---

[82]   See German Association of the Automotive Industrie VDA (2003) and Neuner (1993).

In any case, the upcoming innovations in the field of automobile manufacturing will bring about yet further changes at the interface of suppliers and vehicle manufacturers. The increase of the production costs of a motor vehicle mainly induced by product improvements[83] will probably lead to an additional transfer of R&D and other value generating activities, which are beyond the core competencies of the vehicle manufacturers, to the suppliers. The arising expenses for R&D will not be pre-financed by the vehicle producer anymore, but will be added to the price per unit of the delivered component. The vehicle manufacturer will not provide for a complete amortisation anymore (KPMG, 2003). Overall, the vehicle manufacturer will pass on the cost-pressure to the suppliers, who will need to consolidate further through strategic alliances (PricewaterhouseCoopers, 2003).

Figure 73 describes the expected development of vehicle manufacturers' vertical integration until 2015: There will be an estimated decrease of 10 percentage points of the value added proportion of the vehicle manufacturers. This decline will be explained mainly through the spin-off of tasks from the area of chassis technology (-18 percentage points) and the area of engine technology (-15 percentage points) to the suppliers. Even in the core competencies of the body the value added shares of the vehicle manufacturers are decreasing by 6 percentage points from 72% to 66%. A reduction of costs can be achieved through strategic alliances in the form of cross-border platform developments and by sharing of parts and design. Moreover, new laser-welding technologies and a reinforced use of plastic parts, enabled through the application of the colour matching technology, from different suppliers are hidden cost reduction potentials.

Fig. 73.   Development of vehicle manufacturers' vertical integration

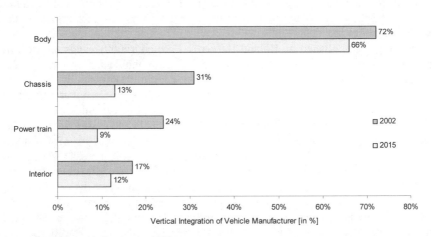

Source: McKinsey&Company, 2003

Since the innovations will exceed the classical limits of supplier segmentation some analyst hypothesise that the traditional supplier pyramid composed of tier 1,

---

[83]   Recent studies expect this cost increase to amount to nearly 30%.

tier 2, and tier 3 suppliers will be replaced by a segment structure of the suppliers. Manufacturers of brake and steering systems for example would network with manufacturers of the chassis technology (Doran and Roome, 2003). Partially, this networking is supposed to reach the consumer via spare parts. Whether the supplier industry will be able to cope with the increased requirements of the cooperation management, will depend mainly on the solution of the financing problem. This financing problem results from a low equity basis of the medium-sized supplier industry. Only with sufficient financial resources it is possible to deal with the financial risks of R&D and product liability, for example through call-backs. Furthermore, it is very doubtful that the vehicle manufacturers will support a technical network of suppliers in terms of corporate and brand-independent standards, which is not controlled by them.

4.5   Trends in Innovation Activities

Many studies deal with "the car and the future". After euphoric forecasts with regard to the introduction of technologies for "automated guided driving" or alternative propulsion technology like the fuel cell more recent studies offer a more sceptical look at the time horizon for the implementation of such technologies. This change can be explained by a multiplicity of reasons like the degree of maturity of these technologies, legal problems of product liability or high opportunity costs in comparison with other technologies. Hence, one should expect the basic features of vehicles to be the same in future: Automated guided vehicle technologies for example will not be avaiable in the near future, innovations will be rather incremental than radical and be hidden to the end customer or be revealed on the second sight.

A study accomplished by Roland Berger & Partners (2000) yields an illustration of upcoming trends in value added for different components of a vehicle induced by innovations (Figure 74). This illustration highlights especially the importance of incorporating IT into automotive innovation. It is expected that 90% of all future innovation in the automobile will be driven by IT (electronics, 2002). This affects both electronics dominated spheres of multimedia and traditional mechanical components as chassis, body or engine. In succession of X-by-wire-systems the fraction of electronics in the construction of chassis will increase from 12 to 40%. Similar developments are expected for safety features e.g. pedestrians' protection, traction control, backward driving cameras, night-view display in windshield, sensor controlled brakes or fuel economy regulation. Even product differentiation will take place more and more through electronics: Engines constructed in the same way could be adjusted to different performances. "Traditional mechanical parts will be either electronically supported or fully replaced by electronics. Components will communicate with one another and change their behaviour based on the information received from other components" (McKinsey & Company, 2003). The value of electronic components in vehicle will rise from 20% today to 40% in 2015. This development won't be without effects on vehicle manufacturers and their component suppliers. Vehicle manufacturers are trying to establish themselves in particular in electronic engine controls, but with minor success so far. In fact it appears that component suppliers specialised on electronic interfaces could occupy this growth segment (McKinsey&Company, 2003).

Fig. 74. Technological innovations

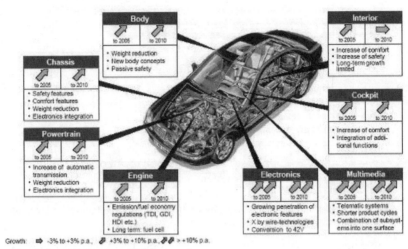

Source: Roland Berger & Partners, 2000.

When and where technologies will be accepted depends first of all on the character of final markets. In order to understand the international diffusion of innovations, it has to be explained beforehand why countries initially prefer different innovation designs. It is commonly expected that the same products are being consumed and similar processes are being applied worldwide due to globalisation. However, national differences can be observed in the applied technologies and product designs. In the USA for example other automobile designs are preferred than in Europe or Japan. The international diffusion of a specific innovation design is complicated through different conditions in each country. This may by rooted in international difference with regard to the fit of local frameworks and technical specifications which then leads to county-specific innovation designs. The riding conditions, the infrastructure, the fuel prices and the customer preferences differ by country. The European consumers e.g. prefer innovation reducing the variable costs of the ownership. As consumers are increasingly more affected by the variable costs of a motor vehicle (e.g. fuel prices), a very high increase in the first registration rate of diesel fuelled passenger cars can be observed.

Fig. 75. Share of diesel cars in first registrations of passenger cars in Western Europe, 2002 in %

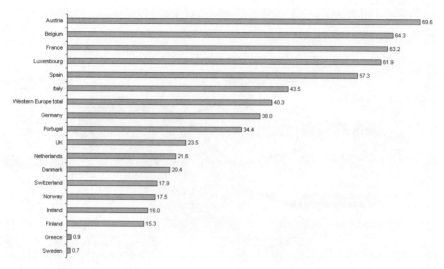

Source: Eurostat and German Association of the Automotive Industry VDA: International Auto Statistics Edition 2003, Frankfurt.

In contrast, diesel cars are not present in the US-American market where the incentive to buy diesel vehicles is so far not profitable due to the low fuel prices. Accordingly, the European and Japanese manufacturers are leading in the production of diesel technologies and due to the high market share in the first registrations of diesel-fuelled passenger cars in Europe they push innovations in the field. When and to what extent the diesel technology will be used in other countries will crucially depend on fuel price development (including taxes) in these countries. In that case, the European automotive market would be a lead market in the field of power train technology.

The Lead Market concept (Beise, 2001) suggests that for many innovations lead markets exist that initiate the international diffusion of a specific design of an innovation. Once a specific innovation design has been adopted by users in the lead market subsequent adoption by users in other countries are more likely. Therefore we define lead markets as regional markets with specific attributes that increase the probability that a locally preferred innovation design becomes internationally successful as well (Beise and Cleff, 2003). In addition, based on first mover advantages producers supplying these markets early will have permanent advantages when the technology spills over to other countries. It indicates that several European countries show the characteristics of a lead market concerning the automobile branch. Porter (1990) describes the demand conditions in Germany as one of the factors explaining the German firms' immense success in export. In addition, French companies seem to have an advantage in designing cars due to the responsiveness of their local customers.

The lead market for automobiles in Germany is characterised through a combination of several lead market factors:

- The propensity to consume with respect to automobiles leads to a comparatively high valuation of this good. The latter also determines the willingness to search, examine and select new products. This fosters the perception of product innovations by the consumer.
- High fuel prices stimulate the early diffusion of new engines with high fuel efficiency. This may result in a price advantage due to the manufacturing experience of large lot sizes for corresponding product innovations.
- The German automotive industry also benefits from a transfer advantage[84], which is maintained through the strong presence of the firms abroad and the established image of the German automotive industry as high-quality suppliers. The transfer advantage reduces the concerns of foreign consumers in terms of adopting new innovation, hence leading to an export advantage.
- The German automobile market is open and overall intensively competitive especially between local manufacturers. In addition, the size of the German automotive industry leads to industry-structure advantages through a dense network of highly specialised and technologically competent component supplier firms from all industrial sectors. Those are – opposed to the industry-structures in the USA and Japan – not bound to certain manufacturers but deliver mostly to several manufacturers. Therefore, innovations in the area of parts and components diffuse especially rapidly between the companies and foster competition further.
- Finally, the lead market role of the automobile manufacture is also strengthened by infrastructure and legal framework (dense motorway network, no speed limits, taxation). This fosters the customers' high pretensions towards driving qualities at high speed as well as safety criteria.

Because lead market consideration seems to be at the heart of competitiveness in complex products we will illustrate the importance of the factors mentioned by the example of ABS.[85] After the Second World War, ABS systems were at first developed by American and British companies, particularly for aeroplanes and racing cars. The German companies, which developed an anti-lock braking system (ABS) ready for start of production in the 1960s did not have any technical advantage at this time. Quite the contrary: The first development steps of German companies as Daimler-Benz and Teldix consisted of testing the existing (foreign) ABS systems (Bingmann, 1993). Due to insufficient technological maturity, it took until the late 1970s that a now electronic system as special equipment for luxury class vehicles was introduced at the market. Figure 76 shows the estimated process of the diffusion of ABS in passenger cars in Germany, Western Europe, USA and Japan.

---

[84]   A country has a transfer advantage if innovations first introduced and accepted in a country give hints to the innovators that this innovation is also accepted by customers in other countries.

[85]   For details see Beise et al. (2002).

Fig. 76.   International diffusion of ABS

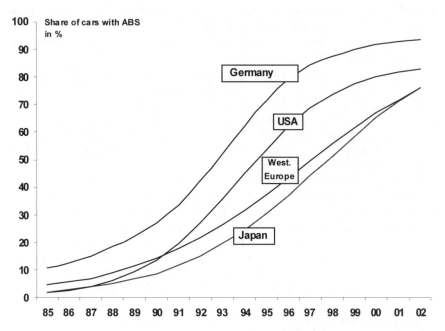

Source: Beise (2001).

The diffusion process in Germany is characterised by marketing and pricing behaviours of the pioneering companies (Daimler-Benz, BMW) as well as by strong competition. First, the additional costs for the ABS equipment were kept below the sales-price in order to establish the ABS at the market. The prices could be cut even further through the use of economies of scale in combination with the expansion of automated production facilities by the suppliers Bosch and Teves. In the meantime other companies also developed anti-block braking systems which boosted competition. Bosch was not a monopolist at the market; since the ABS could not be patented, the know-how of the technique spread out quickly. In the USA the market for ABS developed with a delay of approximately two years. Because the use of ABS was at first lower than in Europe due to the general speed limit and the drier climate so that the penetration of the market succeeded only when cost advantages of mass production allowed for lower prices for ABS. In addition the US market generally suffers from a strict manufacturer's liability. The US automotive manufacturers are retentive concerning the introduction of security innovations because each additive electronics in the vehicle could lead to additional accidents by malfunction and faulty operation in extremely rare cases. The airbag is another example: There was much fear that engine misfires could lead to injuries of the driver. Already few accidents could lead to extremely high compensation payments and losses resulting from the introduction of an innovation. For this reason, US automotive manufacturers normally wait until they observe the experiences from Europe before offering innovations in vehicles on their own. The reason for the sluggish diffusion in Japan was the additional price for ABS in proportion to the basic price of the vehicle (Bingman, 1993).

Due to the first mover effect German companies, particularly Bosch, have a significant world market share on passenger car anti-lock braking systems up to now. This national advantage has been maintained up to the present with regard to further development on electronic brake control systems (e.g. ESP, Sensotronic, ASR). Although the technical know-how was already well-known and the ability of components suppliers in many industrial countries approved the development of anti-lock braking systems in passenger cars, German companies have acquired a lead function, which is due to the early adoption of this technology in Germany (Beise et al., 2002).

It is important to mention that lead markets do have an impact on the value chain. Companies of a lead market take up the specific demand and convert it to a demand of components and preliminary products. This way, lead market impulses are passed upstream along the value chain. Idiosyncratic product innovations, which quickly adopt an innovation design that is never adopted by other countries, limit the competitiveness of firms acting within this country. A firm responding to idiosyncratic markets can achieve a temporary local innovation success but is later pushed to switch to the globally dominant design. A consideration of the lead market aspect in the national innovation policies generally means the following:
1. To support the competition between innovation designs. The different power train technologies (petrol-operated engine, diesel engine, liquid gas engines, electric motor, fuel cell) represent for example different innovation designs. The high competition between the European automotive manufacturers and between the suppliers is particularly characteristic for the European market.
2. To be amenable to the diffusion of new technologies from other countries/regions and the support of technologies on future international trends in the field of the application of these technologies, tends to result in early adoption or adaptation of new technical trends. This could be illustrated by the example of ABS brakes. This move is facilitated when manufacturers and suppliers are global players, which is particularly right for the European suppliers and automotive industry.
3. To advocate open markets between industrial countries, also particularly by supporting the diffusion of regulations and internationally uniform standards.

In Figure 77 innovations in the field of vehicle manufacturing that are expected for different dates of introduction in different regions of the triad are listed. Europe and Japan may be called a lead market for innovations in the field of driving security (chassis and body). The customer have a high interest in those aspects, whether they are willing to pay for particular features remains to be seen. Due to high costs of fuel the driving forces of innovations on the Japanese market will be those in the field of power train technologies. Innovations in driving assistant systems are also expected in Japan and Europe. In North America many innovations are expected to be introduced with a lag of three to five years, due to the legislation of product liability and the extensive cost pressure. And it is expected that the organisation of the value chain and the limited role of suppliers in innovation will also hinder early introduction by US based firms.

Fig. 77.   Innovation road map for different functional themes of the triad

Interior

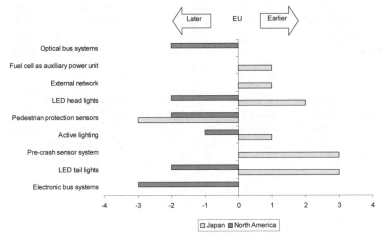

Power Train

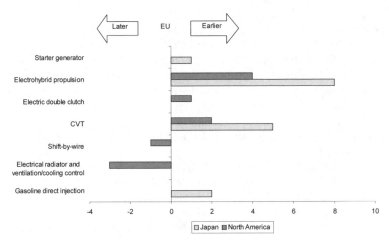

Chassis

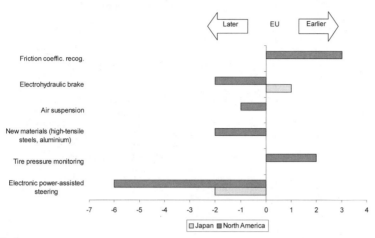

Body

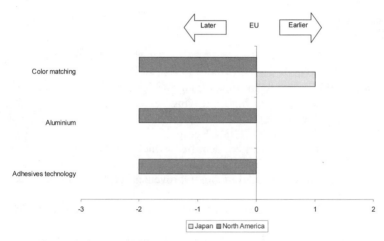

Source: McKinsey&Company, 2003.

Comparing the customer requirement of commercial vehicles with those of passenger cars, there seem to be differences in buyers' profiles, that one may assume differences in innovations' performances, too. For a customer of a passenger car the cost of purchase is most important, while a buyer of commercial vehicles tries to minimise the "total cost of ownership". Constructing lighter car body materials can reduce costs of usage, which in fact results in dynamic innovations in the area of commercial vehicles. This tendency is boosted by regulations governing emissions (EPA04/EPA07 in the USA and EURO 4 in the EU). This will in the medium term lead to innovations in fuel-injection technology and emissions aftertreatment systems (particle filters, exhaust gas recirculation, etc.) and will also affect the passenger car sector.

Fig. 78.   Total cost of ownership (TCO) for commercial vehicle 2002

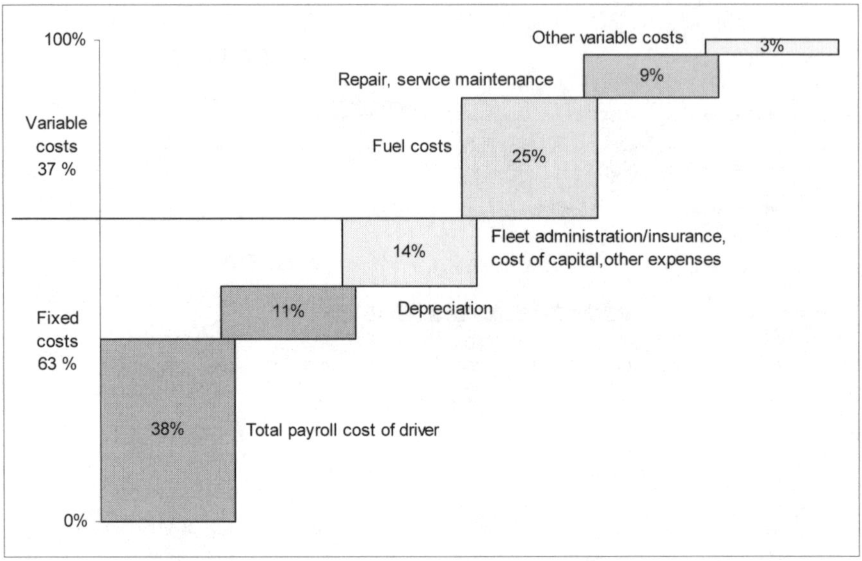

Source: McKinsey&Company, 2003.

Innovations for minimising repair time through self and remote diagnostics and lowering insurance rates through higher driving safety (e.g. electronic driving assistance like night-view display) do not vary from the needs of a passenger car customer (McKinsey&Company, 2003). Recapitulating, electronic engineering dominated paths of innovations can be identified, which are similar for the range of passenger and commercial vehicles. The basic trigger for product innovation in vehicle manufacturing lies particularly in an improvement of the whole passenger car or separate components and for this reason in an improvement of the customers' utility. This excess of innovation is not always related to consumers' willingness to pay an increased price. These innovations will increase the production costs of passenger cars up to 27% in 2015, and this increase has to be compensated, at least partly, through process innovations along the value chain.

4.6   Price and Technological Competitiveness – A Short Summary

The automotive industry is characterised by an increasing competition on a worldwide scale. All leading manufacturers produce and sell in all major regions of the world. Customers are able to chose from a wide variety of automotive products. This is especially the case in the car sector. In order to stay in the market manufacturers need to keep competitive with regard to the price dimension but also with regard to the technological dimension of competitiveness.

EU-15 automotive industry is gradually catching-up in terms of labour productivity which induces an improvement in terms of price competitiveness. However, the catching-up in the area of labour costs has been steep. Taken together EU-15 automotive industry is now under severe pressure with regard to price competitiveness. This is especially true with regard to the US which gains price advantages due to decreasing labour costs connected with some advance in the productivity area. The process of enlargement adds regions with extremely low labour costs to the EU. This will help the automotive industry to regain price competitiveness. Hence, we see increased outsourcing in the assembly as well as in the supplier industries to these new locations. However, the other side of the coin is that traditional locations of car or car-parts production in the EU-15 will face a double pressure resulting from the need of increasing price competitiveness in world markets and low cost production possibilities in the new member states. Hence, although enlargement will help the EU automotive industry to stay competitive enlargement will increase the need and the possibilities for restructuring the value chain.

Given the problems in the area of price competitiveness EU-15 automotive industry invests heavily in product and process innovation, namely R&D. There are several indications that these investments have already improved the technological competitiveness of EU automotive industry. Especially the increasing share of EU automotive industry in patenting in the 1990s nurture the hope that the catching-up of EU automotive industry will regain momentum in the future. A detailed look at the innovation possibilities in the car sectors show that the EU is well equipped for future technological challenges especially in the area of construction of car bodies and chassis. In some other areas of technological innovation the EU lags behind Japan. Especially pronounced is the technological lead of Japan in the areas of active safety features and engine technology.

5 Regulation and Industrial Policy

Thomas Cleff, Oliver Heneric, and Alfred Spielkamp

5.1 The Regulatory Environment

The automotive industry is increasingly affected by EU regulations. In general, these regulations foster competitiveness on the one hand by increasing competition within the sector and may induce new technological solutions and innovations. On the other hand regulation also poses a severe threat as it can be seen as a major driver of additional costs and may point innovation activities into dead ends where global demand trends will not follow. Regulation measures may be imposed by the European Commission by enacting laws and directives[86] in order to control and supervise the economic activities of private enterprises and citizens.

In the range of conditions affecting the competitiveness of the European automobile industry various types of regulations on the national or EU level (e.g. environmental regulation, competition law, employment regulation, social policy, consumer protection, standardisation) affect the competitiveness of the European automobile industry. For example, regulation focuses on the increasing competition within the automotive sector, the competition between modes of transport, social conditions of transport business and/or environmental and safety concerns. For our purpose it is useful to draw a rough distinction between measure and procedures that are supply side oriented, and measures with a focus on the demand side.

On the supply side, regulations have an impact on various parts of the value chain such as procurement, construction, production, distribution, and services. Among these measures are the following legal requirements:

- Block Exemption: Block Exemption regulation governs the distribution of cars and vehicle services.
- Industrial design protection and design patents: Protection of industrial design and the instrument of patenting are vital factors of innovativeness and a shield from unauthorised imitations.
- Registration, Evaluation, Authorisation and Restriction of Chemicals (REACH): The registration would include information on properties, uses and safe ways of handling the products. This safety information will be passed down the supply chain.

---

[86] For our discussion the economic perspective, mainly the interrelationship between regulation and the competitiveness of the automotive sector, is of uppermost interest. Therefore, the terms legislation, fiscal measures, directives, proposals for a regulation or directive are used as "more-or-less" similar instruments in industrial policy, and not in the precise political and/or legal meaning.

- End-of-life vehicle regulation: Vehicle manufacturers are obliged to take back old vehicles, substitute certain specific hazardous substances and increase the level of material recovery.
- The Kyoto claim: In order to reduce CO2 emissions the Commission's strategy to reduce CO2 emissions and improve fuel economy was endorsed.
- CO2 labelling: Labelling has the aim of obliging manufacturers, importers and dealers to inform consumers about fuel consumption and CO2 emissions of new vehicles.
- Fuel cell vehicles: Fuel cell technology is seen as one possible response to meet environmental challenges in the future and to achieve global leadership in this field within the next 20 to 30 years.
- Mobile Air Conditioning (MAC): work on mobile air conditioning focusing on possible options to measure and, if possible, to reduce the additional fuel consumption and related CO2 emissions, and to reduce emissions of the coolant.
- EURO 5: It can be expected that the limits for particle emissions and other gaseous pollutants will be tightened. The EURO 5 emission limit values should be applicable around the year 2010.
- EU type approval: Harmonised type approval is used only for cars (category M1 vehicles) and contains 44 EU directives.[87] An individual EU recycling directive will become part of the EU type approval.
- Safety systems: The active safety systems for all "new" cars will achieve common safety standards, for instance distance control, speed management, a reporting system and devices for the protection of vehicle occupants, pedestrians protection and cyclists.

On the demand side regulation measures affect consumers' behaviour, the willingness to pay, and the usage of motor vehicles. The intervention will probably have an impact on business-to-business as well as business-to-consumer. The selection of the following measures gives an overview of some envisaged policy instruments and legal requirements:

- Charging for external costs of transportation: Encouraging competition between alternative modes of transportation by charging for infrastructure and social costs of transportation.
- Taxation of motor vehicles: For example harmonisation of fuel taxes and restriction on tax differ by fuel category (petrol versus diesel), customer segment (industrial versus private use), and purpose (heating etc.).[88]
- Fostering bio-fuels by tax breaks: A new directive on energy products will allow tax breaks for hydrogen and bio fuels. This proposal is part of a general action that considers a certain percentage (~20%) of energy supply on the market should be covered by bio fuels.

---

[87]   With the UN-ECE Agreement of 1998, a regulatory mechanism was established whereby the US, Europe and Japan, with their widely varying vehicle approval procedures, were permitted to use common regulation.

[88]   It should be mentioned that fuel accounts for around 20% of the operating costs of road haulage companies.

- Rules and penalties: A harmonisation of rules and penalties, e.g. for disregarding road signs, laws on drink-driving or speed limits.
- Working hours: Working hours should not exceed an average level of 48 hours per week or a maximum of 60 hours per week.
- Weekend bans: A harmonisation of weekend bans for trucks on the basis of national rules.
- Driver certificate: To enable national inspectors to check that the driver is lawfully employed, a driver certificate will be introduced.
- Vocational training: A compulsory initial training for "new" drivers in the transport of goods and passengers and ongoing training for all drivers are proposed.

Some of the listed regulation measures directly aim at the automotive sector. Other regulations indirectly affect the automotive sectors by changing consumers' preferences and demand attitudes. Regulations with an impact on the level and structure of costs will rapidly affect the competitiveness of manufacturers and force them to react. Compared with supply side measures, influences on the demand side may take some time before they come into action. When consumers change their buying behaviour or postpone investments because of higher taxes or increased fuel prices cuts in market demand are very likely the consequences. The same result may occur when transportation businesses become less profitable due to rising taxes, infrastructure tolls as well as new restrictions on working hours, weekend travel etc. Declining demand will diminish returns, probably reduce profits as well, and tighten competition between manufacturers.

In the following discussion a small number of regulation measures is selected and analysed according to the impact on the competitiveness of the automotive sector. Besides, we do not carry out a comprehensive evaluation of specific political instruments and procedures, but we provide a brief and compact synthesis of a variety of studies undertaken by other experts and scientists in the field. In this context we highlight possible opportunities and threats facing the European automotive industry. The summarising review will draw attention to the importance of a sound impact assessment of EU legislation concerning the European automotive industry.

5.2   Measures and Procedures Affecting the Supply Side

Given the oligopolistic structure of the final producer segment and the ongoing M&A activities the automotive sector is tightly watched by competition authorities. One of the concerns about market power which hurt European consumers is related to the price differentials in the European car market which prevail despite the internal market. Although recent statistics show a gradual decline in price differentials within the EU there remain significant differences.[89] Recent regula-

---

[89]   As recently reported by DG Competition a Ford Focus is sold for EUR 14,022 in Germany and for EUR 10,447 in Denmark (net of taxes). Similar differences can be

tion tries to stimulate competition by putting restraints on vertical relations between the vehicle manufacturer and the car dealer. Special attention will be paid here to the impact of Block Exemption Regulation and the current discussion about the harmonisation of industrial design for spare parts.

Another field of regulation measures that is addressed on the supply side highlights the environmental impacts of transportation and the automotive industry. According to the Kyoto protocol the European Union is prepared to reduce greenhouse gas emissions by the period of 2008-2012. Close to these actions are new concepts of recycling and the recovery of materials, especially specific chemical substances that underpin the EU sustainable development strategies. Therefore, the impacts on the competitiveness of the automotive sector of the end-of-life directive, the new chemical legislation, and actions to reduce CO_2 emission will be reviewed.

5.2.1   Block Exemption Regulation

The sectors downstream of the vehicle manufacturing comprise all motor vehicle retail enterprises (NACE 50.1), all motor vehicle maintenance and repair enterprises (NACE 50.2) the sale of motor vehicle parts and accessories enterprises (NACE 50.3), the sale of motor bikes, motor bike maintenance and accessories enterprises (NACE 50.4) and the retail sale of automotive fuel (NACE 50.5). The sector consists mainly of small-scale enterprises. In 2000, 42.5% of all employees in the EU worked in enterprises with less than 10 employees. In the future the relevant changes for the automobile industry are expected in the sectors NACE 50.1 to NACE 50.4. Only these sectors will be discussed in the following (the retail and maintenance of motorbikes with a turnover rate of 2.5% is regarded as insignificant).

In 2000, about 2.74 million employees were working in sectors 50.1-50.4 in approximately 505,000 operations throughout the EU-15. Turnover per employee averaged EUR 294,300. According to the number of inhabitants there were 15.4 enterprises per 10,000 inhabitants. In Italy (23.3 enterprises per 10,000 inhabitants) and Portugal (27 enterprises per 10,000 inhabitants) the business density is rather scattered, whereas in Austria (7.3 enterprises per 10,000 inhabitants) and Germany (6.9 enterprises per 10,000 inhabitants) the business density is more concentrated. The high amount for Italy is mainly due to the comparatively large number of repair enterprises (NACE 50.2). The different degrees of concentration have an explicit influence on the value added and the gross operating rate. There is an observed tendency of a rising value added and gross operating rate with increasing concentration of businesses, if the concentration is expressed in employees per enterprise or enterprises per 10,000 inhabitants. Almost 44% of the value of the gross operating rate is explained through the business density of a country.

---

found for most cars. Also price differentials seem to be lower with more expensive cars. In general, prices are converging without a clear tendency whether they converge downwards or upwards.

Fig. 79.   Value added and business concentration

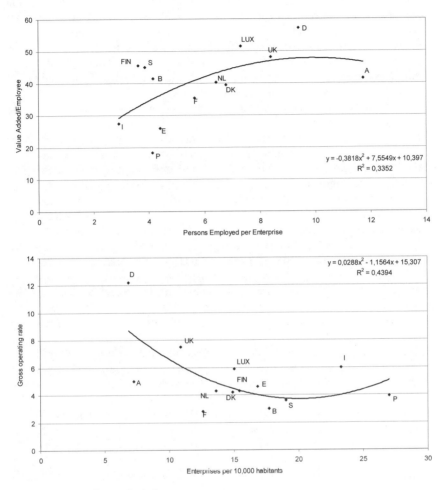

Source: Eurostat. Own calculation.

Accordingly the value added per employee is highest in Germany, Luxembourg and in the U.K. It is lowest in the southern European countries Italy, Portugal and Spain. This is also true for the gross operating rate. Since October 2002 motor vehicle distribution and servicing agreements within the EU have come under the new Block Exemption (regulation no. 1400/2002). The reason for the amendment of a former regulation (regulation 1475/95) was – according to the European Commission – insufficient competition in some sub-areas of the automotive distribution sector. The new Block Exemption is supposed to foster competition between dealers of the same brand and competition on the after-sales market, for example by facilitating cross border sales.

Vehicle manufacturers have to choose between two models of distribution:

1. In the "Selective Distribution Model" no dealer has an allocated sales territory. They can sell to any customers in the EU except to other dealers outside of the manufacturers' network. Direct sales to supermarkets or internet-dealers are not possible. Starting October 1st 2005, dealers are allowed to open up other branches in optional locations in addition to their original location.
2. In the "Exclusive Distribution Model" every dealer has an allocated sales territory. They are not permitted to sell outside the sales territory but are free to sell to operators outside the manufacturers' network.

In both models the sales and service processes will be unbundled. Vehicle manufacturers cannot insist on a mandatory link between sales and after-sales services. "Any person who can fulfil the quality criteria set by the manufacturer can become an authorised repairer and carry out all servicing, warranty and recall work on vehicles of the brand for which they are authorised, without incurring an obligation to sell vehicles" (Emanuel, 2002). Furthermore, an authorised retailer will not need permission to take over another authorised retailer. This is also true for a repairer. However, a cross-specialised acquisition of a sales business by a repairer (or vice versa) requires the consent of the vehicle manufacturer.

The repairer cannot be forced to use original spare parts anymore. Only if repair costs arise which are covered by the vehicle manufacturer, for example warranty work, free servicing and vehicle recall work, the vehicle manufacturer can insist on the use of original spare parts. Other than that, matching quality spare parts of the manufacturers or of independent suppliers can be used. A warranty, which is guaranteed beyond the legal limit, will, of course, oblige vehicle repairers to use original spare parts.

Vehicle manufacturers are similarly confined through the effects of the Block Exemption concerning the sales sector. The prohibition of multi-brand distribution will be abolished, even though vehicle manufacturers can still demand their brand to represent at least 30% of the dealer's turnover. Mere calculation tells us, that only three-brand distributions are possible. However, even though multi-brand dealers are not obliged to employ separate sales forces yet there still exist regulations in terms of the display of brands and Corporate Identities (for example the appropriate equipment of a showroom). This means that in reality we will hardly see more than two-brand distribution due to the need for sufficient capital for the brand display.

It is certainly too early at this point to evaluate the impact of the Block Exemption in all its consequences, above all since last implications of this regulation do not become effective until 2005. But the trends in automobile trade and service should be observed and be rated in the light of possible effects of the Block Exemption.

5.2.1.1   Trends in Retail Sales of Motor Vehicles and Parts of Motor Vehicles

In contrast to other industries characterised by a distinctive competition among different types of business execution i.e. cash & carry markets, supermarkets, discounters, warehouses and mail order firms, the European distribution system of the automobile industry is dominated by companies with almost identical tender in intra- and inter-brand competition (Heß, 1997). In the past, licensed dealers operated as legally independent companies acting locally, selling the producer's vehicles on their own behalf and expense. Exclusive agreements governed, among other things, the size of the sales and exhibition area, the scale of the new cars stock, quantity of demonstration cars, placement of the spare parts storage and the amount of marketing expenditure (Terporten, 1999).

Since the mid-1990s a lasting change in the distribution systems is recognisable: Vehicle manufacturers try to extend their competitive advantage by reorganising their distribution systems, by shaping customer and service-oriented sales channels. At the same time they focus on the realisation of cost reduction potentials in distribution. Because the technical vehicle quality of different manufacturers in one market segment is increasingly equivalent, product quality is not more than a necessary condition for market success. Looking for further success, vehicle manufacturers discovered the "qualified market machinery" for themselves (Terporten, 1999). Customers demand complete packages including financing and repair services. Among other high quality services, vehicle manufacturers demand retailers to observe increasingly exacting standards in staff training, exhibition room equipment as well as diagnostic and repair devices (Heß, 1997). Of course, these arrangements lead to higher costs in automobile retail.

Manufacturers are not willing to give information about the amount of estimated future cost reduction potentials in automobile retail. We are likely to see larger distribution units generated by reorganisation of the distribution channels, and sales and distribution – due to the above-mentioned link between market concentration and gross operating profit – become more efficient. The distributors' earnings are shrinking due to increasing price pressure while, at the same time, the break-even point of their business is rising and becomes more difficult to reach. Whereas it was possible in the seventies to earn high margins in automobile retail, nowadays this business has to be subsidised with funds making it earned in the after sales, service and accessories business. Figure 80 shows that the gross operating rate in automobile retail (NACE 50.1) is well below corresponding values in automobile parts and accessories (NACE 50.3) and considerably lower than in automobile repair (NACE 50.2).

Because of new competitors parts sales decreased, too. Due to the Block Exemption this trend will affect the whole after sales sector so that subsidising other areas to the present degree will no longer be possible.

Many smaller firms will be forced to give up their business. Fewer sales outlets than dealers will disappear. Many sales outlets of resigned dealers might not be closed but continued as branch of a larger retail group having larger capital requirements. The effects on economies of scale for larger dealers will – remember the positive relation between market concentration and gross operating rate formulated above – balance out decreasing margins. For the vehicle manufacturer the distribution costs will be lower with fewer access points (Cap Gemini Ernst & Young, 2003).

Fig. 80.   Gross operating rate of different downstream sectors (NACE 50) 1998

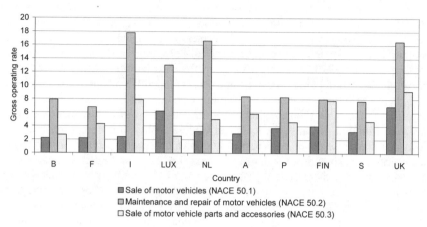

Source: Eurostat. Own calculation.

The question is, how long the process of concentration will last. Here the literature refers to the situation in the USA where "there are one third as many dealerships as in Europe. The top 25 dealers sell 1.3 million new cars per year [...].
AutoNation Inc., the largest dealer group, sells almost half a million vehicles,
through 290 outlets [...]. They appear to achieve much better profitability on new
vehicle sales than their European counterparts" (autopolis, 2000). Many of these
conclusions are made on the basis of the dealer base affiliated to NADA (National
Automobile Dealers Association) and reported by it. But it does not take into
account the bulk of dealers not affiliated to NADA. Nevertheless, a comparison of
national statistics about the quantity of establishments per 10,000 inhabitants
shows, that only Germany, Austria and Italy reach the density of operations of the
USA. In Germany there are 1,593, in Italy 1,430 vehicles in use per establishment,
in the USA this figure is at about 1,168.

The degree of concentration is much lower in other European countries. In Portugal for example, there are only 527 vehicles in use per establishment. This figure
is still above the corresponding Japanese figure at 610.

The changed legal situation under the Block Exemption leads us to expect an
improved position of the retail sector. Particularly cross-border sales and access of
hitherto "outsiders" to a brand's retail business will occur at the expense of those
dealers who were licensed under the old system. Throughout Europe, more than
34% of the dealers fear an increase of inter- and intra-brand competition because
of the Block Exemption leading to an increase of frequency and amount of discounts as well as a decrease of sales margins. Vehicle manufacturers seem to
agree (Cap Gemini Ernst & Young, 2003). Further concentration processes can be
observed in the USA and in Germany, and this development will occur at an even
higher level in countries with lower concentration. Furthermore, Block Exemption

will amplify the process. Smaller operations are very unlikely to survive the opening of the retail market.

Fig. 81.   Establishments per 10,000 inhabitants and cars in use per establishment for retail
of motor vehicles and parts of motor vehicles

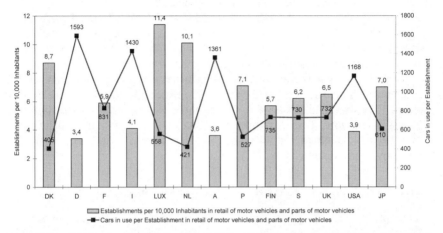

Data: USA (2000), Japan (2002), DK (1995), IRL (1996), I, S (1997) else (1998).
Source: Eurostat and Statistics Bureau: Japan Statistical Yearbook 2004, p. 408 and US
Department of Commerce: Statistical Abstract of the United States: 2002, 122nd Ed. 2002,
p. 636. Own calculation.

In turn, declining sales margins seem to be an advantage for vehicle producers,
but there is a risk that dealers substitute their shrinking margins by including further brands into their sales range. Particularly those brands that were as yet unable
to assert themselves against large dealer networks are expected to benefit from the
higher density of multi-franchise dealers. Particularly Asian vehicle manufacturer
will win over dealers who already sell an upper-end car line (Cap Gemini Ernst &
Young, 2003). European vehicle manufacturers are aware of this risk. Therefore,
they are intensifying brand specific investments. Downstream integration activities of the vehicle manufacturers who establish their own sales outlets can be observed. Especially some "prestige manufacturers have been buying up certain of
their key dealerships in order to retain control of those outlets" (Emanuel, 2002).
For years, vehicle manufacturers have supported the increasing concentration of
the dealer network because of efficiency aspects.

This process would have continued even without the Block Exemption, because
new distribution structures alongside the licensed dealers would have been created, leading to stiffer competition and increasing consolidation pressure on dealers. The new distribution structures are, among others, key accounts, car bro-
ker/online agents, internet[90], new players in the industry, like supermarkets and

---

[90]   Even if the internet was used by some vehicle producers for distributing new cars –
e.g. Fiat offered a special edition of its Barchetta in Italy exclusively via the internet

international mega dealers, as well as smaller non-authorized dealers. In the case of EU re-imports to Germany, for example, every fifth new car is sold by a non-authorized dealer.

These new distribution channels will "in general only be accepted in connection with a minimum of quality related services. The market success of new car retailers who do not also provide brand-specific servicing facilities, test drives [...], and integrated customer service, will probably be very limited" (Dr. Lademann & Partner, 2001). First appraisals of possible changes in market share of different distribution channels induced by the Block Exemption were carried out in simulation studies (Dr. Lademann & Partner, 2001): Internet dealers – like re-importers and distribution channels from outside the industry – have a market share of 2 to 3%, multi-brand dealers account for 8 to 9.5%. Especially franchised dealers will lose out. They will handle only 45 to 50% of the new cars business, which is about 35% less than before. This loss will benefit sales outlets or the direct distribution by vehicle manufacturers. Estimated at about 30 to 35%, their market share will increase by approximately 20%.

5.2.1.2 Trends in Automotive Repair and Maintenance

Another problem for the dealers arises by the unbundling of sales and service. As yet, the bulk of the retailers' margins was earned in service, to some extent sales outlets were subsidised by after sales service. These earnings threaten to decrease when new competitors access the market. This effect is amplified by the fact that the service needs of vehicles are declining, and the loyalty of customers having their service carried out by the dealer has decreased a lot and will continue to do so in future (Dudenhöffer, 1997). This can be observed in those European countries where competition has been stiff in after sales market activities for a long time – like in the UK. In countries where the amount of cars per establishment is higher the gross operating rate is likely to be higher, too, like for example in the Netherlands, Luxembourg or the UK. This may be true for countries where sales and service sectors have been bundled. The opposite is true for countries like Portugal, Italy, Sweden, Denmark and Finland, where the concentration rate of repair and maintenance companies tends to be rather low.

Unlike in Europe, the US service and sales sector is remarkably independent. Franchise dealers in the USA retain only 20% of the overall maintenance market. Even with respect to vehicles not older than one year they hold no more than 40% (autopolis, 2000). The amount of cars in use per establishment in automotive repair and maintenance, however, corresponds to that of Japan or to the European average.

---

and Vauxhall (UK) offered substantial reductions on list prices for internet purchasers (PricewaterhouseCoopers, 2000) – the internet is more often used for used cars than as distribution channel for new cars. As regards new car purchases it is primarily used to increase the customer's knowledge and to make consumers more demanding about benefits such as price and warranty coverage (Cap Gemini Ernst & Young, 2003).

Fig. 82.   Establishments per 10,000 inhabitants and cars in use per establishment in automotive repair and maintenance

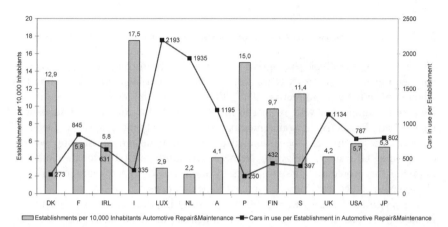

Data: USA (2000), Japan (1999), DK (1995), IRL (1996), I, S (1997) else (1998). Data for Germany not available.
Source: Eurostat and Statistics Bureau: Japan Statistical Yearbook 2004, p. 408 and US Department of Commerce: Statistical Abstract of the United States: 2002, 122nd Ed. 2002, p. 636. Own calculation.

Repair companies will be affected most by the changes under the Block Exemption due to stronger competition from countries where the sales and service sectors have traditionally been bundled. Because of additional retail and service channels, consumers are less likely to be loyal to a specific distribution or service unit. Due to this "fray" for interfaces to the end customer, the repair and maintenance sector is now faced with new customer relationship structures. Customer migration to other repair shops does not only entail the loss of value added from repair service, it also means that new car sales become less likely, so that the value added from new car sales is lost, too: Only 70% of European car owners stay with their combined dealer-service company during the warranty period, a figure which drops to only 46% after that. But it is especially after the warranty period is over that the possibility for a new car purchase increases (Cap Gemini Ernst & Young, 2003). The technology development of cars themselves and corresponding repair technologies will determine the degree to which competition in the repair segment increases. Due to the increasing complexity of vehicle technology, repair services can only be carried out by those companies who can afford the infrastructure required for diagnostic systems and special tools. These are investments that can hardly be generated by smaller companies. Either they simply disappear from the sector or they will have to content themselves with repairs with lower value added.

Due to increased capital requirements, traditional repair companies must generate further earnings from other areas. This might include providing service for other brands as well as using cheaper "matching quality" spare parts (Emanuel, 2002). As vehicle manufacturers continue to pursue their platform and parts sharing policies, repair companies are likely to benefit from synergy effects, too (Cap Gemini Ernst & Young, 2003). Smaller companies, however, are less likely to profit from these opportunities.

5.2.2   Harmonisation of Industrial Design Regulation on Spare Parts

The impact of the Block Exemption regulation can be further increased when the competition in the spare parts market will be boosted even further. At the time when the community directive 98/71/EC on industrial design protection was adopted no agreement with regard to the spare parts for complex products could be reached. Presently in some member states (e.g. France, Austria, Denmark, Sweden) spare parts can be protected by industrial design registration whereas others (e.g. UK, Italy, Belgium, Netherlands) implemented a repair clause not implying the protection of spare parts by industrial design registration. The US also do not protect spare parts by industrial design laws.

The repair market for cars is probably the most important market for spare parts in the EU. Hence, a modification of the industrial design directive is widely discussed in the industry (see ACEA, 2004). Recently, Technopolis assessed the impact of various options for modification of the industrial design directives with regard to the car repair market in Europe.

In summary, this impact assessment concludes that a modification will increase competition in the repair market. However, the concrete impact will vary in different market segments of the spare parts industry (e.g. glass vs. body parts). Despite the increase of competition it is less obvious whether the final consumer will profit by lower repair prices. It may well be the case that the reduction of the market power of the vehicle manufacturers and hence their reduction in profits will be reaped by other actors down the values chain (e.g. repair shops, producers of spare parts). In addition, there are concerns about the impact of the liberalisation of the aftermarket on the quality of spare parts and hence on car safety.

Vehicles manufacturers claim that industrial design on "must match" spare parts is needed to recoup their initial investment in the design of certain parts of cars. They claim that the envisaged modification will endanger the viability of the investment (e.g. extended testing of bumpers) needed to fulfil the recent pedestrian safety regulation and that spare parts and original parts are only two sides of the same coin.

With regard to competitiveness of the EU automotive industry the harmonisation of industrial design will probably have a limited impact. On the one hand, increased competition will put EU vehicle manufacturers and existing suppliers under pressure. This pressure will likely induce innovation which will foster competitiveness. On the other hand, new market entrants in the spare part markets will primarily be based outside the EU and hence some of the rents currently earned by EU industry will move outside the EU. In order to avoid that this redistribution of profits will be increased by an unequal meeting of quality requirements of imported and EU produced "must match" spare parts there is a need for a mechanism which secures that spare parts and original parts meets the same safety standards.

5.2.3   End-Of-Life Vehicle Directive 2000/53/EC

"The common trend in the materials composition of a car towards an increasing use of light-weight materials, especially towards the use of numerous types of plastics and the use of non-ferrous metals like aluminium, copper and magnesium. [...] The plastic content of current models has increased fourfold over the last twenty years and it is expected that it will continue to increase to about 15% in the next years" (Lucas and Schwartze, 2001). About 12 million vehicles reach their end-of-life each year in Europe, around 25% going to landfills as eight million tonnes of waste (PricewaterhouseCoopers, 2002b). In 1997, the European Commission took this fact as an opportunity to make a first proposal for a directive on the disposal of end-of-life vehicles (ELV) (European Commission COM (97) 358). After three years of discussion and an extensive "lobbying campaign", on the 18th of September, the European Parliament passed – with small concessions toward the automotive industry – Directive 2000/53/EC: Vehicle manufacturers are obliged to take back old vehicles, substitute certain specific hazardous substances and increase the level of material recovery up to 85% by 2006 and up to 95% by 2015 (2000/53/EC).

The ELV Directive obliges the vehicle producer to pay for the costs. "Despite voluntary agreements on recycling and recovery of ELVs already in place in several member states, analysts estimate the requirements of the ELV Directive might result in an additional EUR 20 to EUR 150 per vehicle costs for Compliance. [...] Theses costs will be driven through the vehicle value chain to cover activities such as collection, dismantling, recycling or recovery, and destruction of ELV" (PricewaterhouseCoopers, 2002b). In addition to the impact on costs, there are other impacts on the value chain of the vehicle manufacturer, such as new technologies and markets. Concerning product development, vehicle manufacturers have to make sure that materials that reduce the share of recyclability are not used. Vehicle manufacturers criticise the fact that a high recycling ratio collides with other environmental protection measures, such as fuel consumption. "Light-weight construction, one way of fulfilling this objective, is significantly hampered by the enforced recycling ratio, since the cost of plastic parts and composites would be particularly affected by a high material recycling ratio." (Lucas and Schwartze, 2001). Nevertheless, vehicle producers are responsible for the observance of recycling ratios. Because tier 1 suppliers take more responsibility for R&D, but are not obliged to withdraw products, the ELV Directive requires a close cooperation along the value chain activities of the vehicle manufacturer.

The withdrawal of the ELV can take place downstream, through the vehicle manufacturers themselves, or by enterprises specialising in dismantling or shredding. If vehicle manufacturers were to effect withdrawal themselves, a multiplicity of small and medium-sized car-recycling firms would lose their means of existence. If withdrawal is done by dismantling or shredding enterprises, this will allow for increased control and monitoring, such as certificates of destruction. The requirements in dealing with hazardous substances will become more exacting, so that they will only be met by bigger enterprises. No matter how the respective national transposition of the ELV Directive takes place, it will cause the severest problems for medium-sized dismantling or shredding enterprises.

5.2.4   Implications of the New EU Chemicals Legislation (REACH)

On October 29, the European Commission adopted the REACH proposal (Registration, Evaluation and Authorisation of Chemicals) for a new EU regulatory framework for chemicals. Enterprises which manufacture or import more than one ton per year and per manufacturer/importer of a specific chemical substance would be required to register it in a European-wide central database. This database would be managed by the new European Chemicals Agency. Some groups of substances would not have to be registered, like certain intermediates, polymers or other chemicals, managed under different EU legislation. The registration would include information on properties, uses and safe ways of handling the products. This safety information will be passed down the supply chain.

REACH is supposed to provide for coherence on a European level in the different national and sometimes inconsistent rules and regulations on the treatment of old and new materials throughout the whole "life" of a specific substance. As a function of the output, old materials and new materials should be subjected to standardised regulation to replace as many as 40 existing European directives and regulations.

The European Commission and various stakeholders agree on the aims of "protection of human health" and "assumption of more responsibility with regard to the dangers of chemistry products by the industry". However, there is disagreement with regard to the effects of the proposal on the capacity for innovation and the competitiveness of the chemical industry and downstream industries. The conflict is basically about the expenses resulting from additional administrative expenditure and about the time delay due to the procedure of the introduction of new products and processes. The European Commission doubts whether – compared to the already existing directives and the different national admittance regulations – significant additional cost will arise at all: "The direct costs of REACH to the chemical industry are estimated at a total of EUR 2.3 bn over an 11 year period. [...] The costs to downstream users of chemicals are estimated at EUR 2.8 bn to EUR 3.6 bn over a period of 11 and 15 years respectively. [...] The anticipated benefits to environment and human health are expected to be [...] of EUR 50 billion over a 30-year period" (European Commission, 2002).

The European industry and political representatives of some member states are in doubt about the height of the expenses for the enterprises. They argue that a multiplicity of indirect expenses are not taken into account. Costs would not only affect the chemical industry but also the downstream manufacturers of products, using notifiable chemicals as input factors. The effects on the expenses of the customers of the chemical industry would not be considered adequately. The BDI's preliminary estimate is a loss of the value added induced by REACH of 3% for Germany. Which of the two cost estimates is more realistic, is a question that cannot be investigated here. Since the chemical industry is an important supplier for the automotive industry, the focus of this paper is on the implications of REACH for the value chain of the vehicle manufacturing industry: The chemical regulation has – through the application of chemical products in components and intermediate products and the typical supply of hundreds of chemical parts for the aftermarket – a high relevance for the automotive industry, because all actors in the supply chain will be obliged to ensure the safety of a chemical substance they handle. Where a chemical is not used according to the original registration, the new uses or risk reduction measures will have to be reported to the European Chemicals Agency if the volume is higher than 1 ton. Downstream users will have the right to demand from their suppliers that they register substances for all their uses, or the downstream user can choose, for reasons of commercial confidentiality, to do their own Chemical Safety Assessment and Report. The latter requires reinforced financial and temporal expenditure for individual enterprises of the automobile industry.

First of all, this problem mainly concerns tier 1 suppliers who will take on increasing responsibility for the development of new products. Vehicle manufacturers could ask them for complete registration of the "uses" in future. Tier 1 suppliers could in turn demand on their part an appropriate registration from their tier 2 and tier 3 suppliers or directly from the manufacturer of the chemical raw material. Some marginal small and medium sized tier 2 and tier 3 suppliers will have financial problems because of the additional administrative requirements to be met under REACH. For reasons of commercial confidentialities, tier 1 suppliers will sometimes register at their own expense.

Since imported automobiles or automobile parts/modules do not need to fulfil the same requirements as those produced in the EU, vehicle manufacturers and suppliers within the EU will be disadvantaged compared to production outside the EU.

To prevent the loss of market share in export markets and an increased pressure in home markets, vehicle manufacturers and their suppliers are forced to relocate some parts of the value chain outside the EU. The loss of time due to the administrative burden of the registration process will cause a disadvantage in the innovation process for European vehicle manufacturers compared to their Japanese competitors.

5.2.5 The Kyoto Claim: CO2 Emission Reduction – the Manufacturers' Contribution

Containing the threat of climate change is one of the greatest challenges facing the international community. Cars, trucks, buses, and other motor vehicles continue to play a dominant role in causing air pollution worldwide. They are major sources of volatile organic compounds (VOCs) and nitrogen oxides, the precursors to both tropospheric ozone and acid rain; carbon monoxide (CO); toxic air pollutants such as diesel particulate; and chlorofluorocarbons (CFCs) (Walsh, 2000). According to the Kyoto protocol[91] the European Union must reduce greenhouse gas emissions by 8% compared to 1990 levels by the period of 2008-2012. Countries like Germany have to reduce emissions by 21% compared to 1990 levels according to the Kyoto protocol. Since vehicles produced by the automotive industry are major emitters of CO_2, a reaction of the industry was expected.

The European Automobile Manufacturers Association (ACEA), including BMW, DaimlerChrysler, Fiat, Ford, General Motors, Renault, Volkswagen and Volvo[92], negotiated an agreement with the European Commission in 1998 to undertake every effort to reduce CO_2 emissions from passenger cars. ACEA agreed to undertake every effort to reduce CO_2 emissions to 140 grams per kilometre (140g/km) of newly registered cars by 2008. This agreement and the consequences of reducing CO_2 have caused a consistent trend in the reduction of passenger car emissions.

The average specific emissions of the ACEA's car fleet registered in the European Union was 165 g/km in 1990. Broken down by different fuels, petrol-fuelled cars emitted 172 g/km, while diesel-fuelled cars discharged 155 g/km and alternative fuelled cars 177 g/km. Between 1995-2002 the overall reduction achieved in the car fleet was 12.1%. This trend of CO_2 reduction can be attributed to the development of new technologies, which also caused a reduction of fuel consumption. Average consumption (petrol and diesel) fell from 7.6 litres per kilometre (7.6 l/km) to 6.5 l/km. Another positive sign is the increasing share of passenger cars which emit 140 g/km CO_2 or less. ACEA stated that some manufacturers plan to include more models which fulfil the 120 g/km criterion in their product range. The share of these cars in new registrations was at 5% in 2002 compared to 0.7% in 1999. However, it is still an ambitious task to accomplish the commitment by 2008. Therefore the members of ACEA and EUCAR have initiated various R&D programmes to pursue the development of promising technologies for the reduction of CO_2 emissions. This research framework (a so-called "Framework Programme") involves manufacturers, suppliers, research institutes and universities (European Commission, 2003).

---

[91]   The Kyoto Conference took place in 1997. The protocol will enter into force if it is ratified by at least 55 of the 160 signatory countries provided that these countries account in total for at least 55% of the emissions of the industrialised countries. By the end of 2003 more than 100 countries, including the EU and its member states have deposited their instruments of ratification. However, some large countries are still missing.

[92]   Other members are: DAF Trucks NV, MAN Nutzfahrzeuge AG, Dr. Ing. h.c. F. Porsche AG, PSA Peugeot Citroen, Renault SA, SCANIA AB.

Table 31. CO_2 emissions and fuel consumption 1995-2001 (g/km)

ACEA	1995	1996	1997	1998	1999	2000	2001 (3)	2002 (3)	Change 95/02 [%] (4)
Petrol-fuelled vehicles	188	186	183	182	180	177	172	172/171(5)	-8.5/9.0%(6)
Diesel-fuelled vehicles	176	174	172	167	161	157	153	155/152(5)	-11.9/13.6%(6)
All fuels (1)	185	183	180	178	174	169	165	165/163(5)	-10.8/12.1(6)
JAMA (2)									
Petrol-fuelled vehicles	191	187	184	184	181	177	174	172	-9.9%
Diesel-fuelled vehicles	239	235	222	221	221	213	198	180	-24.7%
All fuels (1)	196	193	188	189	187	183	178	174	-11.2%
KAMA(2)									
Petrol-fuelled vehicles	195	197	201	198	189	185	179	178	-8.7%
Diesel-fuelled vehicles	309	274	246	248	253	245	234	*203	-34.3%
All fuels (1)	197	199	203	202	194	191	187	183	-7.1%
EU-15 (2)									
Petrol-fuelled vehicles	189	186	184	182	180	178	173	172	-9.0%
Diesel-fuelled vehicles	179	178	175	171	165	163	156	157	-12.3%
All fuels (1)	186	184	182	180	176	172	167	166	-10.8%

(1) Petrol and diesel-fuelled vehicles only, other fuels and statistically not identified vehicles are not expected to affect these averages significantly. (2) Data from member states are taken for 2002. For the 'change 95/02', 95 data are taken from the associations and 2002 data originate from the member states. New passenger cars put on the EU market by manufacturers not covered by the Commitments would not influence the EU average significantly. (3) The figures for 2001 and 2002 are corrected by 0.7% for the change in the driving cycle. (4) Percentages are calculated from unrounded CO_2 figures; for 2002, data is taken from member states. (5) The first figure is based on data from member states; the second figure is based on data from ACEA. (6) The first figure is based on 2002 data from member states and 1995 data from ACEA; the second figure is based solely on data from ACEA.
Source: European Commission (2004).

The members of the Japan Automobile Manufacturers Association[93] (JAMA) made a commitment to fulfil the 140 g/km level until 2009. The car fleet of JAMA registered in Europe has an average CO_2 emission of 174 g/km which is slightly more than the European manufacturers. They managed to reduce average fuel

---

[93] The members are: Nissan, Honda, Mitsubishi, Suzuki, Mazda, Toyota, Daihatsu, Yamaha, Kawasaki, Isuzu, UD, Fuji Heavy Industries.

consumption from 8.0 l/km to 7.3 l/km. To achieve the target by 2009 the members of JAMA place a focus on new technologies including direct injection and hybrid vehicles.

A different picture is drawn by the Korean Automobile Association[94] (KAMA) which reduced emissions from 197 g/km in 1995 to 183 g/km in 2002. They missed their indicative target range for 2004 which lies between 165 and 170 g/km. But KAMA also agreed to the 2009 commitment, which means a reduction to 140 g/km. To achieve this target, KAMA members focused on various technology developments to catch up with ACEA and JAMA. Their R&D focus is on different engine programmes like the HSDI diesel engine with cooled EGR and VGT (Variable Geometry Turbocharger). They also work on reducing vehicle weight by using aluminium bodies. The bottom line is still that all members have to focus on reducing CO_2 emissions to reach the 2009 target which seems to be a great deal of work at the moment (European Commission, 2003).

In its strategy to reduce CO_2 emissions, the EU does not only rely on the commitment of ACEA, JAMA and KAMA. The community also wants to spread information relating to CO_2 emissions and fuel economy. Consumers need to be informed about the importance and the advantages in order for them to be able to make an informed choice. Fiscal measures will also be part of the strategy, i.e. to offer incentives when consumers buy cars that fulfil the requirements of low CO_2 emissions and fuel consumption (European Commission, 2004).

Hybrid Engines

Automotive engine emissions are recognised as a major source of concentrated pollution, particularly in urban areas. Due to technology and cost reasons, alternative systems have been contemplated for some time and have recently become available in commercial products. Much of the present motivation for such products derives from government regulations and corporate recognition of public consciousness.

The automotive industry widely recognises that widespread use of alternative fuels will be inevitable at some point in the future. Given present limitations in alternative technologies such as batteries and fuel cells, the most viable power train alternatives are hybrid configurations that include a relatively small internal combustion (IC) engine (Assanis et al., 1999). The development goals for this progressive technology include emissions reduction, while obtaining superior fuel economy, as well as the flexibility of using either petroleum or alternative fuels. The first successful hybrid-electric car was engineered by Ferdinand Porsche in 1928. Since then, hobbyists have built such cars but no such car was put into production until 1997, when Honda Insight and Toyota Prius were the commercially available hybrid models. A hybrid car is an automobile that uses more than one power source, almost always an internal-combustion engine driving a generator to provide power to an electric motor. There are two types of hybrid electric vehicles (HEVs), series and parallel. In a series hybrid, all of the vehicle power is provided from one source. For example, with an IC/electric series hybrid, the electric motor

---

[94]   The members are: KIA, GM Daewoo, Renault Samsung, Hyundai, Ssangyong.

drives the vehicle from the battery pack and the internal combustion engine powers a generator that charges the battery. In a parallel hybrid, power is delivered through both paths. In an IC/electric parallel hybrid, both the electric motor and the internal combustion engine power the vehicle.[95]

5.2.6   Fuel Cell

In the awareness that pollution is a problem and that transportation contributes the major part, measures are taken by the jurisdictions of industrial nations, demanding emissions reduction. This will result in a growing demand for zero/ultra-low-emissions vehicles. Thanks to the technological progress in fuel cells, this type of vehicles can be delivered to the market soon, with great opportunities for business and the environment (Lohmueller, 1997).

The history of the fuel cell goes back to 1839, when Sir William Grove discovered that it is possible to generate electricity by reversing the electrolysis of water. Charles Langer and Ludwig Mond engineered the first practical fuel cell in 1889. The first successful fuel cell device was developed by Francis Bacon in 1932. The hydrogen-oxygen cell took advantage of alkaline electrolytes and nickel electrodes – inexpensive alternatives to the catalysts used by Mond and Langer. Being sojourned by a substantial number of technical hurdles, it was not until 1959 that Bacon and company first demonstrated a practical five-kilowatt fuel cell system. Harry Karl Ihrig presented his now famous 20-horsepower fuel cell-powered tractor that same year (SAE International, 2004).

In more recent decades, a number of manufacturers – including major auto manufacturers – and various international and national agencies have supported R&D in the area of fuel cell technology for use in fuel cell vehicles (FCV) and other applications. Fuel cell energy is now expected to replace traditional power sources in coming years – from micro-fuel cells to be used in cell phones to high-powered fuel cells for stock car racing (SAE International, 2004).

The fuel cell, in basic terms, consists of quantities of hydrogen and oxygen which are separated by a catalyst. Inside the cell, a chemical reaction within the catalyst generates electricity. By-products of this reaction may include heat, carbon dioxide and water. Most fuel cells are based on hydrogen extracted from such sources as gasoline or methanol. Each source has its advantages and disadvantages. Eventually, stationary fuel cells may consume hydrogen extracted from biomass, natural gas or even water which could have a tremendous impact on environmental aspects caused by the automotive industry (Plunkett, 2003).

Even though the fuel cell is an invention from the 19th century, the automotive industry could not integrate the fuel cell in a mass product. The oil crisis in the 1970s played a decisive role. Since then the fuel cell idea is no longer confined to some fringe groups, and some European governments started to think about alternatives to oil (Hild, 1998). In 1990 California took a step forward by enacting the "Californian Low Emission Vehicle Program" which prescribed that by 1998 2%

---

[95]   Hybrid Electric Vehicle Programme.

of all vehicles are to be labelled as zero emission. American, European and Japanese manufacturers initiated a focused R&D process due to the importance of California as a sales market. The automotive industry reacted by promoting electric powered vehicles. Due to problems in the development of suitable energy repositories, the focus of R&D changed. The government of California extended the time frame and the manufacturers took a strong focus on fuel cell technology (Nill, 2000). Every global automotive company from among the top ten manufacturers has a research focus on fuel cells. It is not possible to evaluate this technology's competitiveness because fuel cells are practically not available on the market yet. The majority of projects are still in a pilot stage but the technology's potential for a number of different applications is promising. Manufacturers are quite aware of the opportunities associated with fuel cell technology and industry policy could have a positive impact on this development. It is one possible response to environmental challenges, but it is an innovation that must be available at a reasonable price and meet the demands of consumer groups.

5.3   Measures and Procedures Affecting the Demand Side

The progress of mobility and economic development has been linked inextricably in recent years, and new developments in transportation and the related infrastructure have been important qualities of a nation's wealth. Particularly the automotive sector has been a driving force for economic growth and social change. Most developed countries rely on automobiles to provide personal and business mobility. Total expenditure and employment figures of the sector clearly illustrate its importance for the economy.[96]

While investment in infrastructure and the mobility of people, goods and services will have a positive influence on productivity, growth and employment, external (social) costs, especially pollution, are likely to consume resources and affect the economy adversely. Higher living standards in Europe have given rise to demands for environmental protection, quality of work, corporate social responsibility and health protection. While transportation by car enhances the standard of living, it also generates undesired environmental impacts that can lead to human health problems and ecological damage. In many ways, the demand for sustainability is an enormous challenge and leads to legal requirements such as charging for infrastructure and social cost, taxation of motor vehicles in general, and CO2 taxes.

---

[96]   Total expenditure is estimated to be some 1,000 billion EUR or roughly 10% of the European GDP and 10 million employees (European Commission, 2001).

5.3.1   Charging for Infrastructure and Social Costs of Transportation

The automotive industry depends on a highly developed and functioning transportation infrastructure (e.g. uninterrupted road traffic) to assure that their customers can turn their automotive investments into economic profits. The capacity of the roads is already too small even for today's traffic. Mobility is an indispensable part of everyday life for each and every European citizen. A European citizen currently travels an average of 35 kilometres every day. Every year, over 38 tons of goods are transported on his/her behalf over an average distance of 200 kilometres. Europe has a dense road network nearly 4 million kilometres in length. Some 50,000 kilometres of motorways link the centres of the EU countries. With more than 78,000 kilometres, the size of the network of electrified railways in Europe is quite significant, too. In the last twenty years the length of motorways in EU-15 increased by nearly 70%, whereas the length of rail tracks fell slightly under the level of the 1980s.

Fig. 83.   Index of the length of railway lines and motorways in EU-15

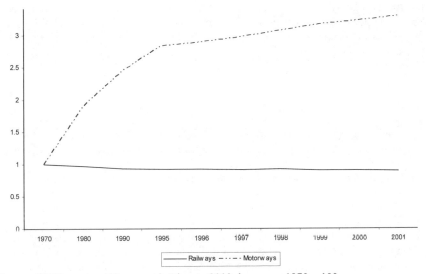

Source: EU Energy and Transport in Figures 2003; base year 1970 = 100.

In its White Paper, the European Commission notes that not only roads in major agglomerations but also large sections of the trans-European transport network are chronically congested. There are daily traffic jams on 7,500 kilometres of Europe's roads – that is, on 10% of the trans-European trunk roads and motorways. Users' preferences for transport by road seem to rely on flexibility, convenience, and independence. Other modes of transport are not able to carry freight from door to door, road transport can.[97]

---

[97]   Trends in the character of transported goods as well as the enlargement of the EU will further stimulate road transport as flexibility and speed will became even more impor-

Many parts of the motorway and trunk road network in Europe do no longer comply with the requirements of modern traffic. Maintenance claims an increasing proportion of infrastructure funding. Congestion seriously jeopardises the competitiveness of the economy. The external costs of congestion on the roads alone amount to some 0.5% of the European Union's GDP. Taking into account further growth in transport, the Commission fears that the costs of traffic jams could rise by 142% to EUR 80 bn a year, which would be equivalent to 1% of GDP in the EU.[98]

Recently, the European Commission has started a debate about the true cost of transportation.[99] The transport sector is blamed for 28% of CO_2 emissions, and the level is expected to increase by 50% in 2010.[100] Every year roughly 41,000 deaths on the road are counted, plus 1.7 million injured people. The direct costs of road accidents are estimated at 45 billion EUR, plus 160 billion EUR of indirect costs or almost 2% of the European GDP.

A "fair" allocation of charges to the user has become of uppermost interest. The concept is based on charging all modes of transport for social and environmental costs by internalising infrastructure costs such as maintenance of road surfaces and tracks, repairs to bridges, noise walls and technical facilities, as well as costs due to air pollution, noise and congestion, i.e. extra time spent on travelling, destroyed crops resulting from emissions of airborne pollutants. Prices are to reflect all used resources.[101]

---

tant in the future. And enlargement will foster road transport as it provides additional possiblities for reengineering value chains in manufacturing to profit from EU-wide costs and competences differentials.

[98] This does not even take into account the massive development needs of the applicant states for their transport networks. The Commission estimates that in these states, 20,000 kilometres of roads and 30,000 kilometres of rail tracks need either building or expanding, which would mean additional costs approaching 100 billion euros.

[99] In 2002 the EU proposed a framework directive setting out the principles and structure of an infrastructure charging system and a common methodology for setting charging levels, offsetting existing taxes, and allowing cross financing. The planned actions are meant to make the tax system more consistent by proposing uniform taxation for commercial road transport fuel by 2003 to complete the single market. See European Commission (2001) and the earlier Green Paper (1995) of the European Commission.

[100] In absolute terms, this would mean a surge from 739 million tons to 1,113 million. There is no doubt about the fact that, in this context, road transportation is the biggest polluter and accounts for 84% of the transport sector's emissions.

[101] Internal costs of transportation are mainly costs of ownership and business operation, i.e. depreciation costs, personnel costs, consumption of fuel, maintenance, insurance, taxes on the purchase, use, and operation of vehicles, tolls and charges for infrastructure. For an in-depth discussion of external costs see Table 62 "Summary of cost estimation and allocation process" in the annex.

A large number of studies have been undertaken in recent years to find a way to internalise social costs.[102] Work has been done on the definition of different cost categories, the identification of cost drivers and with a certain focus on the appropriate method for monetary quantification. Although there is agreement on the ultimate objective – that social costs should be internalised – the strategies and instruments put forward to achieve this differ widely. In the White Paper the cost levels generated by a heavy goods vehicle covering 100 km on a motorway in open country at off-peak times are specified in an interval ranging from EUR 8 to EUR 36, of which a little more than EUR 8 correspond to infrastructure charges. Broken down by different cost categories there are the following average ranges: costs of air pollution (cost of health and damaged crops) from 2.3 to 15 EUR, climate change (floods and damaged crops) from 0.2 to 1.5 EUR, infrastructure from 2.1 to 3.3 EUR, noise (cost of health) from 0.7 to 4 EUR, accidents (medical costs) from 0.2 to 2.6 EUR and congestion (loss of time) from 2.7 to 9.3 EUR (European Commission, 2001).

Table 32. The derivation of charges – road (2001) EUR/vkm

Country	Taxes	Infrastructure net payment *	External cost	Extra charge
Austria	0.14	-0.13	0.36	0.35
Croatia	0.12	-0.06	0.26	0.19
Denmark	0.09	-0.09	0.33	0.33
France	0.14	0.00	0.31	0.17
Germany	0.13	-0.05	0.30	0.22
Greece	0.17	-0.07	0.40	0.30
Hungary	0.11	-0.06	0.35	0.29
Italy	0.09	-0.01	0.30	0.22
Netherlands	0.15	-0.08	0.29	0.22
Poland	0.14	-0.06	0.28	0.20
Slovakia	0.12	-0.06	0.39	0.33
Slovenia	0.12	-0.05	0.54	0.47
Spain	0.12	0.00	0.33	0.21
Sweden	0.09	-0.04	0.24	0.19
Switzerland	0.16	-0.15	0.36	0.35
United Kingdom	0.34	-0.18	0.36	0.20
Weighted average	0.15	-0.05	0.32	0.21

Source: Recordit (2003). * Marginal infrastructure payments minus costs; some rows may not add due to rounding.

In the recent RECORDIT study[103] internal and external costs were estimated for 16 EU countries and as a weighted average. The amount of EUR 0.21 was calcu-

---

[102] Recordit (2003); Link et al. (1999); Maibach et al. (2000); Prognos (2001); Quinet (1997); Verhoef (1994); European Commission (1999); for the US Murphy and Delucchi (1998).

[103] RECORDIT stands for real cost reduction of door-to-door intermodal transport. See Recordit (2003).

lated as extra charge for every kilometre a vehicle travels as net external cost for a 40t vehicle for road transportation by adding up (marginal) infrastructure[104] costs and external costs (i.e. air pollution, noise, accidents, and congestion) and taking into account already paid taxes.[105] The comparable costs for rail transportation are quantified at 0.09 EUR/vkm. In order to maintain the correct balance between road and rail a tax increase or extra charge on road transportation of 0.12 EUR/vkm would therefore compensate for the difference.

When prices or extra charges for the use of different modes of transportation are calculated these figures reflect quite a bandwidth – a sign of understandable uncertainty. The differences occur due to scope of study, accounting system, analytical method, assumptions and data sources. The outcome of additional charging[106] for road transport is critically dependent on the response of the users. By changing the relative price level of road traffic other modes of transport should become more attractive. But, the demand for transportation services does not exclusively depend on the price. Quality and accessibility are further important determinants of demand. Consumers' propensity to demand is determined by two factors: price perception and preferences. The demand for road freight transport will fall if the relative price of transportation rises, and/or the demand for alternative modes of transportation will increase. The latter reaction depends on crossprice elasticities. If users accept the price increase (without reducing demand or shifting to alternative modes), a reduction of operator profits will occur or consumer prices are likely to rise.

Spotlight: Passengers and Freight Transport in the EU up to 2010

Over the last thirty years there has been an immense increase in auto travel in Europe, Japan, and the United States. Between 1970 and 2000, the number of cars in the Community trebled from 62.5 million to nearly 175 million. Though this trend now seems to be slowing down, the number of private cars in the Community is still rising by more than 3 million every year, and following enlargement the figure will be even higher. Today, all Europeans together own more than 180

---

[104]   The calculation of (marginal) infrastructure costs is based on the costs for maintenance and operation by a vehicle movement. The capital costs of infrastructure are regarded as fixed and not included in the analyses. The problem of an adequate charging of full (variable and fix) infrastructure costs for different modes is not solved yet. Therefore, price decisions or new charging systems should be introduced with care. Unless all cost categories are correctly quantified, prices are biased, and do not lead to an optimal solution.

[105]   Some of these external and infrastructure costs are already covered by the charges imposed on the transport vehicle itself, comprising fuel and vehicle taxes and infrastructure charges. The different tax categories contain circulation tax, registration tax, road tolls and charges, fuel tax.

[106]   For the application of the charging system a price differentiation strategy is suggested. There are a number of differentiation criteria such as category of infrastructure, time of the day, distance, size, and weight of the vehicle, etc. that should be taken into account when working with charges.

million cars and over 23 million commercial vehicles for freight transport. In 2002 over 400 cars per 1,000 inhabitants in EU-25 were counted, and in some countries the number is significantly higher (see Figure 43).

The European Commission estimates in its White Paper (European Commission, 2001), that economic growth in the European countries generates almost automatically an increase in transport volume of 38% for goods services and 24% for passengers until 2010. In passenger transport, road accounts for 79% of the market, while air, at 5%, is about to overtake railways, which have reached a ceiling of 6%. In 2000, nearly 80% – 3,789 billion passenger kilometres – of all passenger travel was undertaken by car. In contrast, the contribution of the railways was only 303 billion kilometres, or 6.3%, similar to that of air transport. Road haulage increased by 19% between 1990-1998, whereas rail haulage decreased by 43%. The European Commission assumes that passenger transport will grow by 18.4%, to 5,929 billion passenger kilometres, by 2010 (see Figure 84).

Fig. 84.   Freight transport in the EU up to 2010 in billions of ton kilometres

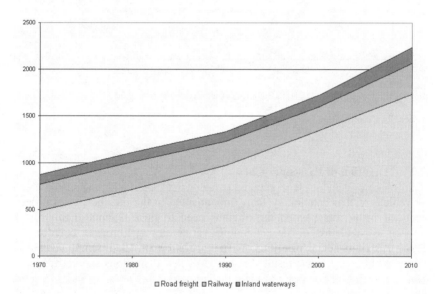

□ Road freight □ Railway ▨ Inland waterways

Source: EU Commission.

Road now makes up 44% of the goods and freight transport market compared with 41% for short sea shipping, 8% for rail and 4% for inland waterways. The movement of goods will grow by 38% by 2010, from 1,700 billion ton kilometres at present to 2,236 billion kilometres (see Figure 85). The latest European Transport Report by Prognos AG also shows that commercial vehicles will carry most of the additional freight between the European states. According to the report, the volume of goods carried by European freight vehicles will rise by a total of 42%

between 2000 and 2015.[107] This increasing demand for transport services will translate into an additional demand for cars and commercial vehicles.

Fig. 85.   Passenger transport in the EU up to 2010 in billions of passenger kilometres

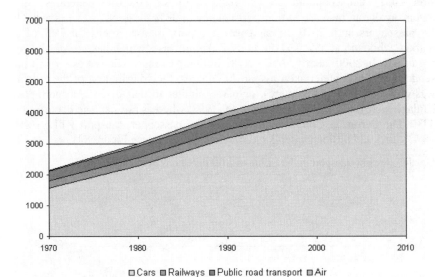

☐ Cars ■ Railways ■ Public road transport ☐ Air

Source: EU Commission.

5.3.2   Taxation of Passenger Cars

The vehicle related taxation systems implemented in the member states reflect a variety of influences beyond the obvious need to raise revenue. Currently the approach to regulation of the automobile varies among European countries, reflecting different social priorities.[108] The operation of 15 different vehicle tax systems within the EU has resulted in tax obstacles, distortions and inefficiencies. From an internal market point of view the car market in the EU is still a long way from a true single market.

Taxes on passenger cars are very diversified in terms of structure and levels. They are based on one or a mix of elements such as fiscal horsepower, engine capacity, weight, kW, price of the car, fuel consumption, or CO2 emissions:
- taxes payable at the time of acquisition, or first putting into service, of a passenger car, defined in most cases as Registration Tax (RT);

---

[107]   See Prognos (2001).

[108]   European Commission COM (2002) 431 final. See also the table in the annex "Summary of tax, environment, transport and emission policy in 2003/4 by country" taken from ACEA (2004).

- periodic taxes payable in connection with the ownership of the passenger car, defined in most cases as Annual Circulation Tax (ACT);
- taxes on fuel (FT);
- any other taxes and charges, such as insurance taxes, registration fees, road user charges, road tolls etc.[109]

Member states having a large car industry tend not to apply a Registration Tax, or they apply a lower registration tax, while car importing member states tend to levy a higher Registration Tax. Tax levels range, in extreme cases, between zero and 198% of pre-tax car price. In absolute terms average Registration Tax ranged, in 1999, between 15,659 EUR in Denmark and 267 EUR in Italy. All member states apart from France apply Annual Circulation Tax at national level. Very different objective factors are used as tax bases (e.g. cm^3, kW, CO2, weight). The average Annual Circulation Tax paid in 1999 ranged from 30 EUR/vehicle in Italy, to 463 EUR/vehicle in Denmark.

Excise duties on motor fuels are seen as an effective fiscal instrument to influence the level of car use, or for internalising environmental and social costs linked to the use of passenger cars, such as infrastructure costs, accident costs, and air pollution costs. Usually, member states applying no, or low Registration Tax, compensate revenue losses by higher fuel tax levels.[110] Motor vehicle taxation levels in the EU – measured as a tax percentage of the net price of the car – vary from 16% in Germany up to 198% in Denmark.[111]

The wide differences in tax systems have a negative impact on the ability of the car industry – and European consumers – to reap the benefits of operating within a single market. Car market fragmentation prevents industry from exploiting economies of scale, or to produce motor vehicles for the entire internal market, applying the same specifications, and does not prevent pre-tax prices from varying significantly within the internal market. Different taxation levels can explain about 20% of the European car price differentials.[112] Industry is often obliged to produce a specific car model with different specifications, in order to soften the pre-tax prices, in particular when the vehicle is destined to high taxing member states. This generates additional costs that undermine the competitiveness of the European car industry.[113] On the other hand, precisely because of the differences in tax

---

[109] Value added taxes (VAT) for motor vehicles are generally subjected to the standard rate of VAT. Value added taxes range from 15% in Luxembourg, 16% in Germany, up to 25% in Denmark and Sweden.

[110] With the only exception of the UK, they all apply lower tax levels on diesel, traditionally used by commercial vehicles. Diesel is taxed on average about 140 EUR/1000 litres lower than unleaded petrol.

[111] See ACEA (2003).

[112] TIS Study (2002).

[113] In parallel, as tax requirements differ, cars marketed in one Member State with specifications designed to meet national requirements and "tax influenced" demand (e.g. brackets of fiscal horsepower, tax policy regarding diesel), are imperfect substitutes of and may not effectively compete with cars sold in a different Member State,

levels, the car industry adapts its pre-tax prices taking into consideration the level of taxation in member states. Pre-tax prices are much higher in those member states applying no, or a low, Registration Tax.

5.3.3   Fiscal Measures in Order to Reduce CO2 Emission – CO2 Taxes

Policies and options for future action in the field of passenger car taxation are envisaged and the priority is to ensure the smooth functioning of the internal market.[114] That means modernised and simplified vehicle taxation systems, and in particular an introduction of new parameters in the tax bases of passenger car related taxes in order to make them partially, or totally, CO2 based. The process should lead to better co-ordination, and an approximation of passenger car taxation systems, by removing tax obstacles and distortions within the internal market. The use of fiscal measures is one of the pillars of the European Union's Sustainable Development Strategy.

In the Commission's opinion vehicle taxation is an important complementary instrument to support the realisation of the EU-target of 120 g CO2/km for new cars by 2008-2010, and to contribute to the accomplishment of the EU engagements under the Kyoto Protocol.[115] Therefore, it is necessary to establish a more direct relation between tax level and the CO2 performance of each new passenger car. Vehicle tax differentiation has been identified as an important parameter for improving the overall fuel-efficiency of new passenger cars. Existing vehicle taxes should be replaced by taxes fully based on CO2 emissions or, alternatively, a CO2 sensitive element should be added to existing Registration Tax and Annual Circulation Tax. Add-on elements would also allow taking into account other national environmental objectives, e.g. the early introduction of EURO 4 or the forthcoming EURO 5 standards.[116]

Both Registration Tax and Annual Circulation Tax should be turned into entirely CO2 based taxes, or at least a CO2 sensitive element should be added to both of them. This structural change is necessary in order to optimise the effect of taxation on the reduction of CO2 emissions from new passenger cars. Taxation should take into account the increasing importance of company cars, and provide a clear and strong incentive to companies to use more CO2 efficient cars. In most member states, existing corporate or income tax structures do not include such an incentive.

The Commission is aware of the potential conflict between the revenue objective of vehicle taxation and other policy objectives. If Registration Tax and An-

---

[114] thereby undermining the benefits which EU consumers should derive from a competitive and integrated market.
In an earlier communication the Commission sets out its views on the fundamental priorities for tax policy in the European Union. See European Commission COM (2001).
[115] COWI (2001).
[116] Com (2002) 431 final.

nual Circulation Tax were restructured in an environmentally friendly direction, revenues from these taxes could show a downward trend as a result of a successful environmental policy. However, this very much depends on the design of the restructured taxes, and on the way car buyers and car drivers react on new tax incentives. In order to ensure stable revenue, and to maintain the incentive function of these taxes, it may be necessary to amend the design and the levels of these taxes. Such amendments would also take into account the potential for revenue losses due to the expected higher fuel efficiency of future passenger car generations.

Spotlight: CO2 Savings and Estimated Technology Cost – The Example of N1[117] Vehicles

The identification and evaluation of technology options has shown that high technological potential remains for reducing CO2 emissions from vehicles over the next 15 years. In addition to the analyses of the CO2 reduction efficiency of the identified technologies, a survey of technology cost was conducted.[118] Costs are given as "costs for the customer" excluding taxes. They are estimated for the year of the implementation of each technology.[119] The table summarises the findings.

A large number of currently available technologies have been identified which could reduce fuel consumption and CO2 emissions of N1 vehicles. The actual costs for the end-consumer differ due to the technology option and are ultimately a question of competition and marketing of the manufacturers. According to manufacturers the priorities of customers when buying N1 vehicles are in the following order: cost of ownership, functionality, robustness, safety and dynamics. Savings from fuel-efficiency have only little impact on the total costs of ownership, and therefore they play a minor role in decision making, both for customers and for manufacturers. The Commission believes that savings could be achieved at a cost ranging between EUR 20 and EUR 50 per ton abated.[120]

---

[117] Commercial vehicles up to 3,500 kg.

[118] RAND Europe/Institut für das Kraftfahrzeugwesen Aachen FKA/Transport&Mobility (2003), Preparation of Measures to reduce CO2 Emissions from N1 Vehicles, final Report.

[119] Technology-specific sources were analysed to derive the information presented in this chapter, and this data was supplemented by generic sources like studies by Energy and Environmental Analysis Inc. (1995, 2001), DG ENTR (2002) and own research.

[120] See European Commission COM (2004) 78 final.

Table 33. Possible CO_2 savings in 2010 and estimated technology cost – N1 vehicles

Technology option	CO_2 savings	Estimated cost (in consumer prices)[121]
Engine		
Injection	-15% to -20%	+ EUR 700 to +EUR 1,000
Valve gear	-10% to -15%	+ EUR 250
Exhausted control system	+2%	+EUR 100 to EUR 3,500
Turbo-charging, downsizing	-25% (class 1)	+20% engine cost
Hybrid	-11% to -20%	+EUR 2500 to + EUR 7,000
Fuel cell	0% to -6%	?
Alternative fuels	-10% to -19%	+ EUR 1,500
Energy management		
Accessories	-1% to -2%	+EUR 50
Starter/generator	-6% to -30%	+EUR 1,000
Drive train		
Transmission	-3% to -18%	+EUR 260 to + EUR 900
Drive train automation	-3% to -15%	+ EUR 100
Body/chassis		
Optimisation aerodynamics	-4%	+EUR 1,500
Optimisation of rolling resistance	-2%	+EUR 100
Lightweight	-4% to -7%	+EUR 1,600

Note: Basis of comparison for the CO_2 saving data is the European driving cycle (EDC).
Source: RAND Europe/FKA/Transport&Mobility (2003).

5.4   Assessment and Implications

The regulation measures described will certainly lead to a greater administrative burden and higher costs for companies in the EU. The extent to which it will be possible to transfer the arising expenses to the consumer will depend on the individual vehicle manufacturer and on the vehicle class. The fact that price elasticity is smaller on European markets compared to the US market should facilitate the transfer of at least part of the costs.

The *Block Exemption Regulation* has repercussions not just for car dealers, but for the entire automotive value chain. It is justifiable to state that this introduces a whole new market order for the automotive sector. The new Block Exemption is supposed to foster competition between dealers of the same brand and competition on the after-sales market. Particularly cross-border sales and access of hitherto "outsiders" to a brand's retail business will occur at the expense of those dealers who were licensed under the old system. Dealers fear an increase of inter- and

---

[121]   The cost estimates are based on a literature review of costs for the end-consumer. It is realistic to assume that the actual costs for the manufacturers are significantly lower. As a rule, it is estimated that the production costs are by a factor of 2 to 3 lower than the prices for the end-consumer. See European Commission COM (2004) 78 final.

intra-brand competition because of increasing discounts as well as a decrease of sales margins. In turn, declining sales margins seem to be an advantage for vehicle producers, but there is a risk that dealers substitute their shrinking margins by including further brands into their sales range. Particularly Asian vehicle manufacturers will win over dealers who already sell an upper-end car line. European vehicle manufacturers are aware of this risk and are intensifying brand specific investments to tighten the links between consumers and European brands.

Impact analyses on *industrial design regulation* conclude that a modification will increase competition in the repair market. However, the concrete impact will vary in different market segments of the spare parts industry. Despite the increase of competition it is less obvious whether the final consumer will profit by lower repair prices. It may well be the case that the reduction of the market power of the vehicle manufacturers and hence their reduction in profits will be reaped by other actors down the value chain (e.g. repair shops, producers of spare parts). Vehicles manufacturers claim that industrial design regulation on "must match" spare parts is needed to recoup their initial investment in the design of certain parts of cars. They claim that the envisaged modification will endanger the viability of the investment (e.g. extended testing of bumpers) needed to fulfil the recent pedestrian safety regulation. With regard to competitiveness of the EU automotive industry the harmonisation of industrial design will probably put EU vehicle manufacturers and existing suppliers under pressure. New market entrants in the spare part markets will primarily be based outside the EU and hence rents currently earned by European industry will move outside the EU.

Since the *End-of-Life Vehicle Directive* concerns manufacturers in Europe as well as abroad, no cost disadvantage will arise for European manufacturers compared to non-EU manufacturers at the beginning. In fact, the propinquity to car-recycling firms presumably constitutes an advantage for the European automotive industry, considering the fact that several Asian manufacturers have not managed to establish a dense network of dealers up to now. Given that the non-EU manufacturers do not intend to ignore the European market in the future, they will invest in the general use of recyclable materials as well.

As regards the Commission's proposal on the *registration, evaluation and authorisation of chemicals (REACH)*, imported automobiles or automobile parts do not have to fulfil the same requirements as those produced in the EU. Vehicle manufacturers and suppliers within the EU will be disadvantaged compared to production outside the EU. They will be forced to relocate some parts of the value chain outside the EU to avoid a loss of market share in export markets and increased pressure in home markets. Due to the administrative burden of the registration process, the loss of time will cause a disadvantage in the innovation process for European vehicle manufacturers compared to Japanese competitors.

The disadvantages for European vehicle manufacturers arising from the legal framework can only be reversed if innovations are created that are also increasingly beneficial or preferable in most countries outside the EU. This would be the case if corresponding regulations were introduced with a certain time-lag in non-EU countries or the final consumers developed a high demand for products which are registered in Europe. Thus there would be an anticipatory demand in the EU, namely at the forefront of an international trend. Vehicle manufacturers and their suppliers within the EU would then not only have a time-to-market advantage for certain product innovations but these products preferred domestically would tend to be the globally dominant design. If no anticipatory demand is created as counterbalance by REACH and thus no innovations emerge with a high probability of becoming the globally dominant design, the already existing cost disadvantages will increase and disadvantages in the process of innovation will be added.

Policy actions as well as the agreement of the industry on *reducing CO2 emissions* have caused a consistent trend in the reduction of passenger car emissions. European car manufacturers have initiated various R&D programmes to pursue the development of promising technologies for the reduction of CO_2 emissions. This research framework involves manufacturers, suppliers, research institutes and universities. Investments in new pollution standards have a direct effect on the performance and cost structure of carmakers that challenges the competitive strength of the industry. But at the same time, dealing with the measures can be the first step towards new markets by introducing new technologies and achieving technology or quality leadership.

In the context of measures to reduce CO_2 emissions an obvious disadvantage for European manufacturers is, that the ACEA manufacturers must meet the intermediate target of 140 g CO_2 per kilometre by 2008, the deadline for JAMA and KAMA is 2009. It is difficult to understand why European industry should face stricter requirements than manufacturers operating outside of Europe.

Public sector pressures to make vehicles safer and more environment-friendly will increase. These pressures will drive *research and innovation* in power trains, fuels, electric vehicles and lightweight materials. The technology of fuel cells opens a lot of opportunities for business and environment. Due to the fact that motor vehicles play a dominant role in causing air pollution manufacturers have to develop products which could face the challenge of reducing CO_2 emission. By reaching the stadium of readiness of marketing new consumer groups could be made available.

Looking for measures to slow down the growth of *road haulage* requires a concept that goes beyond traditional tax policy.[122] A charge only by fuel tax is too simple. It is not the overall level of taxes that has to be changed but the structure of the tax system. In a new system, an integration of external and infrastructure costs is possible. However, European policymakers have not, so far, created the requisite framework for harmonising motor vehicle taxes (which are determined primarily by the tax laws of the member states). Varying value added tax rates and exorbitant taxes on car sales and registrations – over 200% in some countries – are the result. In addition, the wide differences in tax systems have a negative impact on the ability of the car industry – and European consumers – to reap the benefits of operating within a single market. Car market fragmentation prevents industry from exploiting economies of scale, or to produce motor vehicles for the entire

---

[122]   Baum (2000); for the US: Han and Fang (1998); see for the discussion of the interdependencies of economic growth and mobility also Willeke (2003); Diekmann (2001).

internal market, applying the same specifications and does not prevent pre-tax prices from varying significantly within the internal market.

The *differences in national approaches to regulation* lead to a serious design problem for the manufacturers, which are under increasing competitive pressure to make their products for international markets. Conflicting national and regional regulations discourage such global players. Companies producing in the EU can achieve a temporary local innovation success in a first step, but might be forced to switch to the dominant design produced outside the EU later on. The EU becomes an idiosyncratic market. Reasons for this development may be the cost advantages of the innovation designs which are produced in other areas.

There is the risk that industry performance is weakened by numerous regulations that are interpreted and implemented differently in various member states. Dependent on their number and their complexity, legislation measures tend to have cumulative effects on the industry. In some cases regulations seem to be incoherent following different objectives that are contradictory. For example, if cars are to be largely composed of polymer composites, how are they going to be recycled? If the zero-emission vehicle is going to use batteries, how are the toxic heavy metals usually associated with batteries kept out of the environment? And how is vehicle safety maintained, when the vehicle's mass is reduced by 50%? Is the reduction of landfill consumption through increased recycling worth the net increase in energy used to run recyclable vehicles? In each case, there are critical issues among the technologies available to meet the initiative, the cost of their implementation, and their impact both on traditional measures of vehicle performance and on these newer indicators of performance. Hence, the complicated web of regulation and policies often results in trade-offs between different objectives of the regulation. Even more, different regulation aiming at the same goal (e.g. reducing the environmental impact) may lead to contradictory impacts.

While changes in taste and technology require constant re-configurations in the automotive value chain, some regulatory acts make this task more difficult and costly through increasing bureaucracy. Since these *regulations strain predominantly domestic producers* and not necessarily importing competitors they endanger the competitiveness of the European automotive sector. Cost competition will continue to encourage World Car concepts that amortise development efforts over more production units.

The automotive sector is touched by other regulation and policies through a web of intense *forward and backward linkages* with the rest of the economy. The relation between regulation and competitiveness is far from being straightforward. Regulation can enhance competitiveness but also endanger competitiveness of the industry.

Consequences of regulatory burdens of the industry are very likely an upwards trend of costs, especially of doing business in Europe, and a misallocation of resources, because of investments devoted to meet regulatory requirements instead of investments in R&D and new markets.

From the industry point of view an *improving of the EU automotive regulatory environment* will strengthen the competitiveness of the automotive sector. The competitiveness of the automotive industry depends on a stable, coherent, cost-effective regulatory framework. Government regulations that are not harmonised across borders will continue to limit (at least to some degree) the attainable gains from this strategy, giving companies good reasons to ask for improved regulatory co-ordination. Therefore, the automotive industry has always been in favour of harmonising motor vehicle standards as well as taxation in the EU, and world-wide. To meet these challenges the European Commission developed assessment tools. Impact assessment is intended to integrate, reinforce, streamline and replace separate impact assessment mechanisms. The extended impact assessment[123] fo-cuses on the economic, social and environmental as well as regulatory impacts of a proposal. It also includes an analysis of subsidiary and proportionality. Finally, an extended impact assessment process normally includes a consultation with interested parties and relevant experts according to the Commission's minimum standards for consultation.

Industry supports market driven changes where drivers of innovation and com-petitiveness are competition and market demand. The *challenge for policy makers* is to act as moderators rather than regulators. Of course, markets show weaknesses or imperfections where regulation measures can help to make business people think about their social responsibilities. But, in the end, companies are guided by business objectives. They will work out strategies and adopt instruments as long as their business can profit from them. Given the connection of government regu-lation and product competition, car companies that can develop and implement innovations in their supply chains are likely to benefit significantly in finding low-cost ways to meet requirements and put customer-desired features on vehicles.

---

[123]   For the impact assessment approach see European Commission COM (2002), Euro-pean Commission COM (2002); European Commission COM (2003).

6   Challenges and Opportunities for the European Automotive Industry

Oliver Heneric, Georg Licht, and Wolfgang Sofka

(EU)   L62
L11

The current trends in automotive production suggest a shift away from large stan-dardised fleets towards differentiated offers that follow customer tastes and needs closely. Hence, value chain operations have to follow. The importance of econo-mies of scale in production diminishes in favour of modular flexible production techniques. Large scale production is still a major instrument in achieving cost efficiency but this does no longer apply to the complete car but to a basic platform instead. Therefore, high potential car factories are smaller and more flexible pro-duction sites that operate at the centre of an optimised supply and distribution network. This development stands in sharp contrast to the gigantic production sites of the past. The modern production facilities are designed to operate profitably at almost all levels of capacity utilisation, no matter whether these fluctuations are triggered by macroeconomic trends or changes in taste.

The changing role of suppliers has been highlighted before. They were tradi-tionally responsible to achieve primarily cost efficiency in the automotive value chain while vehicle manufacturers focused on customer responsiveness. As sup-pliers move towards manufacturing whole modules the line between suppliers and manufacturers blurs, especially since suppliers also become responsible for mod-ule innovation and development. On the one hand, this development suggests increasing strategic power for the so-called first tier suppliers. Still, we doubt whether they will be able to leverage this role accordingly. Automobiles are com-plex products combining a vast amount of functions. Vehicle manufacturers still control the composition of this bundle. Albeit, customers buy the car, not an as-sembly of components and vehicle manufacturers control the prime element of this customer focus: the brand. Customers don't buy some car with a 100 hp en-gine, four seats and a radio, they buy a Porsche Cayenne, a VW Golf or a Renault Espace. Hence, producing larger portions of the car does not automatically qualify suppliers to design and build a whole car. The complete car is more than the sum of its parts. Hence, vehicle manufacturers will remain in the driver seat in the automotive production. They will decide what to produce and where to produce and the value chain will have to follow. While some experts predict a serious concentration among suppliers in the future, we share this vision only for a few dominant first tier suppliers. Vehicle manufacturers in the past have done an ex-cellent job in managing complex value chains while ensuring quality. Hence, there is no immediate indication that transaction costs could be internalised by moving from a market co-ordination mechanism towards intra-organisational solutions. Additionally, the need for individualised and flexible production could open up opportunities for small, specialised suppliers which are inadequately described as second tier suppliers since they do not bring mere screws to the table but innovative designs and technology.

Fortunately, Europe has able vehicle manufacturers and they have established a strong bond with domestic customers. These loyal customers in the largest car market in the world are a strong competitive advantage that can hardly be copied or assailed by foreign competitors. Developing and introducing a new car model requires still considerable resources (time, finances and human capital). This engagement translates into substantial risk whether the investments can be recouped by future sales. Hence, developing a new automotive product isolated from its prospective market appears to be not a feasible option. Customer feedback and interaction is necessary to yield a successful product. Therefore, the large sophisticated demand in Europe is a strong pillar of the competitive advantage of the European automotive industry. Then again, it is also true that European automotive producers need to invest abroad to generate access to tacit customer and market information to be successful in foreign markets. As long as these foreign engagements are driven by the search for knowledge and customer responsiveness abroad they make the European automotive industry stronger not weaker.

Besides, Europe has a strong position in international automotive trade. Still, most of this advantage is due to value chain re-configurations within Europe. European automotive producers achieve new potentials in efficiency by shifting production responsibilities to regions with lower costs, notably labour costs. Fortunately, after the fall of the iron curtain in Europe the new member states have emerged as great production opportunity for the European automotive industry. Especially Poland, the Czech Republic, the Slovak Republic and Hungary show the promising combination of a traditional expertise in the sector, affordable labour and the proximity to the large European markets. Although some hopes in the new member states as sales markets have not materialised yet, the engagement of the automotive industry there has turned out to be a win-win situation The changes in the production system described above facilitate such border crossing value chains. Since this value chain optimisation can be achieved within the enlarged boundaries of the European Union it is highly preferable to developments in other industries which seek comparative advantages outside of Europe. Still, those trans-European value chains need to be facilitated by an adequate infrastructure and up-to-date competencies in logistics.

6.1   A Summary of Strengths and Weaknesses, Opportunities and Threats

6.1.1   Strengths

Large home market: The EU is the largest single market for passenger cars and the second largest for commercial vehicles. It is best positioned to leverage economies of scale and scope.

Loyal European customers: European producers profit the most from positive demand factors in domestic markets since European customers predominantly prefer European brands.

Sophisticated demand: EU customers enjoy their cars beyond practical use. Many treat it as a status symbol or a hobby. Advanced feedback from loyal customers propels product quality.

Modular value chain: The value chain configuration of the European automotive industry supports flexibility and risk sharing. European producers have achieved excellence in value chain management, system standardisation and quality control.

Qualified labour: The European Automotive Industry is above all labour intensive and needs highly qualified personnel to produce highly complex, high performance, quality products. Today, the automotive products are more complex and sophisticated than ever. This implies a strong know-how base for technological innovation and a flexible labour force for organisational innovation in the value chain.

High innovation capacity: High expenditures for innovation and especially R&D in the automotive sector indicate that expectations on substantial industry dynamics in the future are high. The prominent share of the European automotive industry on these global engagements signals confidence that it will succeed in the competition for innovative products and services.

Strong position in trade: Europe holds dominant world market shares in most automotive product categories. Major indicators (revealed comparative advantages) signal that this performance can be translated in sustainable competitive potential for the future.

Responsiveness for foreign demand: The European automotive industry is highly active in leveraging knowledge, customer and market information from abroad. Those benefits can only be fully exploited by operating on site. This engagement opens up new trade opportunities for intermediate products and parts from the European home base.

Promising position in China: With China's membership in the World Trade Organisation, it is expected that the automotive industry will be one of China's largest and most powerful industries in the next twenty years. All the major car manufacturers have already established assembly plants and are still planning to build up new production capacities. The Volkswagen Group is a step ahead according to their first mover advantage.

Affordable labour in new member states: The privatisation of state-owned enterprises allowed international companies to acquire existing production plants and to employ their qualified labour force. The establishment of the automotive industry in the new member states was positively influenced by the technical labour pool. The Czech Republic for example owns 8 technical universities which establish a basis of engineers.

New member states as efficient production locations in stable European regulatory framework: New chances and possibilities arrive by the enlargement process of the EU. The 10 new member states offer a profitable production environment due to their regional labour cost and tax policy. The positive side effect is the stable regulatory framework of the European Union which backs up investments of the automotive industry.

Road transportation as major component of value chains: Road transportation is the backbone of the European transportation system. Hence, it is deeply embedded in the value chains of almost all industries. This fact translates into investments, learning curve effects and sunk costs that generate significant barriers to entry for alternative modes of transportation and subsequently stable demand for vehicles. In addition, the demand for mobility of European citizens is steadily increasing which in turn also stimulates demand for affordable cars.

6.1.2   Weaknesses

Productivity: EU still lags behind the US and Japan in terms of labour productivity despite a significant catch-up process in the last decades. In addition, the speed of catching-up slowed in the 1990s. Also, this productivity disadvantage is not outweighed by lower labour costs. On the contrary, the catching-up with regard to labour cost compared to the US is almost complete and hourly labour costs in EU-15 are larger than in Japan and Korea.

High labour costs and inflexible labour market regulation: Modern automotive production relies on high levels of flexibility and quality. To achieve these ambitious goals highly qualified employees are a prerequisite. This manpower is expensive and automotive companies want to utilise it as productive as possible. Stringent regulative corsets through unions or the legislator make it difficult to synchronise the usage of the input factor labour with the dynamics of the automotive markets. Since other production locations catch up in educated labour forces with less regulation the European competitive position is eroding.

Knowledge loss due to forced joint ventures: In some countries, e.g. China, the automotive industry has to face the challenge of a loss of knowledge by getting market access. Some legal requirements force manufacturers to hold a minority stake of local companies. An insecure legal position concerning intellectual property rights leads not only to a knowledge loss but also to a loss of competitive advantage. The framework of FDI and IPR is being improved in the major emerging markets (e.g. China). But additional rules are being set which will especially affect decisions of internationally active supplier companies.

Slow growth in the home market: The growth of the European automotive markets has been flat in recent years compared to promising markets especially in South America and Asia. In addition some advanced automotive markets (e.g. the US in the 1990s) show more positive sales trends than EU markets. As other markets continue to grow the demand advantages from the large European market diminish over time.

Political influence on value chain decisions: Success stories in automotive production have become the synonyms for economic success in many industrialised European countries. The European Union hosts a lot of famous automotive production sites that are far more than just manufacturing locations. They have become icons of national pride. That makes it politically difficult to give up those plants in favour of modern and more efficient facilities. Albeit, this is needed for the European automotive industry to become more competitive on a global scale. Hence, authorities that stand in the way of this process of creative destruction jeopardise the future success of the industry.

Myopic demand feedback for premium segment in the home market: While demand in the home market is a strong unassailable competitive advantage, European customers might not be the best proxy for demand in emerging markets. These growth markets might emphasise affordability and robustness over de-luxe models incorporating high-tech and comfort. Only recently EU car manufacturers start to address the challenge of mass motorisation in low income, emerging economies.

6.1.3   Opportunities

Strong position in world markets: While success in trade certainly indicates an excellence in production it does also generate valuable know-how in terms of assessing, opening and servicing foreign markets. This expertise in bridging soft skill gaps between countries (e.g. cultural differences) can hardly be obtained without actually operating in that field. Accordingly, Europe as a major player in international markets has established stable channels that constitute a competitive advantage.

Engagement in China: The Chinese automotive market is growing very rapidly. Among other things the country derives benefit from a FDI rate of about 60 billion USD a year. Market size, terms of investment and an improving infrastructure are the base for foreign automotive companies. The potential of the Chinese market does attract not only manufacturers but also the whole supplier industry.

Trend towards free trade: As the World Trade Organisation expands its membership and activities are under way for a new round of trade liberalisation, Europe as a major player in automotive trade should be among the prime beneficiaries from the opening of new markets and the intensification of existing relationships. For example China after entering the WTO is on the way to lower import tariffs and remove of non-tariff trade barriers for car imports. However, local content policies will stimulate the movement of all parts of the value chain and hence increase the danger of leaking out the knowledge of suppliers and of supply chain organisations (flexibility in production).

New technologies: The technology of fuel cells opens up a lot of opportunities for business and environment. Due to the fact that motor vehicles play a dominant role in causing air pollution manufacturers have to develop products which could address the challenge of reducing CO_2 emission and increasing oil prices. In addition, European automotive firms are leading in some transitional drive train technologies which can turn out profitable before the fuel cell technology is ripe for the mass market.

6.1.4   Threats

Idiosyncratic innovation: It could be a danger for the European automotive industry that major innovations are not pushed by regulation oriented at the long-term development in the global market. Instead in some cases regulation may push innovation in dead end streets, or an inconsistent regulatory framework may hamper competitiveness. In many cases the regulation in the US, especially in California which is one of the most important markets for the industry, is one step ahead. Even the announcement of the "California Low Emission Vehicle Programme" in 1990 gave a major impulse for fuel cell research.

Regulation jeopardises value chain flexibility: While changes in taste and technology require constant re-configurations in the automotive value chain, in some countries the regulatory framework makes this task more difficult and costly. If these regulations strain predominantly domestic producers and not necessarily importing competitors they endanger the competitiveness of the European automotive sector.

Deficits in road infrastructure: Obviously, rising levels of road congestion and lacking road maintenance in combination with increasing traffic volumes make road transportation and hence vehicle demand less attractive. Additionally, the shortcomings in road transportation links make the distributed automotive production system of Europe less competitive.

Overcapacities: In recent years European, North American and Japanese markets have seen a weak development in demand. In Europe and Japan the market has been sluggish for nearly a decade. On the other hand a rapid capacity build-up in emerging Asian markets and East-European markets can be observed. Both developments may induce overcapacity in a worldwide perspective and stimulate price competition. Due to high labour costs and the lagging labour productivity EU producers are not very well equipped for price competition in the standard car segment. Together with a sluggish development in established markets this may induce additional pressures for consolidation of the industry e.g. via mergers. However, it remains to be seen whether the current slump in most established markets will continue. There are examples (e.g., UK, US in the 1990s) of revitalising established markets when the macroeconomic framework is more favourable.

Macroeconomic trend in Europe: The recent economic downturn in most of Europe has also affected the demand for automotive products. Producers have largely stimulated demand through extensive sales tactics (e.g., rebates). Still, a prolonged economic downturn at home would threaten the global competitiveness of the European automotive industry.

Groundbreaking innovations challenge existing excellence in production: The European manufacturers distinguish themselves with an excellent position in different markets. Due to the fact that R&D is getting more important and it is still the key source for new products, the threat of oversleeping groundbreaking innovations is still on the agenda. Success can breed failure, as manufacturers are in danger of being locked in traditional products and technologies and ignore revolutionising developments outside their traditional field of expertise. Some of those major breakthroughs are on the horizon in the automotive sector (e.g. the fuel cell). They have the potential to make conventional value chain configurations obsolete and subsequently open up opportunities for new competitors.

Major innovation competition from Japanese producers: The Japanese automotive manufacturers do have a very competitive position with respect to global vehicle production. As much as three companies (Toyota, Honda and Nissan) are part of the top then manufacturers. Therefore they are a strong counterpart to the European and American companies. In some fields like hybrid engine they lead the market a long way ahead of other manufacturers.

6.2   The Forward Vision: A Scenario Approach

The previous SWOT analysis outlined the major driving forces in the competitiveness of the European automotive industry. While those items were presented separately they will obviously interact dynamically. While optimists will point towards combinations of strengths and opportunities, sceptics might stress weaknesses and threats. At first glance one would suggest to consider all possible combinations of factors. Without doubt this approach is the only true comprehensive concept. But, it is certainly not the most efficient one. Dozens of potential cases would almost certainly blur the essential information. Additionally, one could hardly assume that all factors interact at the exact same point in time. A truly comprehensive approach would therefore also have to include different time paths increasing the complexity of this concept even more. Subsequently, a more practicable framework is required.

While not all feasible combinations of future outcomes can be covered it is useful to define at least the range of possible developments. Hence, two scenarios were developed that represent borderline cases: A best and a worst case. Both try to look approximately 10 to 15 years into the future and are stimulated by the results of the prior analysis. Still they should under no circumstances be interpreted as predictions or forecasts. The real outcome will most likely lie between those two extremes. Additionally, given the time horizon there will almost certainly be new issucs influencing competitiveness that have not been considered yet. Nevertheless, this scenario analysis will highlight mechanisms and dynamics that may go unnoticed otherwise. They are designed to emphasise basic mechanisms and cross dependencies with the main objective of stimulating discussions on the issue.

6.2.1   The Worst Case: Killing the Engine

While the current turbulence on the world oil markets subside over time, following 2006 oil prices do not significantly come down again and stay – inflation adjusted – at the current level or climb to new record levels. The high prices spark new investments in oil drilling and new natural resources are opened up for oil extraction that were previously deemed economically unattractive. These new sources take time to develop and imply higher costs than traditional ones, stocks of which are limited. As a result supply on international oil markets grows slowly. On the other hand, demand explodes. In the USA conservation remains an issue of personal virtue and European demand shrinks only gradually. Hence, the largest traditional blocks of oil demand from industrialised countries remain almost unchanged. New market players especially from the growing Asian economies – notably China – move fast towards Western living standards. This includes necessarily energy consumption and mobility, which both translate into an increasing demand for oil.

Not surprisingly, significantly higher fuel prices raise car customer's interests in low consumption cars or even alternative fuel concepts. While there is a consensus that eventually hydrogen will be the fuel of the future predictions on its arrival on the mass market are shifted ten years ahead, again. Therefore, the need for a robust transitional solution arises. Given the popularity of diesel engines in Europe and the challenges of having two complete power train modes in one car as in hybrid cars, European manufacturers bet heavily on diesel. While a continued diesel boom in the European markets proofs them right, the rest of the world watches bewildered from the fences. By 2007 the US government following intense European diplomatic pressure, approves more favourable regulations on diesel fuel standards. As expected, the law stalls in congress as members of parliament consider those standards a valuable barrier to foreign competition for US carmakers whose expertise in producing diesel engines is in fact limited. The new diesel standards are signed into law by 2009. While the diesel engines have become highly efficient and meet strong environmental standards by then, US customers simply won't buy. The previous lax diesel fuel standards have severely eroded its image in the public opinion as stinking and dirty. More US customers know diesel as a jeans brand rather than a fuel. Besides, diesel infrastructure among US gas stations runs thin. Diesel is largely only available for trucks on truck gas pumps.

Recognising this shortcoming European manufacturers decide to copy tactics from telecommunications companies by subsidising diesel gas pumps in hope of selling more diesel fuelled cars. As a result, hundreds of gas stations change their setting, but not thousands. The infrastructure still appears to be frayed and peripheral. Diesel cars remain a niche product in northern America. US manufacturers license hybrid technology from Japanese competitors which reduces petrol consumption without shifting towards diesel. The deep gap between demand in the home market and their largest export market makes it difficult for European manufacturers to realise economies of scale. A few extend their relatively autonomous operations in the NAFTA region but they can't compete on size and hence costs. Meanwhile, Japanese manufacturers benefit heavily from this development since they moved early in the hybrid technology and can offer market ready technology right when customers ask for it. Royalty incomes from licenses in the US market combined with a strong diesel expertise for the European market make them the dominant player. European hopes of exporting the diesel trend to China fade, too, as Chinese officials advocate hybrid technology because of the learning effects when the hydrogen engine eventually arrives and because of environmental concerns in congested cities where hybrid engines pose an advantage. By 2015 European manufacturers have lost their position in world trade and focus primarily on the home market.

The large hopes European manufacturers had in the Chinese market evaporate. In accordance with previous statements the Chinese producers turn to automotive exporters by 2007. On the back of the large and steadily growing home market and without a viable alternative due to massive overcapacities and sunk investments, China becomes the world's third largest automotive exporter by 2010. By then Chinese manufacturers have emerged as highly productive producers who excel in absorbing foreign expertise from the various joint ventures with foreign producers. In an orchestrated effort Chinese producers transfer know-how and competitive resources out of the joint ventures into companies which are completely under Chinese control. Especially through the neglect of enforcing international intellectual property laws and some subtle measures of official interference in company decisions the joint venture operations loose ground on the market place. An only superficially rooted brand awareness among Chinese customers and a broad "Buy Chinese" ad campaign accelerate the process. While most trade tariffs are gone by now, non-tariff trade barriers, like special Chinese standards and regulations, make it difficult to serve the huge market through exports. The European Commission brings the case before the World Trade Organisation. In a headline making decision the WTO rules in favour of the European Union and authorises severe countervailing measures, 4 years later. Unfortunately, the global automotive value chains have moved on during that time span and the European Union settles the case with China in an agreement that gives other industries better protection from the same fate. As a result, the European automotive producers were not able to generate a large export market for themselves. To the contrary, low price imports from China are now threatening their home market and export markets in Eastern Europe.

On the production side European producers find it also difficult to compete. Innovation intensity and investment remains strong but most of these activities are spurred by regulatory requirements not by the market. Accordingly, they generate costs but rarely sales. Design – the traditional mainstay of European cars – is now not only limited by the dominant platform production concept but also by regulatory requirements that limit the freedom and creativity of European car designers. A product differentiation strategy becomes less feasible. In congruence, as European automotive customers are offered less design options, price becomes the crucial argument at the dealership. Necessarily customer loyalty towards home brands suffers. Hence, with the exception of a few niche players all manufacturers turn towards cost cutting. In a reverse of the previous small and flexible production trend, European manufacturers rely again on economies of scale. High costs for transportation, especially through fuel prices, and an inadequate infrastructure with chronically congested roads make it difficult to sustain elaborated multi-plant multi-location value chains. European manufacturers have to refocus their production system. Most of them decide to leave only marketing and R&D facilities in Europe. The labour intensive production operations are at first completely shifted towards the new member states (NMS). As labour costs start rising there too, they move further east. Naturally, some member states are hit harder than others. The burden weighs especially heavy on the largest member states. Some traditional production sites in these countries are harshly affected by this restructuring process. They are far more than just some production site but a symbol of national pride and prowess. As a result, keeping production and jobs there becomes the issue of intense political debate and union activism. In the end the respective governments respond with considerable subsidies. Those measures hamper the necessary restructuring process while jeopardising efficiency and hence competitiveness. As the outside pressures mount and the subsidised manufacturers struggle with high costs and inefficient production the idea of a mega-merger among European automotive producers begins to take shape. Afraid of foreign control, politicians fuel the idea of a European auto champion which realises the ultimate economies of scale and smoothes the reductions in workforce. This move succeeds in stabilising the European automotive production system but the shifts in market power leave the European customers worse off and stimulate import competition.

By 2019 the European automotive landscape has changed dramatically. Only three European producers service primarily their home market with more or less comparable commodity cars. Some smaller players survive serving niches in the domestic and foreign luxury car segments. They account for roughly 60% of the home market. 25 % are held by Japanese brands, the rest stems from low price imports from South Korea and China. Nearly 90% of all cars in Europe drive on diesel now. Almost 90% of diesel cars worldwide are sold in the EU. The world market for automotive products is dominated by Japanese manufacturers, while NAFTA and European producers have hardly any export success stories to tell. The vast majority of automotive production is performed on the Eastern border of the EU. EU employment in the sector is down to 350000 jobs that require market contact. The race is on for the new hydrogen engine that will shuffle the cards in automotive competitiveness anew.

6.2.2   European Automotive Industry: Taking the Pole Position

Within the next ten or fifteen years the European automotive industry has to face a lot of challenges but the industry as well as the policy makers do manage the impacts of globalisation and the upcoming principal legal stipulations.

The dependence on fossil fuels will still be a major topic on the automotive agenda but the alliance between OEM, suppliers, governments and petroleum exporting countries will be successful in terms of finding a balance between energy efficiency, sustainable oil markets, taxation and pricing. Nevertheless, the fossil reserve assets are still a limiting factor which could determine an oil price (IPE Brent Crude) in the long run at 30USD up to 32USD per barrel. In the past, the European automotive industry anticipated this trend and put a main focus on innovations concerning power engines having a high propensity to save energy. The situation of the USA is diametrically opposed. The American high level consumption of oil will still affect their economic system. Therefore, the chance of broadening diesel fuel not only for trucks but also for passenger cars is even more a possible option nowadays. The European automotive industry does have a competitive edge concerning efficient and clear diesel technologies. The hybrid technology, fostered by Japanese manufacturers, could not really achieve acceptance of a bigger share of customers and technical progress in the area remains limited. It remains an idiosyncratic innovation concept used in some densely populated areas only, which will not have a global breakthrough. Consequently, diesel as an alternative will modify the ecosystem of the USA in terms of building up new diesel distribution channels. Due to the European technological advantage, other countries will pale in comparison which leads to an absolute export advantage of products including diesel technology. The European strategy of concentrating on diesel and fuel cell by neglecting the hybrid technology turns out to hit the right position. The groundbreaking innovation in commercialising fuel cell technology is not that far away. European governments call for zero emission cars by 2015 which heightens the pressure on the manufacturers' R&D efforts. The European industry is taking benefit by falling back on research experience from previous projects. By 2015, the fuel cell is not only one of the standardised products offered by European manufacturers but also the beginning of a new age of technology.

The European automotive industry, which is highly sensitive to the general economic situation, will experience a general positive economic trend. The risk of remaining static in relation to sales is a future challenge for each OEM, supplier and region. Europe will set a trend by developing the product differentiation strategy even further and discovering tailor-made cars for new consumer groups. Regarding the age pyramid, people will be far older than twenty years ago i.e. passenger cars need to have different features which satisfy the needs of older people. Even the female car drivers will have a bigger stake in the future which forces the manufacturers to emphasise feminine components of passenger cars.

With the accession of ten countries to the European Union the economic community has grown in size as well as being more heterogeneous. The NMS will report the fastest rates of growth of various economic indicators. Besides the fact that countries still give a very different picture concerning e.g. government deficit or debt, the improving economic situation will have a positive impact. Regions in the NMS which are lagging behind benefit from special EU enlargement programmes. The European automotive industry is taking advantage of a stable regulatory framework of the European Union and relatively low wages. To economise on cheap labour in the NMS, automotive production including the supply chain shifts from west to east. Therefore, the phenomenon of automotive clusters is not static but rather dynamic. New clusters will emerge in the NMS.

On the one hand the enlargement process had its previously climax by the accession of the NMS. On the other hand, the process of a further economic enlargement taking Russia and China into account is an incontrovertible fact. The European manufacturers managed to have a foot in the door of these new markets. It is a question of time when Russia is joining the WTO. Trade barriers will vanish into thin air. Hence, the propensity of export of the European automotive industry will be assisted by this development and assure the access to new markets. The living standard in emerging markets like China and Russia take a tremendous turn. Commodities and luxury goods are accessible to larger consumer groups. The local value of cars shifts from a status symbol to a constant factor in the basket of commodities. OEM's and suppliers could take benefit of extraordinary possibilities for accelerating output and sales.

By 2020 2.5 million people will work in the automotive industry in Europe. The tripartition of Europe, Japan and the US in global car markets remains but weights shift. Europe controls now 55% of the world automotive output followed by Japan and the US. The fuel cell is part of almost every modern car by now. Pollution is no longer an issue as are traffic related deaths and injuries due to the development of active and passive safety features. The automotive sector is still the backbone of Europe's economy and other sectors are truly prospering in its shadow.

6.3   Policy Issues

In conclusion, it has been shown that the European automotive industry is currently in a strong position compared to its major rivals. Albeit this assessment is only a snapshot in time and there are major challenges and opportunities ahead. From our perspective the fate of the industry will primarily depend on the excellence and expertise of the individual companies. Improving productivity to revitalise the catching-up process is key for future European competitiveness. This is primarily the task of the automotive industry where companies must continue to invest in product and process innovation. Still, there is an important role for policy to play as an enabler and facilitator but more importantly by setting framework conditions and fostering stable macroeconomic growth. The main issues for policy arising from the report are as follows:

Excellence in Regulation

The European Union is increasingly important in setting the rules of the game. The number of regulations affecting the automotive industry has increased steadily in the last decade. Regulations follow different objectives and have different origins or starting points. Regulation at EU level augments and sometimes standardises regulation at the national level. The EU automotive industry is facing an increasingly intense web of regulations. The regulatory frame in many cases hurts the productivity catching-up process. Although impact assessment of regulatory policies is now the rule for all new regulations there will always be a dispute on whether a particular regulation will foster productivity and hence competitiveness or not. In order to revitalise the catching-up process future regulation must take long-term competitiveness as a top criterion when judging the economic impact of regulation. The regulatory framework for the EU automotive industry should be assessed and checked with regard to the consistency of this framework. In addition, future regulations have to take into account that EU automotive companies in order to exploit economies of scale and scope must be able to sell similar products in Europe and on the world market. Idiosyncratic regulation may tempt companies to invest in innovation which will only be successful in Europe and not on the worldwide market. Those regulations will hamper further steps in catching-up to Japan and the US. Regulation also has to take into account that the development of new cars needs considerable time. As early as four years before market introduction the basic setup of a new car has to be determined. Any regulation introducing changes in core elements will induce significant additional cost affecting the whole value chain and hence will result in inefficient cars. So, the regulatory framework must be stable over the life-time of a car and changes in the regulatory framework must be forward-looking for nearly a decade to be efficient.

Enhancing Competition at Home

We welcome every measure to increase fair competition on the European home market. Strong competition on the home market is the best prerequisite for success abroad. While the process of creative destruction might hurt in the short run it fosters international competitiveness. Given that merger and acquisition will continue to be a major characteristic of the industry which is driven by the need to economise on scale and scope the framework for M&A activity in EU automotive industry should be strengthened and no short sighted national champion policy should be advocated. The productivity miracle in the French automotive industry in the second half of the 1990s may also be related to the privatisation of the French automotive industry.

The market is the single best mechanism to allocate resources efficiently and distribute incomes appropriately. Shielding Europe's automotive industry from world market trends through regulation would jeopardise its competitiveness. Fostering competition is not constrained to the car sector. Also the supplier and car parts industry will be stimulated to improve its productivity and competitiveness when market forces work at an international scale. Whenever possible we advocate a market based system to implement regulatory interventions.

Macroeconomic Framework

A stable macroeconomic framework is a keystone for success of the EU automotive industry. The sluggish growth in the 1990s in most European countries contributes to slow down the productivity catching-up. Revitalising growth in Europe will be crucial for the future of the automotive industry as one of Europe's key industrial sectors. The macroeconomic reform agenda is long and has been widely discussed elsewhere. Despite considerable steps in the last years there is still room for more flexible labour markets, improvements in existing company taxation systems, et cetera. In addition, there is a role for the Commission in order to help countries to gradually converge national frameworks in these areas so that location decisions of companies are based on prevailing differences in factor prices and factor endowments and not on differences in an ever changing regulatory framework.

In addition improvements in the macroeconomic framework are needed in order to make the EU more attractive to automotive R&D and innovation. The R&D support systems at least in some EU countries favour large firms. However, given the structural shifts in the automotive industry the need for R&D investment for small and medium-sized suppliers has increased considerably. In addition, the

R&D tax credit reform in Japan with highly favourable terms for SMEs will foster R&D investment. Hence, EU countries should carefully look for innovations in their R&D support systems.

Infrastructure Upgrade

There are two major lines of argument in favour of upgrading the road infrastructure. Firstly, a functioning road system is the necessary base for automotive usage. The large home market is one of the major sustainable competitive advantages of the automotive industry. In the long run Europeans will only buy cars if they provide them with the desired degree of mobility and flexibility. Both factors depend highly on a functioning infrastructure.

Secondly, road transports are the backbone of the European transportation system. While there is a certain rationale for internalising external costs, it should not be forgotten that lowering external costs of transport might also generate additional costs to the transport system and hence to broader industrial processes. The lack of alternative modes of transportation especially in the new member states as well as the requirements in flexibility and availability of logistics in a modern economy (including the automotive industry) make it necessary to strengthen the European road infrastructure. Neglecting Europe's prime pillar in transportation, the road, would jeopardise its competitiveness as a whole.

In addition, future transport needs, fuelled by new logistics, more intense division of labour and new characteristics of products, will require flexible modes of transport. Especially in this dimension road transport has some advantage against alternative modes of transport in terms of speed and flexibility.

Even now, the road infrastructure regularly turns out to be insufficient. The full integration of new member states will stimulate an additional demand for transportation. Hence, there is a strong need for additional investment in transport infrastructure.

EU Enlargement

With the accession of ten countries to the European Union in 2004, the economic community has grown in size but even more in heterogeneity. The expectations for the economic development of the new member countries are relatively positive, even if crucial reforms continue to be pursued. The new member states offer very important site-related factors for the automotive industry which are fundamental for their competitiveness. Therefore, a future need of high skilled labour has to be satisfied and a structure of important knowledge centres like universities have to be starched.

Promoting Free Trade

It has become clear that the European automotive industry is competitive on international markets. Still, this strength can only be fully utilised internationally if barriers to free trade are removed. While these include traditional tariffs and quotas, major non tariff barriers to free trade, e.g., the lack of international standards or the intellectual property rights framework, should also be considered. Especially in these fields the automotive industry needs support from policy. Moving towards a higher degree of free trade especially with major emerging markets would certainly foster the competitiveness of the automotive industry.

Societal Goal: Reducing Emissions

The automotive industry recognises the importance of climate change. The industry has taken and will continue to take actions to contribute to long-term solutions. As a result of past industry investments, vehicle fuel efficiency has been steadily improving for many years. But these improvements have been more than offset by society's increasing demand for mobility (both people and freight) resulting in rising greenhouse gas emissions from road transport.

Cars will still be one of the most popular means of conveyance. Therefore, future efforts of the automotive industry have to focus on R&D to reach goals like zero emission or fuel cell as a standardised product within the next twenty years. Here, long-term but strict regulation is needed and new emission standards are called for. In addition, in the past tax policies proved to be important to set incentives for consumers to buy low emission cars. Hence, this strategy will probably prove successful in the future.

Main Book Title:

7 Summary and Conclusions (EU)

L11
L62 030
F23

Oliver Heneric, Georg Licht, and Wolfgang Sofka

The automotive industry is a major pillar of the European economic and social system. It provides jobs for more than 2 million Europeans. One out of ten European automotive workers lives in the new member states, underlining the importance of this sector in the EU enlargement process. They produced 17 million cars in 2002 (42% of global production) and 14% of all trucks produced worldwide. The European automotive industry spends heavily to ensure its future success: More than EUR 30 bn were invested in 2001 (EU-15). 38% of the R&D expenses of the three leading automotive regions (Japan, USA and EU) are spent in EU-15. These investments show up not only in sales and employment: 60% of all EPO patent applications in the automotive field stem from EU-25. This share is way above the EU share in overall EPO patenting.

Some of the best known global automotive players have their roots in Europe. German and French companies hold four spots in the global production top ten. Additionally, Europe has some strong niche players especially in the premium segment. Not surprisingly a strong European network of sophisticated suppliers has developed. The role of suppliers in the production process is increasing because of technological innovation and especially through organisational innovations in the value chain. Again, EU enlargement facilitates this development by combining affordable labour with the proximity to traditional European automotive clusters. Globalisation is a driving force in the industry as reflected by the fact that new supplier and manufacturing locations are predominantly built up in Eastern Europe. The other side of globalisation is the success on international markets. The industry is traditionally strongly positioned in trade and invests abroad, too. Especially emerging markets like China and the Russian Federation have become promising sources of growth and profits.

However, EU automotive industry still lags behind the US and Japan with regard to productivity. The catching-up process of the EU automotive industry has slowed down in the last decade despite a steep productivity increase in productivity in some member states. More recently, there are some signs of revitalising the catching-up to the US probably driven by the recent crisis in the US automotive market.

The level of labour costs presents an increasingly serious problem for the automotive industry in some EU member states. Still labour cost per hour worked in the EU are somewhat below the US but significantly larger than in Japan and especially in Korea. In addition, German labour costs even beat the US level. The US automotive industry managed to keep labour costs down and decreased real product labour costs in the last decade. The reverse is true for EU and Japan. Given the current level of labour productivity this development puts jobs in the EU-15 under pressure. In this context the EU enlargement has provided automotive firms in high wage countries with new opportunities to profit from low labour costs via restructuring and relocating significant parts of their value chain and will do so in the future. This will help the EU-15 automotive industry to stay competitive albeit the jobs prospects are less promising than in the past.

Excessive labour costs and their negative impact on price competitiveness are especially dangerous in the light of structural overcapacity in the global automotive industry. Seen in a global context capacity utilisation rates are still high in the EU and there were also some positive signs during 2004. However, despite overcapacity in global automotive production new capacity will enter the market soon especially in emerging countries like China but also in the new member states. This will fuel price competition globally especially in the mass market segments of the automotive industry.

Besides, Europeans are avid car buyers. They used a total of 209 million cars in 2002 (38% of all cars globally), making it the largest single market in the world. Apart from cars, the truck sector has also a considerable size of more than 30 million vehicles in use in 2002. However, due to low economic growth the demand for cars and trucks was sluggish in Europe and Japan in the last decade. Presently, there is no convincing sign for a stable turnaround.

Taking into account the tripartition of the global automotive market European automotive success should not be taken for granted. Japanese manufacturers are equally strong in investing in automotive innovations and US producers leverage not only the large home market but have also pursued internationalisation strategies for years. Besides, there are major technological challenges ahead including the most prominent example: the fuel cell.

This complex set of competitive forces might potentially influence the competitiveness of the European automotive industry. The crucial driving forces have been outlined before. In a nutshell, the European automotive industry is clearly on the move. There are major curves and curbs ahead. All Europeans compete in the same global race. It's time for accelerating, release the brakes.

Appendix

Fig. 86. Illustration on slopes of short and long-term trends

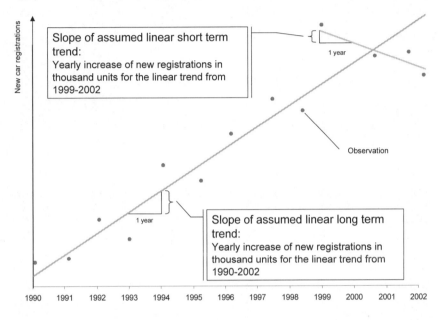

Source: ZEW.

Table 34. Slope of assumed linear trend in new registrations or sales for passenger cars in EU-25, in thousand units

Country	Slope of linear long-term trend (1990-2002)	Slope of linear short-term trend (1999-2002)
Austria	-0.1	-12.0
Belgium	4.3	-9.9
Cyprus	n/a	0.9
Czech Republic	2.1	0.8
Denmark	3.2	-11.3
Estonia	n/a	0.3
Finland	3.3	-8.3
France	6.9	11.1
Germany	-10.6	-168.4
Greece	12.9	1.0
Hungary	3.0	17.2
Ireland	11.5	-12.0
Italy	26.3	-19.1
Latvia	n/a	-1.6
Lithuania	n/a	-14.2
Luxembourg	0.4	1.0
Malta	n/a	-0.6
Netherlands	8.7	-37.0
Poland	-4.2	-114.8
Portugal	2.2	-24.9
Slovak Republic	1.8	4.2
Slovenia	0.3	-9.7
Spain	50.5	-16.7
Sweden	9.6	-16.6
UK	67.7	133.5
EU-25	n/a	-307.1
EU-15	196.7	-189.7

Source: ZEW calculation using ACEA, VDA, Eurostat data; n/a=not available.

Table 35. Slope of assumed linear trend in new registrations or sales for passenger cars in third countries, in thousand units

Country	Slope of linear long-term trend (1990-2002)	Slope of linear short-term trend (1999-2002)
Argentine	1.6	-74.4
Australia	14.9	-41.0
Belarus	n/a	-0.3
Brazil	61.9	77.1
Bulgaria	7.0	7.3
Canada	4.6	40.2
China	82.1 [1]	177.6
Croatia	n/a	3.2
India	44.1	15.2
Indonesia	n/a	3.6
Japan	-43.7	89.2
Malaysia	n/a	40.7
Mexico	25.2	79.1
New Zealand	n/a	1.2
Norway	4.0	-4.3
Romania	-9.0	-1.8
Russian Federation	85.6 [1]	11.1
Serbia and Montenegro	n/a	2.1
South Africa	2.2	14.0
South Korea	24.7	101.9
Switzerland	1.0	-6.5
Taiwan	n/a	-26.4
Thailand	n/a	20.0
Turkey	-10.5	-92.9
Ukraine	n/a	8.0
USA	-16.2	-220.9

[1] Due to data availability long-term trend was only estimated from 1995-2002.
Source: ZEW calculation using ACEA, VDA, Eurostat data; n/a=not available.

Table 36. Slope of assumed linear trend in new registrations or sales for commercial vehicles in EU-25, in thousand units

Country	Slope of linear long-term trend (1990-2002)	Slope of linear short-term trend (1999-2002)
Austria	0.3	-1.6
Belgium	2.1	-2.6
Cyprus	n/a	0.3
Czech Republic	1.2	0.1
Denmark	1.4	-0.6
Estonia	n/a	0.3
Finland	0.1	-0.5
France	8.6	9.9
Germany	1.7	-17.9
Greece	-0.9	-1.2
Hungary	1.1	1.5
Ireland	2.4	-0.4
Italy	11.0	23.6
Latvia	n/a	-0.3
Lithuania	n/a	-0.2
Luxembourg	0.2	0.3
Malta	n/a	-0.1
Netherlands	3.4	-7.7
Poland	-3.6	-8.5
Portugal	2.8	-9.9
Slovak Republic	-0.1	0.5
Slovenia	0.3	0.0
Spain	9.8	-12.7
Sweden	1.8	-0.5
UK	7.9	12.0
EU-25	n/a	-24.3
EU-15	52.5	-9.9

Source: ZEW calculation using ACEA, VDA, Eurostat data; n/a=not available.

Table 37. Slope of assumed linear trend in new registrations or sales for commercial vehicles in third countries, in thousand units

Country	Slope of linear long-term trend (1990-2002)	Slope of linear short-term trend (1999-2002)
Argentina	3.6	-27.9
Australia	11.2	58.2
Belarus	n/a	0.5
Brazil	8.4	1.5
Bulgaria	n/a	1.5
Canada	37.5	18.7
China	216.8 [1]	274.6
Croatia	n/a	2.4
India	1.5	7.0
Indonesia	n/a	63.2
Japan	-113.2	-116.1
Malaysia	n/a	8.6
Mexico	8.1	14.2
New Zealand	n/a	1.6
Norway	1.1	-0.8
Romania	-0.2	0.5
Russian Federation	-7.4 [1]	0.7
Serbia and Montenegro	n/a	-0.3
South Africa	0.5	6.2
South Korea	-15.7	12.2
Switzerland	0.3	0.4
Taiwan	n/a	11.7
Thailand	n/a	40.8
Turkey	5.1	-21.9
Ukraine	n/a	-3.0
USA	433.0	104.7

[1] Due to data availability long-term trend was only estimated from 1995-2002.
Source: ZEW calculation using ACEA, VDA, Eurostat data; n/a=not available.

214   Appendix

Table 38. Passenger cars in use, new registrations and per 1,000 inhabitants, 2002

Country	Passenger cars in use in 1,000 units 2002	Passenger cars first registrations or sales in 1,000 units 2002	Passenger cars per 1,000 inhabitants 2002
Austria	3,987.09	279.49	489.88
Belgium	4,747.37	469.00	462.30
Cyprus	280.10	24.50	368.99
Czech Republic	3,648.91	147.75	357.70
Denmark	1,892.90	111.60	352.23
Estonia	407.30	25.70	297.95
Finland	2,180.03	117.03	419.15
France	29,160.00	2,145.07	490.23
Germany	44,657.30	3,252.90	541.58
Greece	3,647.83	268.49	342.33
Hungary	2,629.53	172.34	258.71
Ireland	1,425.00	156.12	365.67
Italy	33,706.15	2,277.95	586.46
Latvia	586.20	37.80	247.94
Lithuania	1,133.50	71.30	325.72
Luxembourg	282.43	43.40	636.11
Malta	195.40	10.30	499.23
Netherlands	6,854.70	510.74	425.63
Poland	11,028.85	308.16	285.55
Portugal	3,885.00	226.09	374.28
Slovak Republic	1,326.89	65.31	246.68
Slovenia	899.17	52.60	465.19
Spain	18,732.63	1,331.88	462.01
Sweden	4,044.93	254.59	452.41
UK	28,483.96	2,563.63	476.12
EU-25	209,823.17	14,923.74	409.20
USA	130,628.68	8,103.22	452.63
Japan	54,539.80	4,441.35	427.98
Argentina	5,445.00	59.08	144.00
Australia	9,965.00	540.24	506.79
Belarus	1,512.40	2.75	152.78
Brazil	17,004.00	1,229.55	96.60
Bulgaria	2,174.10	121.50	285.26
Canada	17,543.66	934.06	558.47
China	5,570.00	1,126.03	4.34
Croatia	1,244.25	94.77	280.43
India	6,945.00	719.94	6.64
Indonesia	3,235.00	26.92	15.52
Malaysia	5,085.00	360.05	207.30
Mexico	12,964.70	706.06	127.86
New Zealand	2,228.86	58.16	574.30
Norway	1,899.80	88.72	418.64
Romania	3,246.00	88.80	145.44
Russian Federation	22,100.00	941.91	152.22
Serbia and Montenegro	1,570.30	22.65	147.35
South Africa	3,977.26	239.06	89.25
South Korea	9,737.43	1,249.11	204.40
Switzerland	3,700.95	293.03	507.61
Taiwan	4,989.34	246.05	221.54
Thailand	2,985.00	126.25	47.45
Turkey	4,600.14	90.62	68.34
Ukraine	5,442.80	107.10	112.50

Source: ZEW calculation using ACEA, VDA, EUROSTAT data; for Cyprus, Estonia, Latvia, Lithuania and Malta only 2001 data was used.

Table 39. Commercial vehicles in use and new registrations 2002

Country	Commercial vehicles in use in 1,000 units 2002	Commercial vehicles first registration or sales in 1,000 units 2002
Austria	338.79	30.61
Belgium	626.86	56.20
Czech Republic	413.53	21.72
Denmark	402.41	35.59
Estonia	80.50	5.30
Finland	316.32	17.86
France	5,984.00	456.34
Germany	3,481.65	264.83
Greece	1,078.15	19.95
Hungary	396.08	35.12
Ireland	232.00	38.33
Italy	3,884.32	305.04
Latvia	99.72	5.06
Lithuania	100.32	6.91
Luxembourg	35.07	4.94
Malta	44.70	1.70
Netherlands	1,038.60	94.84
Poland	2,031.83	31.71
Portugal	1,240.00	84.68
Slovak Republic	171.32	8.19
Slovenia	65.29	4.98
Spain	4,258.89	302.04
Sweden	408.96	34.56
UK	3,390.37	318.27
EU-25	30,237.62	2,184.57
USA	92,689.39	9,037.31
Japan	17,480.40	1,334.38
Argentina	1,487.00	23.27
Australia	2,195.00	284.07
Belarus	17.56	12.43
Brazil	4,332.00	241.57
Bulgaria	279.90	15.00
Canada	644.30	797.56
China	14,960.00	2,122.03
Croatia	138.70	13.04
Cyprus	117.95	8.03
India	2,940.00	178.45
Indonesia	1,815.00	290.18
Malaysia	1,055.00	74.90
Mexico	5,683.41	298.00
New Zealand	428.05	16.57
Norway	430.70	27.55
Romania	634.00	22.14
Russian Federation	4,540.00	178.95
Serbia and Montenegro	137.10	13.44
South Africa	1,731.09	127.84
South Korea	2,894.41	248.81
Switzerland	290.14	23.98
Taiwan	908.79	152.83
Thailand	4,365.00	282.99
Turkey	1,274.41	83.97
Ukraine	1,092.80	2.96

Source: ZEW calculation using ACEA, VDA, EUROSTAT data; for Cyprus, Estonia, Latvia, Lithuania and Malta only 2001 data was used.

Table 40. Regression results for the hedonic function

Hedonic function: $$\ln(price_i) = \alpha + \sum_j \beta_j \ln(X_i) + \sum_k \beta_k D_i + \varepsilon$$

with:
price   Price in EUR
X   Continuous quality variable
D   Dummy quality variable
i   Number of car model
j   Number of continuos quality variable
k   Number of dummy quality variable

Linear regression results (R^2=0.9089):

Variable name	Description	Coefficient	t-value
_cons	Constant	4.71	24.57
abgas	exhaust gas cleaning system (dummy)	0.02	2.05
abs	anti-lock braking system (dummy)	0.05	4.22
asr	traction control ASR (dummy)	0.05	3.92
autmat	automatic (dummy)	0.13	5.13
breifend	wide base tires (dummy)	0.11	10.02
diesel	diesel engine (dummy)	0.08	7.97
edelholz	decorative wood interior (dummy)	0.05	4.49
fheberd	power windows (dummy)	0.02	1.88
form_2	station wagon (dummy)	0.04	4.6
form_3	van (dummy)	0.08	3.01
form_4	convertible or coupe (dummy)	0.17	8.48
klimad	air conditioning (dummy)	0.06	6.82
lnccm	cylinder capacity in ccm (log)	0.37	11.33
lnkw	engine performance in kw (log)	0.48	14.92
polster_3	imitation leather (dummy)	0.02	0.6
polster_4	real leather (dummy)	0.10	3.9
radio	radio (dummy)	-0.02	-1.52
tempomat	speed control (dummy)	0.03	1.47
tuerd	more than 3 doors (dummy)	0.06	5.94

Note: Using (logarithmic) prices in EUR as dependent variable and (logarithmic) quality characteristics as independent variables.

Table 41. Regression results for the hedonic function

Hedonic function: $\ln(\text{price}_i) = \alpha + \sum_j \beta_j \ln(X_i) + \sum_k \beta_k D_i + \sum_l \beta_l B_i + \varepsilon$

with:

price	Price in Euros
X	Continuous quality variable
D	Dummy quality variable
B	Dummy brand variable
i	Number of car model
j	Number of continuos quality variable
k	Number of dummy quality variable
l	Number of dummy brand variable

Linear regression results ($R^2 = 0{,}9507$):

Variable name	Description	Coefficient	t-value
_cons	constant	4.97	30.62
abgas	exhaust gas cleaning system (dummy)	0.03	2.83
abs	anti-lock braking system (dummy)	0.05	4.36
asr	traction control ASR (dummy)	-0.01	-0.66
autmat	automatic (dummy)	0.11	5.08
breifend	wide base tires (dummy)	0.08	8.63
diesel	diesel engine (dummy)	0.06	6.64
edelholz	decorative wood interior (dummy)	0.06	5.68
fheberd	power windows (dummy)	0.03	3.86
form_2	station wagon (dummy)	0.05	7.11
form_3	van (dummy)	0.12	3.52
form_4	convertible or coupe (dummy)	0.13	8.45
klimad	air conditioning (dummy)	0.06	7.91
lnccm	cylinder capacity in ccm (log)	0.36	12.28
lnkw	engine performance in kw (log)	0.37	14.89
polster_3	imitation leather (dummy)	0.03	0.93
polster_4	real leather (dummy)	0.09	3.88
radio	radio (dummy)	0.02	2.36
tempomat	speed control (dummy)	0.04	2.36
tuerd	more than 3 doors (dummy)	0.08	9.26
audi	Audi (dummy)	0.48	14.54
bmw	Bmw (dummy)	0.44	12.9
chrysler	Chrysler (dummy)	0.17	2.66
citroen	Citroen (dummy)	0.28	7.97
daimler	Daimler (dummy)	0.56	13.07
deawoo	Deawoo (dummy)	0.18	4.89
fiat	Fiat (dummy)	0.22	6.38
ford	Ford (dummy)	0.29	8.83
honda	Honda (dummy)	0.31	8.41
hyundai	Hyundai (dummy)	0.17	4.93

Variable name	Description	Coefficient	t-value
jaguar	Jaguar (dummy)	0.53	11.22
mazda	Mazda (dummy)	0.28	8.09
mitsubishi	Mitsubishi (dummy)	0.28	7.59
nissan	Nissan (dummy)	0.25	7.17
opel	Opel (dummy)	0.29	8.84
peugeot	Peugeot (dummy)	0.30	8.39
porsche	Porsche (dummy)	1.00	16.48
proton	Proton (dummy)	0.14	4.06
renault	Renault (dummy)	0.25	7.13
rover	Rover (dummy)	0.21	5.55
saab	Saab (dummy)	0.41	7.67
seat	Seat (dummy)	0.27	8.1
skoda	Skoda (dummy)	0.15	4.64
suzuki	Suzuki (dummy)	0.22	6.25
toyota	Toyota (dummy)	0.28	8.44
volkswagen	Volkswagen (dummy)	0.35	10.93
volvo	Volvo (dummy)	0.40	12.38

Note: Using (logarithmic) prices in Euros as dependent variable and (logarithmic) quality characteristics as independent variables while introducing additional brand dummies.

Table 42. Automotive exports of OECD[1] countries in 1991 (in mn USD)

Country	78 Automotive products	781 Motor cars	782 Trucks	783 Buses, road tractors	784 Parts and accessories	Other road vehicles	Total merchandise
Germany	61,999	35,990	5,156	1,506	8,773	10,575	389,204
France	25,377	13,363	2,023	649	8,114	1,227	200,153
UK	15,096	7,221	855	137	5,471	1,411	162,276
Italy	13,748	5,878	2,077	331	4,139	1,324	162,892
Belgium/Luxembourg	18,367	13,407	1,646	973	1,860	482	111,170
Netherlands	5,150	1,458	1,035	1,049	952	656	112,862
Denmark	856	218	132	33	278	195	32,912
Ireland	175	62	33	3	57	20	22,538
Greece	20	7	1	2	7	4	6,783
Spain	13,081	9,577	764	145	2,469	127	53,476
Portugal	955	240	396	34	242	42	15,748
Sweden	5,949	2,942	757	101	2,008	140	49,734
Finland	922	598	102	57	103	62	22,730
Austria	2,316	501	763	63	765	223	40,531
Switzerland	740	181	192	21	262	85	58,661
Norway	313	9	47	7	194	57	15,756
Iceland	0	0	0	0	0	0	1,385
Turkey	151	57	6	26	57	5	10,923
Poland							
Czech Republic							
Slovak Republic							
Hungary							
Canada	26,423	14,419	6,179	542	5,208	76	98,307
USA	31,898	11,403	3,985	591	14,612	1,308	353,953
Mexico	4,302	3,623	168	4	491	16	16,462
Japan	70,507	44,991	8,418	980	11,652	4,466	308,999
South Korea							
Australia	634	343	38	2	234	18	21,083
New Zealand	32	0	0	0	28	4	7,909
OECD	299,011	166,488	34,772	7,254	67,975	22,521	2,276,445
EU-15 excluding intra EU-15 trade	40,071	21,563	3,715	1,333	8,495	4,965	475,245
OECD excluding intra EU-15 trade	175,072	96,588	22,748	3,506	41,232	10,998	1,368,683

1) OECD without Poland, Czech Republic, Slovak Republic, Hungary und Korea.
Source: OECD: ITCS – International Trade By Commodity Statistics, Rev. 3, 2001, 2002.
NIW calculation.

Table 43. Automotive exports of OECD countries in 1995 (in mn USD)

Country	78 Automotive products	781 Motor cars	782 Trucks	783 Buses, road tractors	784 Parts and accessories	Other road vehicles	Total mer- chandise
Germany	83,138	48,608	6,102	4,159	12,573	11,697	497,525
France	31,380	15,233	2,415	2,240	10,324	1,167	270,581
UK	19,448	11,325	1,149	162	5,206	1,606	214,494
Italy	19,053	8,019	2,641	127	6,051	2,215	223,963
Belgium/Luxembourg	24,500	18,025	1,654	1,299	3,074	448	152,079
Netherlands	7,371	2,622	1,121	1,379	1,573	675	153,245
Denmark	999	134	114	40	500	211	44,489
Ireland	191	22	19	2	108	40	39,961
Greece	62	13	11	10	20	8	8,998
Spain	21,157	14,877	1,168	531	4,171	410	82,981
Portugal	2,084	1,134	488	32	353	76	22750
Sweden	8,713	4,265	216	401	3,688	144	70,259
Finland	1,167	572	186	79	223	107	39,424
Austria	4,205	1,678	686	153	1,358	330	56,821
Switzerland	777	110	195	33	348	90	79,609
Norway	536	11	106	7	339	73	19,693
Iceland	0	0	0	0	0	0	1,686
Turkey	727	251	42	143	182	108	19,388
Poland	1,128	659	182	9	124	155	20,696
Czech Republic	1,399	708	154	54	363	120	15,603
Slovak Republic	0	0	0	0	0	0	0
Hungary	683	186	20	115	250	111	11,833
Canada	41,749	25,607	6,757	2,082	7,138	165	154,964
USA	47,509	16,211	4,818	1,415	23,279	1,785	487,487
Mexico	12,098	7,491	1,828	10	2,494	275	67,307
Japan	78,127	42,238	9,088	1,162	19,670	5,968	433,352
South Korea	10,122	7,243	796	364	667	1,052	126,367
Australia	835	392	79	17	302	44	30,748
New Zealand	50	1	1	0	40	9	11,200
OECD	419,206	227,634	42,036	16,025	104,420	29,091	3,357,503
EU-15 excluding intra EU-15 trade	67,552	40,500	5,089	2,051	12,950	6,961	716,470
OECD excluding intra EU-15 trade	263,292	141,608	29,155	7,463	68,148	16,918	2,196,402

Source: OECD: ITCS – International Trade By Commodity Statistics, Rev. 3, 2001, 2002. NIW calculation.

Table 44. Automotive exports of OECD countries in 1998 (in mn USD)

Country	78 Automotive products	781 Motor cars	782 Trucks	783 Buses, road tractors	784 Parts and accessories	Other road vehicles	Total merchandise
Germany	97,574	60,268	7,389	3,298	16,181	10,437	524,008
France	36,136	19,419	3,064	1,370	10,892	1,390	287,327
UK	24,630	14,489	1,415	242	7,158	1,326	256,085
Italy	19,568	6,886	2,769	125	7,505	2,284	234,698
Belgium/Luxembourg	25,547	17,590	2,059	1,652	3,527	720	160,371
Netherlands	9,866	4,240	1,245	1,925	1,480	976	153,015
Denmark	1,115	187	138	28	503	258	42,453
Ireland	419	206	64	10	77	63	60,402
Greece	81	18	12	5	27	19	9,028
Spain	26,366	16,327	3,475	328	5,568	668	101,589
Portugal	3,704	2,596	506	39	480	82	23,727
Sweden	9,475	4,085	223	504	4,475	187	75,634
Finland	1,323	742	149	75	240	118	42,347
Austria	5,561	2,347	756	247	1,832	378	60,030
Switzerland	907	135	197	33	467	76	77,652
Norway	526	16	116	6	318	71	20,374
Iceland	0	0	0	0	0	0	1,837
Turkey	827	140	31	211	359	86	24,240
Poland	2,010	1,011	343	34	415	208	26,502
Czech Republic	3,857	2,053	286	79	1,241	198	27,227
Slovak Republic	1,994	1,507	23	3	397	64	10,462
Hungary	1,412	547	11	120	567	167	22,078
Canada	46,513	28,619	6,130	2,806	8,682	275	177,975
USA	56,469	16,703	7,374	1,753	28,325	2,313	621,534
Mexico	19,502	10,962	3,591	331	4,188	431	106,501
Japan	78,012	50,832	7,661	1,050	12,742	5,726	375,742
South Korea	11,753	8,604	794	498	1,281	575	131,340
Australia	1,170	731	73	8	343	16	30,968
New Zealand	78	7	16	0	43	12	10,455
OECD	486,395	271,268	49,911	16,779	119,312	29,126	3,695,601
EU-15 excluding intra EU-15 trade	76,895	43,223	5,922	2,942	17,087	7,720	789,437
OECD excluding intra EU-15 trade	301,927	165,093	32,569	9,874	76,453	17,938	2,454,324

Source: OECD: ITCS – International Trade By Commodity Statistics, Rev. 3, 2001, 2002. NIW calculation.

Table 45. Automotive exports of OECD countries in 2001 (in mn USD)

Country	78 Automotive products	781 Motor cars	782 Trucks	783 Buses, road tractors	784 Parts and accessories	Other road vehicles	Total merchandise
Germany	105,058	67,455	7,477	3,289	17,311	9,526	550,485
France	38,899	21,803	3,263	1,096	11,627	1,109	288,640
UK	20,125	11,842	1,235	216	6,032	799	252,855
Italy	19,346	6,922	2,969	81	7,207	2,167	241,782
Belgium/Luxembourg	28,395	20,140	2,535	1,287	3,543	890	182,159
Netherlands	9,120	3,592	1,257	1,836	1,420	1,013	163,342
Denmark	1,227	387	115	45	446	235	43,912
Ireland	625	385	100	13	66	61	73,264
Greece	84	37	12	3	15	17	8,551
Spain	26,707	16,943	2,732	317	6,051	664	106,314
Portugal	3,829	2,768	308	30	648	75	23,878
Sweden	8,186	4,074	372	468	3,043	229	70,681
Finland	1,518	969	152	76	215	106	43,389
Austria	6,566	2,856	1,046	281	1,926	457	63,899
Switzerland	940	131	192	29	515	73	80,813
Norway	551	28	119	10	331	62	21,444
Iceland	2	0	1	0	0	0	1,910
Turkey	2,297	973	385	335	539	65	29,078
Poland	3,238	1,415	377	110	1,088	248	34,426
Czech Republic	5,318	2,921	105	82	2,026	185	32,499
Slovak Republic	2,330	1,760	22	3	473	72	12,363
Hungary	2,714	1,467	19	122	903	203	29,316
Canada	52,712	31,761	9,008	1,533	10,050	360	203,695
USA	56,703	18,364	6,076	988	29,165	2,110	668,292
Mexico	27,869	15,297	6,450	189	5,578	357	141,501
Japan	80,827	52,892	5,272	960	15,603	6,100	385,623
South Korea	15,363	12,029	690	522	1,906	216	149,390
Australia	2,192	1,575	61	28	465	63	32,237
New Zealand	86	1	1	0	73	11	11,308
OECD	522,828	300,787	52,353	13,949	128,266	27,473	3,947,048
EU-15 excluding intra EU-15 trade	85,650	50,707	6,287	2,862	18,764	7,030	842,432
OECD excluding intra EU-15 trade	338,792	191,320	35,065	7,774	87,479	17,154	2,676,328

Source: OECD: ITCS – International Trade By Commodity Statistics, Rev. 3, 2001, 2002.
NIW calculation.

Table 46. Automotive imports of OECD[1] countries in 1991 (in mn USD)

Country	78 Automotive products	781 Motor cars	782 Trucks	783 Buses, road tractors	784 Parts and accessories	Other road vehicles	Total mer- chandise
Germany	39,736	23,980	3,912	583	5,021	6,240	340,264
France	20,172	10,976	2,458	1,064	4,180	1,495	200,832
UK	17,949	9,644	541	132	6,457	1,175	183,768
Italy	18,996	13,481	1,805	354	2,545	812	152,794
Belgium/Luxembourg	12,062	6,561	1,111	583	3,173	634	97,443
Netherlands	9,613	5,075	1,178	359	1,909	1,092	107,624
Denmark	1,918	815	489	36	322	256	30,684
Ireland	993	565	166	36	148	78	19,000
Greece	2,417	1,540	354	83	306	134	19,214
Spain	9,612	4,553	1,006	314	3,059	679	78,352
Portugal	3,448	1,620	498	89	1,069	172	22,816
Sweden	3,886	1,768	277	101	1,429	311	44,422
Finland	1,668	756	230	6	558	117	18,251
Austria	6,067	3,835	669	158	979	426	46,635
Switzerland	5,889	4,271	495	130	503	490	60,732
Norway	1,261	503	268	88	235	167	23,990
Iceland	151	85	37	4	15	10	1,687
Turkey	907	259	118	85	394	52	17,035
Poland							
Czech Republic							
Slovak Republic							
Hungary							
Canada	23,101	10,425	2,325	302	9,485	564	105,253
USA	72,676	46,728	8,379	599	15,265	1,706	432,702
Mexico	1,176	299	152	62	511	152	30,261
Japan	6,684	5,187	185	13	933	367	161,026
South Korea							
Australia	3,324	1,735	675	50	673	190	35,777
New Zealand	778	517	132	10	74	45	7,718
OECD	264,485	155,178	27,459	5,241	59,243	17,364	2,238,280
EU-15 excluding intra EU-15 trade	26,354	16,270	1,805	62	3,695	4,522	450,834
OECD excluding intra EU-15 trade	142,302	86,279	14,570	1,406	31,782	8,265	1,327,016

1) OECD without Poland, Czech Republic, Slovak Republic, Hungary und Korea.
Source: OECD: ITCS – International Trade By Commodity Statistics, Rev. 3, 2001, 2002.
NIW calculation.

Table 47. Automotive imports of OECD countries in 1995 (in 1,000 USD)

Country	78 Automotive products	781 Motor cars	782 Trucks	783 Buses, road tractors	784 Parts and accessories	Other road vehicles	Total merchandise
Germany	44,155	23,247	3,412	1,584	7,250	8,661	393,283
France	27,157	14,389	2,998	2,441	5,656	1,672	244,888
UK	28,249	15,289	2,263	412	9,197	1,088	241,726
Italy	18,821	13,299	1,453	666	2,491	911	176,352
Belgium/Luxembourg	16,118	7,636	888	629	6,231	734	126,684
Netherlands	12,029	6,686	1,238	408	2,589	1,107	137,533
Denmark	3,574	1,735	782	66	547	444	41,752
Ireland	1,449	907	246	45	181	70	28,086
Greece	2,216	1,279	250	58	462	168	23,350
Spain	13,047	5,608	949	343	5,585	562	96,652
Portugal	3,869	2,066	518	69	1,026	190	29,125
Sweden	5,031	1,865	345	52	2,507	263	55,992
Finland	1,928	888	386	14	529	111	25,154
Austria	7,581	4,299	705	322	1,695	559	61,677
Switzerland	6,867	4,976	594	206	547	545	75,108
Norway	2,624	1,240	623	114	384	262	30,912
Iceland	119	77	20	2	14	7	1,692
Turkey	1,522	328	177	192	768	57	29,701
Poland	1,556	467	113	64	753	160	24,837
Czech Republic	1,367	627	204	96	316	124	17,989
Slovak Republic							
Hungary	914	418	219	42	160	75	13,553
Canada	29,602	10,010	2,907	1,090	14,718	878	148,941
USA	102,640	66,366	9,953	2,239	21,156	2,925	675,039
Mexico	3,832	442	119	16	3,104	151	65,480
Japan	12,542	10,015	174	18	1,455	881	254,762
South Korea	1,910	267	216	3	1,304	121	115,490
Australia	6,248	3,212	1,379	154	1,168	335	53,206
New Zealand	1,678	1,140	321	30	117	69	12,985
OECD	358,647	198,780	33,451	11,378	91,908	23,130	3,201,950
EU-15 excluding intra EU-15 trade	30,648	16,328	1,804	121	7,231	5,164	588,030
OECD excluding intra EU-15 trade	204,071	115,913	18,822	4,389	53,193	11,753	2,107,726

Source: OECD: ITCS – International Trade By Commodity Statistics, Rev. 3, 2001, 2002.
NIW calculation.

Table 48. Automotive imports of OECD countries in 1998 (in mn USD)

Country	78 Automotive products	781 Motor cars	782 Trucks	783 Buses, road tractors	784 Parts and accessories	Other road vehicles	Total merchandise
Germany	46,662	24,824	4,222	530	10,373	6,713	406,272
France	27,722	14,547	3,292	1,508	6,552	1,823	258,715
UK	38,366	23,211	2,917	543	10,039	1,656	296,875
Italy	25,343	18,059	2,058	725	3,180	1,321	189,580
Bel-gium/Luxembourg	19,856	10,067	1,533	482	6,925	848	144,307
Netherlands	14,027	7,230	1,764	340	3,322	1,371	140,051
Denmark	3,877	1,954	724	97	529	573	42,281
Ireland	3,117	2,245	497	41	240	94	39,791
Greece	2,594	1,519	341	57	487	190	25,708
Spain	20,956	9,996	1,653	555	7,877	875	121,331
Portugal	5,365	2,827	871	106	1,342	219	33,110
Sweden	6,557	3,394	410	76	2,334	343	58,691
Finland	2,623	1,377	420	26	637	163	28,036
Austria	8,110	4,187	798	379	1,939	807	63,622
Switzerland	6,552	4,862	508	154	538	489	74,690
Norway	3,432	1,855	727	88	419	343	35,505
Iceland	244	170	37	6	18	13	2,474
Turkey	3,678	1,395	692	325	1,179	88	40,061
Poland	4,407	1,380	321	174	2,206	327	42,451
Czech Republic	2,099	620	210	170	925	175	27,487
Slovak Republic	1,608	536	123	82	819	48	11,198
Hungary	1,792	628	362	106	584	111	23,792
Canada	35,717	12,264	3,786	1,366	16,982	1,319	184,917
USA	123,588	82,656	10,859	3,233	23,455	3,385	835,478
Mexico	10,004	2,122	792	123	6,660	307	118,973
Japan	8,059	5,568	120	20	1,591	760	214,294
South Korea	752	16	27	1	648	60	72,241
Australia	7,368	4,110	1,385	182	1,307	385	56,914
New Zealand	1,339	988	186	10	92	64	11,637
OECD	435,814	244,606	41,634	11,506	113,198	24,870	3,600,481
EU-15 excluding intra EU-15 trade	43,708	25,588	2,719	249	8,782	6,370	686,457
OECD excluding intra EU-15 trade	254,347	144,758	22,852	6,288	66,205	14,243	2,438,569

Source: OECD: ITCS – International Trade By Commodity Statistics, Rev. 3, 2001, 2002. NIW calculation.

Table 49. Automotive imports of OECD countries in 2001 (in mn USD)

Country	78 Automotive products	781 Motor cars	782 Trucks	783 Buses, road tractors	784 Parts and accessories	Other road vehicles	Total merchandise
Germany	44,555	24,330	3,235	664	10,754	5,571	418,768
France	30,652	16,463	3,702	991	7,658	1,839	269,158
UK	38,801	24,680	2,955	433	9,260	1,473	307,981
Italy	27,675	19,129	2,339	913	3,652	1,642	204,639
Belgium/Luxembourg	22,982	12,820	1,755	529	6,981	898	165,221
Netherlands	12,848	7,480	1,351	263	2,417	1,336	146,372
Denmark	2,857	1,427	510	45	401	475	40,354
Ireland	2,952	2,143	423	37	234	115	45,536
Greece	2,163	1,297	247	73	349	197	23,391
Spain	24,225	11,720	1,634	627	9,401	841	132,715
Portugal	5,149	2,608	914	144	1,298	185	34,426
Sweden	5,823	2,385	443	78	2,547	370	54,486
Finland	2,225	1,015	351	16	698	145	27,552
Austria	8,107	3,671	653	443	2,785	555	65,272
Switzerland	6,938	4,987	661	206	580	504	78,693
Norway	2,860	1,550	580	65	352	312	31,189
Iceland	134	82	22	5	13	12	2,206
Turkey	1,814	588	268	89	815	54	35,598
Poland	3,932	2,000	376	196	1,132	228	44,172
Czech Republic	2,899	741	256	227	1,480	195	32,795
Slovak Republic	1,683	506	118	100	896	63	12,082
Hungary	2,461	880	370	101	968	142	31,751
Canada	37,311	14,694	4,194	701	16,503	1,220	198,534
USA	158,632	109,968	16,571	1,930	25,195	4,968	989,500
Mexico	15,839	4,318	1,251	140	9,692	438	155,101
Japan	9,638	6,241	134	41	2,118	1,105	260,529
South Korea	1,667	250	102	21	1,195	99	106,478
Australia	7,332	4,487	1,134	127	1,141	443	54,634
New Zealand	1,573	1,107	276	15	106	69	12,078
OECD	485,728	283,569	46,825	9,220	120,620	25,494	3,981,210
EU-15 excluding intra EU-15 trade	46,117	25,016	2,678	392	11,716	6,315	773,232
OECD excluding intra EU-15 trade	300,831	177,414	28,992	4,356	73,903	16,166	2,818,573

Source: OECD: ITCS – International Trade By Commodity Statistics, Rev. 3, 2001, 2002. NIW calculation.

Table 50. Trade surplus in automotive products, 1991 (in mn USD)

Country	78 Automotive products	781 Motor cars	782 Trucks	783 Buses, road tractors	784 Parts and accessories	Other road vehicles	Total mer-chandise
Germany	22,262	12,010	1,243	923	3,751	4,334	48,941
France	5,204	2,388	-435	-415	3,934	-268	-679
UK	-2,853	-2,423	314	5	-986	236	-21,493
Italy	-5,249	-7,604	272	-23	1,593	512	10,098
Belgium/Luxembourg	6,305	6,846	535	390	-1,314	-152	13,727
Netherlands	-4,463	-3,617	-143	690	-956	-436	5,238
Denmark	-1,062	-597	-358	-2	-44	-61	2,228
Ireland	-818	-503	-132	-33	-91	-58	3,537
Greece	-2,397	-1,533	-353	-81	-300	-130	-12,432
Spain	3,470	5,024	-242	-169	-590	-552	-24,876
Portugal	-2,494	-1,380	-102	-55	-827	-129	-7,068
Sweden	2,063	1,174	480	0	579	-171	5,312
Finland	-746	-158	-128	50	-456	-55	4,480
Austria	-3,751	-3,334	94	-94	-214	-203	-6,103
Switzerland	-5,149	-4,090	-303	-109	-241	-405	-2,071
Norway	-948	-494	-221	-82	-41	-110	-8,234
Iceland	-151	-85	-37	-4	-15	-10	-303
Turkey	-756	-202	-112	-59	-337	-47	-6,112
Poland							
Czech Republic							
Slovak Republic							
Hungary							
Canada	3,322	3,994	3,854	239	-4,278	-489	-6,946
USA	-40,777	-35,325	-4,394	-8	-652	-398	-78,749
Mexico	3,126	3,324	16	-58	-20	-136	-13,799
Japan	63,823	39,804	8,233	968	10,719	4,099	147,973
South Korea	0	0	0	0	0	0	0
Australia	-2,689	-1,393	-637	-49	-439	-172	-14,694
New Zealand	-746	-517	-132	-10	-46	-41	191
OECD	34,526	11,310	7,313	2,013	8,732	5,156	38,165
EU-15 excluding intra EU-15 trade	13,717	5,293	1,910	1,271	4,800	443	24,412
OECD excluding intra EU-15 trade	32,770	10,309	8,178	2,100	9,450	2,733	41,667

Table 51. Trade surplus in automotive products, 1995 (in mn USD)

Country	78 Automotive products	781 Motor cars	782 Trucks	783 Buses, road tractors	784 Parts and accessories	Other road vehicles	Total merchandise
Germany	38,983	25,361	2,690	2,575	5,323	3,035	104,242
France	4,222	844	-583	-201	4,668	-505	25,693
UK	-8,801	-3,964	-1,114	-250	-3,991	518	-27,232
Italy	233	-5,281	1,189	-539	3,560	1,303	47,611
Belgium/Luxembourg	8,381	10,389	766	671	-3,157	-286	25,395
Netherlands	-4,658	-4,064	-117	971	-1,016	-432	15,712
Denmark	-2,575	-1,601	-668	-27	-47	-234	2,738
Ireland	-1,259	-885	-227	-43	-73	-30	11,875
Greece	-2,155	-1,267	-239	-48	-442	-159	-14,353
Spain	8,110	9,270	218	188	-1,413	-152	-13,671
Portugal	-1,785	-931	-30	-37	-673	-113	-6,376
Sweden	3,682	2,399	-129	348	1,181	-118	14,267
Finland	-762	-317	-200	65	-306	-4	14,270
Austria	-3,376	-2,621	-20	-169	-337	-229	-4,856
Switzerland	-6,090	-4,866	-399	-173	-199	-454	4,501
Norway	-2,088	-1,230	-517	-107	-45	-189	-11,219
Iceland	-119	-77	-20	-2	-14	-7	-7
Turkey	-795	-76	-135	-49	-585	51	-10,313
Poland	-428	193	69	-56	-629	-5	-4,142
Czech Republic	32	80	-50	-42	47	-4	-2,386
Slovak Republic	0	0	0	0	0	0	0
Hungary	-231	-231	-198	72	90	36	-1,720
Canada	12,147	15,597	3,851	992	-7,580	-713	6,022
USA	-55,131	-50,156	-5,135	-823	2,123	-1,140	-187,551
Mexico	8,266	7,049	1,708	-6	-610	125	1,828
Japan	65,584	32,223	8,915	1,144	18,216	5,087	178,591
South Korea	8,211	6,976	580	361	-636	931	10,877
Australia	-5,413	-2,819	-1,300	-137	-866	-291	-22,458
New Zealand	-1,628	-1,139	-320	-30	-78	-60	-1,786
OECD	60,559	28,855	8,585	4,648	12,512	5,960	155,553
EU-15 excluding intra EU-15 trade	36,903	24,172	3,284	1,930	5,720	1,797	128,439
OECD excluding intra EU-15 trade	59,221	25,695	10,333	3,074	14,954	5,165	88,676

Table 52. Trade surplus in automotive products, 1998 (in mn USD)

Country	78 Automotive products	781 Motor cars	782 Trucks	783 Buses, road tractors	784 Parts and accessories	Other road vehicles	Total mer-chandise
Germany	50,912	35,445	3,167	2,768	5,808	3,724	117,737
France	8,413	4,872	-228	-137	4,340	-433	28,612
UK	-13,736	-8,722	-1,502	-301	-2,881	-330	-40,790
Italy	-5,775	-11,173	711	-601	4,325	963	45,118
Belgium/Luxembourg	5,691	7,522	525	1,169	-3,398	-128	16,064
Netherlands	-4,161	-2,990	-519	1,585	-1,842	-394	12,964
Denmark	-2,762	-1,767	-586	-69	-26	-314	172
Ireland	-2,698	-2,039	-434	-31	-163	-31	20,611
Greece	-2,513	-1,501	-329	-52	-460	-171	-16,680
Spain	5,410	6,331	1,823	-228	-2,309	-207	-19,742
Portugal	-1,661	-232	-365	-67	-861	-137	-9,383
Sweden	2,918	691	-187	428	2,142	-156	16,943
Finland	-1,300	-635	-271	49	-397	-45	14,310
Austria	-2,549	-1,840	-42	-133	-107	-429	-3,592
Switzerland	-5,644	-4,727	-311	-122	-72	-413	2,961
Norway	-2,905	-1,839	-611	-83	-101	-272	-15,131
Iceland	-244	-170	-37	-6	-18	-13	-637
Turkey	-2,850	-1,255	-661	-114	-820	-1	-15,821
Poland	-2,397	-369	23	-140	-1,792	-119	-15,948
Czech Republic	1,758	1,434	76	-91	316	23	-260
Slovak Republic	386	971	-100	-79	-422	16	-735
Hungary	-380	-81	-351	14	-17	56	-1,714
Canada	10,796	16,355	2,344	1,440	-8,300	-1,044	-6,942
USA	-67,119	-65,953	-3,485	-1,479	4,870	-1,072	-213,943
Mexico	9,499	8,840	2,799	209	-2,472	123	-12,472
Japan	69,953	45,265	7,541	1,030	11,151	4,966	161,448
South Korea	11,001	8,588	767	497	633	515	59,099
Australia	-6,198	-3,379	-1,312	-174	-964	-369	-25,946
New Zealand	-1,261	-980	-170	-10	-49	-52	-1,182
OECD	50,581	26,662	8,276	5,273	6,114	4,256	95,120
EU-15 excluding intra EU-15 trade	33,187	17,635	3,204	2,693	8,304	1,350	102,980
OECD excluding intra EU-15 trade	47,580	20,335	9,716	3,586	10,248	3,695	15,755

Table 53. Trade surplus in automotive products, 2001 (in mn USD)

Country	78 Automotive products	781 Motor cars	782 Trucks	783 Buses, road tractors	784 Parts and accessories	Other road vehicles	Total merchandise
Germany	60,503	43,125	4,242	2,625	6,557	3,955	131,717
France	8,247	5,341	-439	105	3,969	-730	19,482
UK	-18,676	-12,838	-1,719	-217	-3,227	-674	-55,126
Italy	-8,329	-12,207	630	-832	3,555	525	37,143
Belgium/Luxembourg	5,412	7,320	780	758	-3,438	-8	16,939
Netherlands	-3,728	-3,888	-94	1,573	-996	-323	16,970
Denmark	-1,630	-1,041	-395	0	45	-239	3,558
Ireland	-2,327	-1,758	-323	-24	-168	-54	27,728
Greece	-2,079	-1,260	-235	-70	-334	-180	-14,840
Spain	2,483	5,223	1,098	-310	-3,350	-178	-26,401
Portugal	-1,319	160	-606	-114	-650	-110	-10,547
Sweden	2,363	1,689	-71	390	496	-141	16,195
Finland	-707	-46	-199	59	-482	-39	15,837
Austria	-1,540	-815	394	-162	-859	-97	-1,372
Switzerland	-5,999	-4,857	-469	-176	-66	-431	2,119
Norway	-2,309	-1,522	-462	-55	-20	-250	-9,745
Iceland	-132	-82	-21	-5	-13	-12	-295
Turkey	482	385	116	246	-276	11	-6,520
Poland	-694	-585	2	-86	-44	20	-9,745
Czech Republic	2,419	2,180	-151	-146	546	-10	-296
Slovak Republic	647	1,254	-96	-97	-423	10	282
Hungary	253	587	-351	21	-65	61	-2,435
Canada	15,400	17,067	4,815	832	-6,453	-860	5,161
USA	-101,929	-91,604	-10,495	-942	3,970	-2,858	-321,208
Mexico	12,031	10,979	5,198	49	-4,114	-81	-13,600
Japan	71,189	46,651	5,138	919	13,485	4,995	125,094
South Korea	13,696	11,780	588	501	711	117	42,912
Australia	-5,140	-2,911	-1,073	-99	-677	-380	-22,397
New Zealand	-1,487	-1,106	-275	-15	-33	-58	-770
OECD	37,100	17,218	5,527	4,729	7,647	1,980	-34,162
EU-15 excluding intra EU-15 trade	39,533	25,691	3,609	2,470	7,048	715	69,199
OECD excluding intra EU-15 trade	37,961	13,906	6,073	3,418	13,576	988	-142,245

Table 54. World market share in automotive products, OECD countries[1] in 1991, in %

Country	78 Automotive products	781 Motor cars	782 Trucks	783 Buses. road tractors	784 Parts and accessories	Other road vehicles	Total merchandise
Germany	20.7	21.6	14.8	20.8	12.9	47.0	17.1
France	8.5	8.0	5.8	8.9	11.9	5.4	8.8
UK	5.0	4.3	2.5	1.9	8.0	6.3	7.1
Italy	4.6	3.5	6.0	4.6	6.1	5.9	7.2
Belgium/Luxembourg	6.1	8.1	4.7	13.4	2.7	2.1	4.9
Netherlands	1.7	0.9	3.0	14.5	1.4	2.9	5.0
Denmark	0.3	0.1	0.4	0.5	0.4	0.9	1.4
Ireland	0.1	0.0	0.1	0.0	0.1	0.1	1.0
Greece	0.0	0.0	0.0	0.0	0.0	0.0	0.3
Spain	4.4	5.8	2.2	2.0	3.6	0.6	2.3
Portugal	0.3	0.1	1.1	0.5	0.4	0.2	0.7
Sweden	2.0	1.8	2.2	1.4	3.0	0.6	2.2
Finland	0.3	0.4	0.3	0.8	0.2	0.3	1.0
Austria	0.8	0.3	2.2	0.9	1.1	1.0	1.8
Switzerland	0.2	0.1	0.6	0.3	0.4	0.4	2.6
Norway	0.1	0.0	0.1	0.1	0.3	0.3	0.7
Iceland	0.0	0.0	0.0	0.0	0.0	0.0	0.1
Turkey	0.1	0.0	0.0	0.4	0.1	0.0	0.5
Poland							
Czech Republic							
Slovak Republic							
Hungary							
Canada	8.8	8.7	17.8	7.5	7.7	0.3	4.3
USA	10.7	6.8	11.5	8.1	21.5	5.8	15.5
Mexico	1.4	2.2	0.5	0.1	0.7	0.1	0.7
Japan	23.6	27.0	24.2	13.5	17.1	19.8	13.6
South Korea							0.0
Australia	0.2	0.2	0.1	0.0	0.3	0.1	0.9
New Zealand	0.0	0.0	0.0	0.0	0.0	0.0	0.3
EU-15 excluding intra EU-15 trade	22.9	22.3	16.3	38.0	20.6	45.1	34.7

World market share: Share of national exports in total OECD exports.
1) OECD without Poland, Czech Republic, Slovak Republic, Hungary und Korea.
Source: OECD: ITCS – International Trade By Commodity Statistics, Rev. 3, 2001, 2002.
NIW calculation.

Table 55. World market share in automotive products, OECD countries in 1995, in %

Country	78 Automotive products	781 Motor cars	782 Trucks	783 Buses. road tractors	784 Parts and accessories	Other road vehicles	Total merchandise
Germany	19.8	21.4	14.5	26.0	12.0	40.2	14.8
France	7.5	6.7	5.7	14.0	9.9	4.0	8.1
UK	4.6	5.0	2.7	1.0	5.0	5.5	6.4
Italy	4.5	3.5	6.3	0.8	5.8	7.6	6.7
Belgium/Luxembourg	5.8	7.9	3.9	8.1	2.9	1.5	4.5
Netherlands	1.8	1.2	2.7	8.6	1.5	2.3	4.6
Denmark	0.2	0.1	0.3	0.2	0.5	0.7	1.3
Ireland	0.0	0.0	0.0	0.0	0.1	0.1	1.2
Greece	0.0	0.0	0.0	0.1	0.0	0.0	0.3
Spain	5.0	6.5	2.8	3.3	4.0	1.4	2.5
Portugal	0.5	0.5	1.2	0.2	0.3	0.3	0.7
Sweden	2.1	1.9	0.5	2.5	3.5	0.5	2.1
Finland	0.3	0.3	0.4	0.5	0.2	0.4	1.2
Austria	1.0	0.7	1.6	1.0	1.3	1.1	1.7
Switzerland	0.2	0.0	0.5	0.2	0.3	0.3	2.4
Norway	0.1	0.0	0.3	0.0	0.3	0.3	0.6
Iceland	0.0	0.0	0.0	0.0	0.0	0.0	0.1
Turkey	0.2	0.1	0.1	0.9	0.2	0.4	0.6
Poland	0.3	0.3	0.4	0.1	0.1	0.5	0.6
Czech Republic	0.3	0.3	0.4	0.3	0.3	0.4	0.5
Slovak Republic	0.0						0.0
Hungary	0.2	0.1	0.0	0.7	0.2	0.4	0.4
Canada	10.0	11.2	16.1	13.0	6.8	0.6	4.6
USA	11.3	7.1	11.5	8.8	22.3	6.1	14.5
Mexico	2.9	3.3	4.3	0.1	2.4	0.9	2.0
Japan	18.6	18.6	21.6	7.3	18.8	20.5	12.9
South Korea	2.4	3.2	1.9	2.3	0.6	3.6	3.8
Australia	0.2	0.2	0.2	0.1	0.3	0.2	0.9
New Zealand	0.0	0.0	0.0	0.0	0.0	0.0	0.3
EU-15 excluding intra EU-15 trade	25.7	28.6	17.5	27.5	19.0	41.1	32.6

World market share: Share of national exports in total OECD exports.
Source: OECD: ITCS – International Trade By Commodity Statistics, Rev. 3, 2001, 2002.
NIW calculation.

Table 56. World market share in automotive products, OECD countries in 1998, in %

Country	78 Automotive products	781 Motor cars	782 Trucks	783 Buses. road tractors	784 Parts and accessories	Other road vehicles	Total merchandise
Germany	20.1	22.2	14.8	19.7	13.6	35.8	14.2
France	7.4	7.2	6.1	8.2	9.1	4.8	7.8
UK	5.1	5.3	2.8	1.4	6.0	4.6	6.9
Italy	4.0	2.5	5.5	0.7	6.3	7.8	6.4
Belgium/Luxembourg	5.3	6.5	4.1	9.8	3.0	2.5	4.3
Netherlands	2.0	1.6	2.5	11.5	1.2	3.4	4.1
Denmark	0.2	0.1	0.3	0.2	0.4	0.9	1.1
Ireland	0.1	0.1	0.1	0.1	0.1	0.2	1.6
Greece	0.0	0.0	0.0	0.0	0.0	0.1	0.2
Spain	5.4	6.0	7.0	2.0	4.7	2.3	2.7
Portugal	0.8	1.0	1.0	0.2	0.4	0.3	0.6
Sweden	1.9	1.5	0.4	3.0	3.8	0.6	2.0
Finland	0.3	0.3	0.3	0.4	0.2	0.4	1.1
Austria	1.1	0.9	1.5	1.5	1.5	1.3	1.6
Switzerland	0.2	0.0	0.4	0.2	0.4	0.3	2.1
Norway	0.1	0.0	0.2	0.0	0.3	0.2	0.6
Iceland	0.0	0.0	0.0	0.0	0.0	0.0	0.0
Turkey	0.2	0.1	0.1	1.3	0.3	0.3	0.7
Poland	0.4	0.4	0.7	0.2	0.3	0.7	0.7
Czech Republic	0.8	0.8	0.6	0.5	1.0	0.7	0.7
Slovak Republic	0.4	0.6	0.0	0.0	0.3	0.2	0.3
Hungary	0.3	0.2	0.0	0.7	0.5	0.6	0.6
Canada	9.6	10.6	12.3	16.7	7.3	0.9	4.8
USA	11.6	6.2	14.8	10.4	23.7	7.9	16.8
Mexico	4.0	4.0	7.2	2.0	3.5	1.5	2.9
Japan	16.0	18.7	15.3	6.3	10.7	19.7	10.2
South Korea	2.4	3.2	1.6	3.0	1.1	2.0	3.6
Australia	0.2	0.3	0.1	0.0	0.3	0.1	0.8
New Zealand	0.0	0.0	0.0	0.0	0.0	0.0	0.3
EU-15 excluding intra EU-15 trade	25.5	26.2	18.2	29.8	22.3	43.0	32.2

World market share: Share of national exports in total OECD exports.
Source: OECD: ITCS – International Trade By Commodity Statistics, Rev. 3, 2001, 2002.
NIW calculation.

Table 57. World market shares in automotive products, OECD countries in 2001, in %

Country	78 Automotive products	781 Motor cars	782 Trucks	783 Buses. road tractors	784 Parts and accessories	Other road vehicles	Total mer-chandise
Germany	20.1	22.4	14.3	23.6	13.5	34.7	13.9
France	7.4	7.2	6.2	7.9	9.1	4.0	7.3
UK	3.8	3.9	2.4	1.6	4.7	2.9	6.4
Italy	3.7	2.3	5.7	0.6	5.6	7.9	6.1
Belgium/Luxembourg	5.4	6.7	4.8	9.2	2.8	3.2	4.6
Netherlands	1.7	1.2	2.4	13.2	1.1	3.7	4.1
Denmark	0.2	0.1	0.2	0.3	0.3	0.9	1.1
Ireland	0.1	0.1	0.2	0.1	0.1	0.2	1.9
Greece	0.0	0.0	0.0	0.0	0.0	0.1	0.2
Spain	5.1	5.6	5.2	2.3	4.7	2.4	2.7
Portugal	0.7	0.9	0.6	0.2	0.5	0.3	0.6
Sweden	1.6	1.4	0.7	3.4	2.4	0.8	1.8
Finland	0.3	0.3	0.3	0.5	0.2	0.4	1.1
Austria	1.3	0.9	2.0	2.0	1.5	1.7	1.6
Switzerland	0.2	0.0	0.4	0.2	0.4	0.3	2.0
Norway	0.1	0.0	0.2	0.1	0.3	0.2	0.5
Iceland	0.0	0.0	0.0	0.0	0.0	0.0	0.0
Turkey	0.4	0.3	0.7	2.4	0.4	0.2	0.7
Poland	0.6	0.5	0.7	0.8	0.8	0.9	0.9
Czech Republic	1.0	1.0	0.2	0.6	1.6	0.7	0.8
Slovak Republic	0.4	0.6	0.0	0.0	0.4	0.3	0.3
Hungary	0.5	0.5	0.0	0.9	0.7	0.7	0.7
Canada	10.1	10.6	17.2	11.0	7.8	1.3	5.2
USA	10.8	6.1	11.6	7.1	22.7	7.7	16.9
Mexico	5.3	5.1	12.3	1.4	4.3	1.3	3.6
Japan	15.5	17.6	10.1	6.9	12.2	22.2	9.8
South Korea	2.9	4.0	1.3	3.7	1.5	0.8	3.8
Australia	0.4	0.5	0.1	0.2	0.4	0.2	0.8
New Zealand	0.0	0.0	0.0	0.0	0.1	0.0	0.3
EU-15 excluding intra EU-15 trade	25.3	26.5	17.9	36.8	21.4	41.0	31.5

World market share: Share of national exports in total OECD exports.
Source: OECD: ITCS – International Trade By Commodity Statistics, Rev. 3, 2001, 2002.
NIW calculation.

Table 58. Revealed Comparative Advantage (RCA) for OECD countries[1], 1991

Country	78 Automotive products	781 Motor cars	782 Trucks	783 Buses, road tractors	784 Parts and accessories	Other road vehicles
Germany	31	27	14	81	42	39
France	23	20	-19	-49	67	-19
UK	-5	-16	58	16	-4	31
Italy	-39	-89	8	-13	42	42
Belgium/Luxembourg	29	58	26	38	-67	-41
Netherlands	-67	-129	-18	102	-74	-56
Denmark	-88	-139	-138	-14	-22	-34
Ireland	-191	-239	-178	-257	-112	-155
Greece	-376	-437	-488	-290	-278	-257
Spain	69	113	11	-39	17	-130
Portugal	-91	-154	14	-59	-111	-103
Sweden	31	40	89	-11	23	-91
Finland	-81	-45	-103	198	-191	-85
Austria	-82	-189	27	-77	-11	-51
Switzerland	-204	-313	-91	-177	-62	-172
Norway	-97	-361	-132	-216	23	-66
Iceland	-650	-597	a	a	-745	-1,156
Turkey	-135	-107	-253	-74	-149	-196
Poland						
Czech Republic						
Slovak Republic						
Hungary						
Canada	20	39	105	65	-53	-194
USA	-62	-121	-54	19	16	-7
Mexico	191	310	71	-212	57	-162
Japan	170	151	317	368	187	185
South Korea						
Australia	-113	-109	-236	-284	-53	-183
EU-15 excluding intra EU-15 trade	37	23	67	301	78	4

1) OECD without Poland, Czech Republic, Slovak Republic, Hungary and Korea.
a) Export of country = 0.
Source: OECD: ITCS – International Trade By Commodity Statistics, Rev. 3, 2001, 2002.
NIW calculation.

Table 59. Revealed Comparative Advantage (RCA) for OECD countries 1995

Country	78 Automotive products	781 Motor cars	782 Trucks	783 Buses, road tractors	784 Parts and accessories	Other road vehicles
Germany	40	50	35	73	32	7
France	4	-4	-32	-19	50	-46
UK	-25	-18	-56	-81	-45	51
Italy	-23	-74	36	-190	65	65
Belgium/Luxembourg	24	68	44	54	-89	-68
Netherlands	-60	-104	-21	111	-61	-60
Denmark	-134	-263	-199	-58	-15	-81
Ireland	-238	-407	-290	-360	-87	-92
Greece	-263	-366	-220	-80	-219	-205
Spain	64	113	36	59	-14	-16
Portugal	-37	-35	19	-53	-82	-67
Sweden	32	60	-69	181	16	-83
Finland	-95	-89	-118	126	-131	-48
Austria	-51	-86	5	-66	-14	-44
Switzerland	-224	-387	-117	-188	-51	-185
Norway	-114	-430	-132	-230	33	-83
Iceland	-633	-622	a	a	-691	-502
Turkey	-31	16	-101	13	-101	107
Poland	-14	53	66	-183	-162	15
Czech Republic	17	26	-14	-43	28	11
Slovak Republic						
Hungary	-16	-67	-224	113	58	53
Canada	30	90	80	61	-76	-171
USA	-44	-108	-40	-13	42	-17
Mexico	112	280	270	-51	-25	58
Japan	130	91	343	362	207	138
South Korea	158	321	121	469	-76	207
Australia	-146	-155	-231	-165	-80	-148
New Zealand	-337	-737	-617	a	-93	-190
EU-15 excluding intra EU-15 trade	59	71	84	263	39	10

a) Export of country = 0.
Source: OECD: ITCS – International Trade By Commodity Statistics, Rev. 3, 2001, 2002. NIW calculation.

Table 60. Revealed Comparative Advantage (RCA) for OECD countries 1998

Country	78 Automotive products	781 Motor cars	782 Trucks	783 Buses, road tractors	784 Parts and accessories	Other road vehicles
Germany	48	63	31	157	19	19
France	16	18	-18	-20	40	-38
UK	-30	-32	-58	-66	-19	-7
Italy	-47	-118	8	-197	65	33
Belgium/Luxembourg	15	45	19	113	-78	-27
Netherlands	-44	-62	-44	164	-90	-43
Denmark	-125	-235	-166	-125	-5	-80
Ireland	-242	-281	-247	-183	-156	-82
Greece	-242	-337	-231	-140	-185	-124
Spain	41	67	92	-35	-17	-9
Portugal	-4	25	-21	-66	-69	-64
Sweden	11	-7	-86	164	40	-86
Finland	-110	-103	-145	64	-139	-74
Austria	-32	-52	0	-37	0	-70
Switzerland	-202	-362	-98	-159	-18	-190
Norway	-132	-419	-128	-220	28	-102
Iceland	-618	-622	-618	a	-549	-656
Turkey	-99	-180	-261	7	-69	49
Poland	-31	16	54	-117	-120	2
Czech Republic	62	121	32	-76	30	14
Slovak Republic	28	110	-162	-314	-66	35
Hungary	-16	-6	-340	20	4	48
Canada	30	89	52	76	-63	-153
USA	-49	-130	-9	-32	48	-8
Mexico	78	175	162	111	-35	45
Japan	171	165	360	339	152	146
South Korea	215	567	277	617	8	166
Australia	-123	-112	-234	-256	-73	-258
New Zealand	-273	-478	-236	-332	-65	-156
EU-15 excluding intra EU-15 trade	43	38	64	233	53	5

a) Export of country = 0.
Source: OECD: ITCS – International Trade By Commodity Statistics, Rev. 3, 2001, 2002.
NIW calculation.

Table 61. Revealed Comparative Advantage (RCA) for OECD countries 2001

Country	78 Automotive products	781 Motor cars	782 Trucks	783 Buses, road tractors	784 Parts and accessories	Other road vehicles
Germany	58	75	56	133	20	26
France	17	21	-20	3	35	-58
UK	-46	-54	-67	-50	-23	-41
Italy	-52	-118	7	-259	51	11
Belgium/Luxembourg	11	35	27	79	-78	-11
Netherlands	-45	-84	-18	183	-64	-39
Denmark	-93	-139	-158	-9	2	-79
Ireland	-203	-219	-192	-149	-174	-111
Greece	-224	-254	-205	-227	-212	-144
Spain	32	59	74	-46	-22	-2
Portugal	7	43	-72	-121	-33	-53
Sweden	8	28	-43	153	-8	-74
Finland	-84	-50	-129	108	-163	-77
Austria	-19	-23	49	-43	-35	-17
Switzerland	-203	-367	-126	-197	-15	-196
Norway	-127	-364	-121	-145	31	-124
Iceland	-418	-514	-279	-577	-436	-594
Turkey	44	71	56	153	-21	39
Poland	6	-10	25	-33	21	33
Czech Republic	62	138	-89	-101	32	-4
Slovak Republic	30	122	-169	-364	-66	12
Hungary	18	59	-290	27	1	44
Canada	32	75	74	76	-52	-125
USA	-64	-140	-61	-28	54	-46
Mexico	66	136	173	39	-46	-11
Japan	173	174	328	277	161	132
South Korea	188	354	157	288	13	44
Australia	-68	-52	-239	-99	-37	-142
New Zealand	-284	-680	-580	-374	-31	-175
EU-15 excluding intra EU-15 trade	53	62	77	190	39	2

Source: OECD: ITCS – International Trade By Commodity Statistics, Rev. 3, 2001, 2002. NIW calculation.

Table 62. Summary of cost estimation and allocation process

Topic	Infrastructure	Congestion	Environmental costs	Accidents
Cost definition	Damage cost (maintenance and repair), some services and operations.	Cost of time delays and any increased operating costs caused by an extra transport unit joining the traffic flow (accidents or maintenance).	Deterioration in human health, crop damage etc. resulting from vehicle generated air, noise and water pollution.	Vehicle repair and medical costs and the cost of "suffering" associated with accidents.
Cost categories	Road type (motorway, national, state, regional roads, urban streets) track speed limit and formation, existing categories (main/minor lines/electrified, single/double).	Infrastructure type, vehicle type, user characteristics and time of travel (peak/inter peak/off peak).	Population characteristics, types of ecological systems, proximity to emissions sources.	Road type, time of day, vehicle type and driver/passenger characteristics.
Cost driver categories	Axle weight (proxy: vehicle type); train weight and speed (proxy: freight/passenger wagon load, high-speed/inter-city/regional/urban), state of maintenance of infrastructure.	Infrastructure characteristics, traffic mix and flow, accidents and road maintenance, rail/air delays.	Vehicle type (motorcycle, car, bus, HGV), with/out catalyst, by fuel type and quality (petrol, unleaded, diesel, LPG), engine type (diesel/electric), road type, vehicle speed and time of travel (proxy: road, vehicle type). Upstream power source (e.g. electrified rail)	Infrastructure condition, speeds, vehicle/driver characteristics and history, traffic density (or proxy: vehicle, road type).
Cost attribution method	Engineering relationships between axle weight/speed and damage (e.g. 4x the power rule), then applying top down, disaggregated infrastructure costs according to this rule.	Bottom-up but generalised area speed-flow relationships for road types and values of time for user type (business/worker/personal), journey purpose (work/leisure) similar process for rail/air delays. (Rail) scarcity costs also considered and valued through bidding or negotiation.	Bottom-up impact pathway approach linking emissions to costs: concentrations of pollutants; dose-response relationships of impacts.	Disaggregated data of medical and hospital costs and estimates of suffering, weighted by a risk factor and attributed to user categories (vehicle type) [chiefly using insurance premiums as the mechanism].
Monetary valuation	Financial costs directly incurred.	Wage rate/WTP estimates of values of time	Financial costs, e.g. crop damage, estimates of health risk often based on WTP, using standard SCBA discount rates.	Financial costs of repair/medical care, WTP often used for estimating non-material costs (injury and other suffering).

Most examples in this table refer to road and rail, however, the principles apply equally to other transport modes. HGV = heavy goods vehicle; LPG = liquid petroleum gas; WTP = willingness-to-pay; SCBA = social cost benefit analysis.
Source: European Commission (1999).

Table 63. USDOT strategic plan – summary of outcomes, targets and performance measures

Outcomes	Targets and performance measures
Safety	
Reduction in transportation-related deaths Reduction in transportation-related injuries	Highway safety targets: By 2008, reduce highway fatalities to 1.0 per 100 million vehicle miles travelled; reduce large truck fatalities to 1.65 per 100 million truck miles travelled.
	Highway safety performance measures
	Highway fatality rate
	Large truck-related fatality rate
	Alcohol-related fatality rate
	Percentage of front occupants using safety belts
	Aviation safety targets: By 2008, reduce commercial aviation fatal accidents to 0.01 per 100 thousand departures; and reduce general aviation fatal accidents to 325.
	Aviation safety performance measures
	Commercial air carrier fatal accident rate
	Number of general aviation fatal accidents
	Number of highest severity operational errors
	Number of category A and B runway incursions
	Rail safety target: By 2008, reduce train accidents and incidents to 16.14 per million train miles.
	Rail safety performance measures
	Train accident and highway rail incident rate
	Rail-related fatality rate
	Train accident rate
	Grade crossing accident rate
	Transit safety target: By 2008, reduce transit fatalities to 0.488 per 100 million passenger miles.
	Transit safety performance measures
	Transit fatality rate
	Transit injury rate
	Pipeline safety target: By 2008, reduce total incidents for gas and hazardous liquid pipelines to 307.
	Pipeline safety performance measure
	Number of incidents of natural gas and hazardous liquid pipelines
	Hazardous materials safety target: By 2008, reduce the number of serious hazardous materials incidents to 488.
	Hazardous materials safety performance measures
	Number of serious hazardous materials transportation incidents

Outcomes	Targets and performance measures
Mobility	
Improved infrastructure in all modes	Improved infrastructure target: By 2008, increase the percentage of vehicle miles travelled on pavement with acceptable ride quality to 94.9%.
	Improved infrastructure performance measures
	Percent of travel on the NHS meeting pavement performance standards for acceptable ride
	Percent of deck area on deficient NHS bridges
	Average condition of transit motor bus fleet
	Average condition of transit rail vehicle fleet
Reduced congestion in all modes	Reduced congestion target: By 2008, decrease the growth in percent of urban area road travel occurring in congested conditions by 0.2% annually.
	Reduced congestion performance measures
	Percent of total annual urban area travel that occurs in congested conditions
	Number of metropolitan areas where integrated Intelligent Transportation Systems (ITS) infrastructure is deployed
Increased reliability throughout the system	Increased reliability targets: By 2008, increase the percent of flights arriving on time to 83.64%.
	Increased reliability performance measures
	Percent of flights arriving on time
	Large hub airport efficiency rate
	Average daily large hub airport arrival capacity
Increased access for all Americans	Increased access target: By 2008, increase bus and transit rail fleets' compliance with the "Americans with Disabilities Act (ADA)" to 100%.
	Increased access performance measures
	Percent of bus fleets ADA compliant
	Percent of rail stations ADA compliant
	Number of employment sites made accessible through Job Access and Reverse Commute grants

Outcomes	Targets and performance measures
	Connectivity
Reduced barriers to trade in transportation goods and services	The 2008 target for the performance measure below is under development:
More efficient movement of cargo throughout the international supply chain	Reduced barriers performance measure
	Number of passengers in international markets with open skies aviation agreements
Enhanced international competitiveness of U.S. transport providers and manufacturers	Efficient cargo movement target
Harmonized and standardised regulatory and facilitation requirements	Through 2008, maintain the U.S. St. Lawrence Seaway lock availability at 99%
The most competitive, cost effective and efficient environment for passenger travel	Efficient cargo movement performance measure
	Percentage of days in the shipping season that the U.S. portion of the St. Lawrence Seaway is available for shipping
Expanded opportunities for all businesses especially women owned and disadvantaged businesses	2008 targets for the performance measures below are under development:
	Efficient cargo movement performance measures
	Travel time in freight significant corridors
	Border crossing delay
	Enhanced competitiveness performance measures
	Number of overseas airport slots opened to competition through aviation agreements
	Harmonized requirements performance measures
	Number of regulatory requirements finalized
	Passenger environment performance measures
	Number of passenger travel markets opened to competition through multilateral or regional agreements
	Expanded opportunity performance measures
	Percent of total dollar value of DOT direct contracts awarded to women owned businesses
	Percent of total dollar value of DOT direct contracts awarded to small disadvantaged businesses

Outcomes	Targets and performance measures
Environment	
Reduced pollution and other adverse environmental effects of transportation and transportation facilities	Reduced pollution and adverse effects target: By 2008, reduce the number of people exposed to significant aviation noise to 396,000.
	Reduced pollution and adverse effects performance measures
Streamlined environmental review of transportation infrastructure projects	Number of people exposed to significant aircraft noise levels
	Number of people in residential communities benefiting from federally funded aviation noise compatibility projects
	Targets are under development for the following performance measures:
	Ratio of wetland acres replaced per acre unavoidably affected by federal-aid highway projects
	Tons of hazardous liquid materials spilled per million ton-miles shipped by pipeline
	12 month moving average number of area transportation emissions conformity lapses
	Percentage of Department of Transportation (DOT) facilities characterised as no further remedial action planned under the Superfund Amendments and Reauthorization Act
	Streamlined review target: By 2008, reduce the median time to complete Environmental Impact Statements (EIS) to 36 months and Environmental Assessments (EA) for DOT funded infrastructure projects to 12 months.
	Streamlined review performance measure
	Median time to complete EISs and EAs for DOT funded projects.
Security	
All modes have implemented steps that would prepare them for a rapid recovery of transportation from intentional harm and natural disasters	Transportation Capability Assessment for Readiness Index Score Target: By 2008, achieve an "A" rating indicating all modes have taken steps needed for a rapid recovery from intentional harm and naturals disasters.
The U.S. transportation system meets national security requirements	Strategic mobility targets: Through 2008, maintain the timely availability of the Departement of Defense (DoD) required shipping capacity at 94% of that required; maintain the timely availability of DoD required commercial port use at 93% of that required.
	Strategic mobility performance measures
	Percentage of DoD-required shipping capacity complete with crews available within mobilization timelines
	Percentage of DoD-designated commercial ports available for military use within DoD established readiness timelines

Source: USDOT (2003), U.S. Department of Transportation – Strategic Plan 2003-2008.

Table 64. NMS motor vehicle production by country and company, 2002

	Number of vehicles
Czech Republic	
Skoda/Volkswagen Group	441,308
Tatra	-
Others	4
Total cars	441,312
Daewoo AVIA	967
Jlaureta	4
Karosa	1,548
KH Motor CENTRUM	45
Magma	30
Praga	31
Skoda M, Hradiste	-
Skoda Tatra	-
Skoda/Volkswagen Group	1,161
SOR Libchavy	218
Tatra	1,761
Others	-
Total commercial vehicles	5,765
Grand total	447,077
Hungary	
Audi	54,048
Opel	-
Suzuki	84,633
Total cars	138,681
Csepel	587
Ikarus/NABI/RABA	1,067
RABA	-
Others	50
Total commercial vehicles	1,704
Grand total	140,385
Poland	
Daewoo	28,880
Fiat	178,044
FSO Polonez	1,144
Opel	85,728
Total cars	293,796
Daewoo/FS Lublin	2,500
FSO Polonez Truck	350
Jelcz	250
MAN/Star SA	1,063
Total commercial vehicles	4,163
Grand total	297,959
Slovak Republic	
VW Bratislava	225,442
Total cars	225,442
Kobit (SEZ KBT)	30
LIAZ Zvolen (Granusan)	-
NOVOP	-
PPS Detva	-
SAO-BUS	1
SLOV-AVIA	79
SLOVBUS	16
TATRA Sipox	8
TAZ Sipox	-

	Number of vehicles
VSS Kosice	132
Others	10
Total commercial vehicles	276
Grand total	225,718
Slovenia	
Revoz (Renault)	126,661
Grand total	126,661
SUM	1,237,800

Source: Ward's Automotive Yearbook, 2003: 98.

Table 65. Production growth in automotive industry

	1996	1997	1998	1999	2000	2001	2002	Total manufacturing avg. annual changes in % 1995-02 [2]	1995-02 [2]	Growth differential [1] 1995-02 [2]
Czech Republic	23.8	45.5	13.5	11.0	32.1	16.2	1.3	19.7	4.2	15.5
Estonia	-7.4	25.7	-10.8	8.2	10.7	27.1	10.2	8.3	7.7	0.6
Hungary	29.0	66.0	46.6	21.5	16.3	3.9	0.8	24.5	10.1	14.4
Latvia	-65.7	-25.0	-11.1	-75.0	100.0	50.0	.	-25.5 [3]	6.2 [3]	-31.7 [3]
Lithuania	-18.6	20.1	40.9	-49.6	64.5	101.7	64.6	21.0	5.8	15.2
Poland	34.0	31.1	20.7	14.8	10.5	-14.0	0.9	12.9	5.7	7.2
Slovak Republic	33.1	17.2	101.5	8.0	24.0	16.4	14.2	27.9	5.3	22.6
Slovenia	-7.1	4.5	35.8	-1.1	10.3	3.7	5.4	6.7	1.7	5.0

Notes: 1) Growth rate motor vehicles, trailers and semi-trailers – growth rate total manufacturing. 2) Basis 1995. 3) 1995-2001.
Source: wiiw Industrial Database; Panorama of Czech Industries, Eurostat, New Cronos, SBS.

Table 66. No. of employees (in 1,000) automotive industry (NACE 34)

	1996	1997	1998	1999	2000	2001	2002	Total manuf. avg. annual changes in % 1995-02[2]	Total manuf. avg. annual changes in % 1995-02[2]	Growth differential [1] 1995-02[2]
Czech Republic	57.5	62.3	67.9	69.1	78.5	84.5	87.0	5.8	-2.5	10.7
Estonia	1.9	1.8	1.6	1.3	1.3	1.5	.	-7.9 [3]	-1.8 [3]	-6.0 [3]
Hungary	24.7	29.2	33.2	32.1	33.2	36.1	36.1	6.4	0.4	6.0
Latvia	2.2	1.5	0.6	0.6	0.4	0.6	.	-23.2 [3]	-1.2 [3]	-22.0 [3]
Lithuania	2.6	2.1	0.9	0.5	0.4	0.3	.	-27.1 [3]	-2.6 [3]	-24.5 [3]
Poland	100.5	105.1	107.9	100.1	96.5	86.1	78.0	-3.4	-3.3	0.0
Slovak Republic	13.3	13.7	14.1	14.2	14.7	15.8	18.2	5.0	-2.7	7.8
Slovenia	7.7	7.3	7.6	7.0	6.6	6.9	7.0	-5.1	-1.2	-3.8

Notes: 1) Growth rate motor vehicles, trailers and semi-trailers – growth rate total manufacturing. 2) Basis 1995. 3) 1995-2001. Source: wiiw Industrial Database; Panorama of Czech Industries, Eurostat, New Cronos, SBS.

Table 67. Labour productivity (production per employee) in automotive industry (NACE 34), 1997-2002 (based on PPP99 conversion factors)

Country	1997	1998	1999	2000	2001	2002	in % of total manuf. 2001	in % of EU-15 2001 (EU 2000)
Czech Republic	159,066	165,606	180,552	209,941	226,613	223,186	222.1	83.6
Estonia	56,530	57,957	78,118	81,864	94,052	.	166.1	34.7
Hungary	232,525	299,446	376,722	423,232	404,146	407,019	325.3	149.1
Latvia	22,318	48,170	12,342	33,428	34,671	.	81.3	12.8
Lithuania	5,637	18,534	16,814	34,573	92,979	.	161.3	34.3
Poland	97,980	115,192	142,549	163,391	157,490	175,410	186.6	58.1
Slovak Rep.	170,603	334,176	360,291	431,881	466,993	463,467	471.4	172.3
Slovenia	162,507	211,529	226,571	265,271	264,204	274,677	319.4	97.5
EU-15				271,110				

Source: wiiw Industrial Database; Panorama of Czech industries, Eurostat, New Cronos, SBS.

Table 68. Labour productivity (production per employee) in automotive industry (NACE 34) 1997-2002 (based on PPPCAP99 conversion factors)

Country	1997	1998	1999	2000	2001	2002	in % of EU-15 2001 (EU 2000)
Czech Rep.	110,307	114,842	125,206	145,587	157,148	154,772	58.0
Estonia	33,023	33,856	45,634	47,822	54,941	.	20.3
Hungary	156,041	200,949	252,807	284,019	271,211	273,138	100.0
Latvia	13,584	29,320	7,512	20,346	21,103	.	7.8
Lithuania	3,207	10,545	9,567	19,671	52,902	.	19.5
Poland	73,172	86,025	106,455	122,020	117,613	130,996	43.4
Slovak Rep.	100,112	196,098	211,422	253,432	274,036	271,967	101.1
Slovenia	138,147	179,821	192,608	225,507	224,600	233,503	82.8
EU-15				271,110			

Source: wiiw Industrial Database; Panorama of Czech industries, Eurostat, New Cronos, SBS.

Table 69. Monthly gross wages (EUR) 1995-2002 in automotive industry

	1995	1996	1997	1998	1999	2000	2001	2002	in % of total manufacturing 2001	in % of EU-15 2001
Czech Rep.	.	317	353	394	425	469	511	575	123.4	17.4
Estonia	197	228	271	316	338	370	375	.	114.1	12.8
Hungary	269	299	344	357	395	449	530	636	133.8	18.1
Latvia	133	135	163	191	157	155	249	.	94.6	8.5
Lithuania	76	80	128	139	148	189	192	.	75.2	6.5
Poland	231	286	325	352	449	515	585	580	115.0	19.9
Slovak Rep.	196	227	267	311	324	407	454	478	145.1	15.5
Slovenia	518	621	664	727	794	849	877	932	106.6	29.9
EU-15						2,934				

Source: wiiw Industrial Database; Panorama of Czech industries; Eurostat, European business, Facts and figures, 2003 edition, p. 224, own calculations.

Table 70. Monthly total labour costs (EUR) 1997-2002 in automotive industry

	1995	1996	1997	1998	1999	2000	2001	2002	in % of total manufacturing 2002	in % of EU-15 2001
Czech Rep.	.	452	502	559	596	664	729	820	117.0	20.4
Estonia										
Hungary	478	506	576	587	632	680	788	923	129.5	22.0
Latvia										
Lithuania										
Poland	335	415	471	510	650	616	700	694	116.6	19.6
Slovak Rep.	274	316	326	404	329	393	878	650	133.3	24.5
Slovenia	751	892	948	1,037	1,133	1,211	1,251	1,329	102.1	35.0
EU-15							3,577			

Source: wiiw Industrial Database; Panorama of Czech industries; Eurostat, European business, Facts and figures, 2003 edition, p. 224, own calculations.

Table 71. Unit labour cost 1997-2002 in automotive industry in %
(at PPP99 conversion; calculated with total labour costs)

	1997	1998	1999	2000	2001	2002	in % of total manufacturing 2001	in % of EU-15 2001 (EU 2000)
Czech Rep.	3.79	4.05	3.96	3.80	3.86	4.41	55.2	27.4
Estonia								
Hungary	2.97	2.35	2.01	1.93	2.34	2.72	40.5	16.9
Latvia								
Lithuania								
Poland	5.77	5.31	5.47	4.53	5.33	4.74	61.6	29.5
Slovak Rep.	2.29	1.45	1.10	1.09	2.26	1.68	41.4	10.5
Slovenia	7.00	5.88	6.00	5.48	5.68	5.81	35.1	36.1
EU-15				16.09				

Source: wiiw Industrial Database; Panorama of Czech industries, Eurostat, New Cronos, SBS.

Table 72. Unit labour cost 1997-2002 in automotive industry in %
(at PPPCAP99 conversion; calculated with total labour costs)

	1997	1998	1999	2000	2001	2002	in % of EU-15 in 2001 (EU 2000)
Czech Rep.	5.46	5.84	5.71	5.47	5.57	6.36	39.5
Estonia							
Hungary	4.43	3.50	3.00	2.87	3.49	4.05	25.2
Latvia							
Lithuania							
Poland	7.72	7.11	7.33	6.06	7.14	6.35	39.5
Slovak Rep.	3.90	2.48	1.87	1.86	3.84	2.87	17.8
Slovenia	8.23	6.92	7.06	6.44	6.68	6.83	42.5
EU-15				16.09			

Source: wiiw Industrial Database; Panorama of Czech industries, Eurostat, New Cronos, SBS.

Table 73. Gross domestic product real change in % against preceding year

	1995	1996	1997	1998	1999	2000	2001	2002	2003[1]	forecast 2004	2005	avg. annual growth rate 1995-2003
Czech Rep.	5.9	4.3	-0.8	-1.0	0.5	3.3	3.1	2.0	2.9	3.0	4	1.6
Hungary	1.5	1.3	4.6	4.9	4.2	5.2	3.8	3.5	2.9	3.5	3.9	3.4
Poland	7.0	6.0	6.8	4.8	4.1	4.0	1.0	1.4	3.7	4.0	4.0	3.5
Slovak Rep.	5.8	6.1	4.6	4.2	1.5	2.0	3.8	4.4	4.2	4.5	5.0	3.4
Slovenia	4.1	3.5	4.6	3.8	5.2	4.6	2.9	2.9	2.3	3.4	3.5	3.3
Estonia	4.3	3.9	9.8	4.6	-0.6	7.3	6.5	6.0	4.8	5.6	5.1	4.6
Latvia	-0.8	3.7	8.4	4.8	2.8	6.8	7.9	6.1	7.4	5.2	5.7	5.3
Lithuania	3.3	4.7	7.0	7.3	-1.8	4.0	6.5	6.8	8.9	5.7	6	4.8

Note: 1) Preliminary.
Source: wiiw Database incorporating national statistics, forecast: wiiw and European Commission (2003) for Baltic States.

Table 74. Gross industrial production real change in % against preceding year

	1995	1996	1997	1998	1999	2000	2001	2002	2003[1]	forecast 2004	forecast 2005	avg. annual growth rate 1995-2003
Czech Rep.	8.7	2.0	4.5	1.6	-3.1	5.4	6.5	4.8	5.8	5.5	6	3.0
Hungary	4.6	3.4	11.1	12.5	10.4	18.1	3.6	2.7	6.4	9	10	7.4
Poland [2]	9.7	8.3	11.5	3.5	3.6	6.7	0.6	1.9	6	7	7	4.6
Slovak Rep.	8.3	2.5	2.7	5.0	-2.7	8.6	6.9	6.5	5.3	6	7	3.8
Slovenia	2.0	1.0	1.0	3.7	-0.5	6.2	2.9	2.4	1.4	2	2.5	2.0
Estonia	1.9	2.9	14.6	4.2	-3.4	14.6	8.9	5.9	10.2	.	.	6.3
Latvia	-3.7	5.5	13.8	3.1	-5.4	4.7	9.2	5.8	6.5	.	.	4.7
Lithuania	5.3	5.0	3.3	12.1	-9.9	2.2	16.0	3.1	16.1	.	.	5.0

Notes: 1) Preliminary. 2) Sales.
Source: wiiw Database incorporating national statistics, forecast: wiiw.

Table 75. Vehicles in use in the NMS (as of 31 Dec.), 1999-2002 in 1,000

		1995	1997	1998	1999	2000	2001	2002
Czech Rep.	Passenger cars	3,113.5	3,382.4	3,484.0	3,431.5	3,431.6	3,523.3	3,648.9
	Trucks	182.3	355.1	365.9	367.8	369.0	388.4	413.5
	Buses	21.9	20.7	19.9	19.0	18.3	18.4	21.3
	Total	3,317.7	5,755.3	5,867.8	5,817.2	5,818.9	5,931.0	6,085.8
Hungary	Passenger cars	2,176.9	2,297.1	2,218.0	2,255.5	2,364.7	2,482.8	2,629.5
	Trucks	258.1	342.3	336.9	364.1	366.4	380.1	396.1
	Buses	21.5	18.6	18.5	17.7	17.9	17.9	17.9
	Total	2,456.5	2,658.0	2,573.4	2,637.4	2,749.0	2,880.8	3,043.5
Poland	Passenger cars	7,517.3	8,533.5	8,890.8	9,282.8	9,991.3	10,503.1	11,028.9
	Trucks	1,386.9	1,513.0	1,658.0	1,767.9	1,880.4	1,979.1	2,031.8
	Buses	85.4	81.8	80.8	78.7	82.4	82.0	83.1
	Total	8,989.6	10,128.3	10,629.6	11,129.4	11,954.0	12,564.2	13,143.8
Slovak Rep.	Passenger cars	1,015.8	1,135.9	1,195.7	1,247.0	1,274.2	1,292.8	1,326.9
	Trucks	148.4	149.1	144.2	149.1	153.2	161.5	171.3
	Buses	11.8	11.2	12.3	11.1	10.9	10.6	10.6
	Total	1,176.0	1,296.2	1,352.1	1,407.1	1,438.3	1,465.0	1,508.8
Slovenia	Passenger cars	698.2	760.4	812.9	848.3	868.3	884.2	899.2
	Trucks	37.7	38.5	55.0	56.8	60.1	62.5	65.3
	Buses	2.5	2.4	2.3	2.3	2.3	2.2	2.2
	Total	738.4	801.3	870.2	907.4	930.6	948.8	966.7

Table 76. Motorisation rate: number of passenger cars per 1,000 inhabitants

	1995	1996	1997	1998	1999	2000	2001	2002
Cyprus	301	308	317	334	342	355	369	369[1]
Czech Rep.	301	325	344	358	359	335	345	358
Estonia	257	275	293	310	317	338	298	298[1]
Hungary	218	220	224	216	221	232	244	259
Latvia	131	152	174	196	215	234	248	248[1]
Lithuania	193	212	238	265	294	317	326	326[1]
Malta	490	448	491	464	482	497	499	499[1]
Poland	195	209	221	230	240	259	272	286
Slovak Rep.	189	197	211	222	229	236	240	247
Slovenia	351	366	385	403	417	426	433	465

1) 2001.
Source: Statistical yearbook on candidate countries, 2000, 2002, 2003; wiiw Handbook of Statistics 2003; VDA International Auto Statistics.

Table 77. FDI stocks in the new member states 2002

	Inward FDI stock in manuf., EUR mn	Employees in manuf., persons	FDI stocks per employee, EUR
CZ			
Manufacturing (D)	11,539	1,037,000	11,128
Motor vehicles (34)	1,933	86,961	22,232
H			
Manufacturing (D)	13,523	746,963	18,104
Motor vehicles (34)	3,236	45,153	7,166
PL			
Manufacturing (D)	16,379	221,319	7,401
Motor vehicles (34)	2,280	151,147	15,087
SK			
Manufacturing (D)	2,713	379,841	7,143
Motor vehicles (34)	148	18,155	8,146
SLO			
Manufacturing (D)	1,696	229,713	7,384
Motor vehicles (34)	53	6,971	7,632
EST			
Manufacturing (D)	759	120,128	6,153
Motor vehicles (34)	24	1,482	24,085
LV			
Manufacturing (D)	407	146,953	2,878
Motor vehicles (34)	2	645	1,483
LT			
Manufacturing (D)	1,119	232,900	3,322
Motor vehicles (34)	43	6,300	6,807

Source: wiiw FDI database.

Table 78. NMS exports, imports and trade balance for road vehicles (SITC 78), 1995-2002 in USD mn

	1995	1996	1997	1998	1999	2000	2001	2002
			Exports of road vehicles (SITC 78)					
Cyprus	1.7	1.8	2.7	2.6	2.4	2.2	1.8	1.9
Czech Rep.	1,593.2	2,034.5	2,815.3	3,859.7	4,043.1	4,541.9	5,321.1	8,011.1
Estonia	113.6	115.8	213.1	133.3	98.4	141.7	180.5	213.0
Hungary	681.7	557.1	1,089.3	1,411.6	2,250.9	2,459.6	2,712.7	2,979.3
Latvia	49.0	30.5	25.1	19.1	10.2	10.7	13.6	19.1
Lithuania	99.4	205.8	263.2	249.3	102.3	154.4	318.6	439.5
Malta	1.4	2.3	2.5	3.3	2.2	3.0	3.0	.
Poland	1,127.7	1,324.3	1,492.9	2,009.2	2,263.0	3,069.8	3,222.8	3,771.7
Slovak Rep.	369.0	677.4	1,011.4	1,993.7	1,892.7	2,449.5	2,334.0	2,899.6
Slovenia	952.3	1,014.4	997.6	1,298.2	1,107.8	1,068.9	1,069.4	1,271.0
			Imports of road vehicles (SITC 78)					
Cyprus	360.4	340.0	275.2	388.3	369.3	413.7	437.9	502.5
Czech Rep.	1,567.8	1,972.5	2,131.4	2,126.5	2,224.1	2,365.7	2,921.4	4171.6
Estonia	188.5	225.2	493.3	392.5	246.7	337.5	418.5	519.5
Hungary	910.0	991.1	1,144.9	1,791.8	2,408.3	2,362.0	2,459.8	3039.2
Latvia	118.9	112.8	193.6	283.5	211.6	224.4	298.5	346.8
Lithuania	240.7	405.6	575.8	632.0	298.8	380.3	647.4	813.4
Malta	169.1	162.5	129.3	126.4	149.9	137.7	131.1	.
Poland	1,556.3	2,622.3	3,673.2	4,406.7	4,326.1	4,029.6	3,911.4	4,888.5
Slovak Rep.	459.4	1,077.7	1,171.6	1,613.9	1,232.6	1,395.1	1,692.8	1,940.9
Slovenia	1,194.4	1,197.3	1,141.7	1,343.2	1,371.8	1,103.8	1,083.7	1,162.6
			Trade balance of road vehicles (SITC 78)					
Cyprus	-358.7	-338.2	-272.5	-385.7	-366.9	-411.5	-436.1	-500.6
Czech Rep.	25.4	62.0	683.9	1,733.2	1,819.0	2,176.2	2,399.7	3,839.5
Estonia	-74.9	-109.4	-280.2	-259.2	-148.3	-195.8	-238.0	-306.5
Hungary	-228.3	-434.0	-55.6	-380.2	-157.4	97.6	252.9	-59.9
Latvia	-69.9	-82.3	-168.5	-264.4	-201.4	-213.7	-284.9	-327.7
Lithuania	-141.3	-199.8	-312.6	-382.7	-196.5	-225.9	-328.8	-373.9
Malta	-167.7	-160.2	-126.8	-123.1	-147.7	-134.7	-128.1	
Poland	-428.6	-1,298.0	-2,180.3	-2,397.5	-2,063.1	-959.8	-688.6	-1,116.8
Slovak Rep.	-90.4	-400.3	-160.2	379.8	660.1	1,054.4	641.2	958.7
Slovenia	-242.1	-182.9	-144.1	-45.0	-264.0	-34.9	-14.3	108.4

Source: UN trade database, wiiw calculations.

Table 79. Automotive industry (NACE 34) export sales/sales, in %

	1995		1996		1997		1998		1999		2000		2001	
	DE	FIE	DE	FIE	DE	FIE	DE	FIE	DE	FIE	DE	FIE	DE	FIE
CZ	.	.	.	.	47.1	67.3	46.2	76.3	40.7	79.7	50.0	69.7	52.4	81.1
H	37.7	81.0	50.0	84.5	28.4	87.4	24.5	89.8	29.7	93.0	49.2	94.8	50.5	92.5
PL	7.7	47.2	10.4	30.6	10.6	26.3	11.6	29.1	13.7	34.5	14.9	52.0	14.3	63.6
SK	.	.	.	.	.	.	.	.	.	.	.	.	.	.
SL	45.1	72.7	53.8	73.2	55.2	78.5	58.8	80.2	64.5	74.5	73.8	79.9	62.4	82.1

Note: DE: domestic enterprises; FIE: foreign invested enterprises.
Source: wiiw FIE database.

Table 80. Exports of road vehicles and sub-groups in total manufacturing exports of the NMS 1995-2002, in %

	SITC rev. 3	1995	1996	1997	1998	1999	2000	2001	2002	Relative change
Cyprus										
road vehicles	78	0.5	0.5	0.8	0.8	0.8	0.7	0.6	0.6	42.2
passenger motor veh. ex. buses	781	n/a	n/a	n/a	n/a	n/a	n/a	n/a	n/a	n/a
goods, special pur. veh.	782	n/a	n/a	n/a	n/a	n/a	n/a	n/a	n/a	n/a
road motor veh. n.e.s.	783	n/a	n/a	n/a	n/a	n/a	n/a	n/a	n/a	n/a
parts, bodies, tractors	784	0.5	0.5	0.8	0.8	0.7	0.7	0.6	0.6	34.7
Czech Rep.										
road vehicles	78	8.0	10.0	13.1	14.2	15.7	16.2	16.4	19.1	137.3
passenger motor veh. ex. buses	781	3.6	4.6	6.3	7.6	8.3	8.8	9.0	11.5	215.3
goods, special pur. veh.	782	0.9	0.9	1.5	1.1	0.7	0.7	0.3	0.2	-71.1
road motor veh. n.e.s.	783	0.3	0.4	0.3	0.3	0.3	0.3	0.3	0.3	-10.4
parts, bodies, tractors	784	2.5	3.3	4.2	4.6	5.7	5.8	6.3	6.6	169.3
Estonia										
road vehicles	78	7.0	6.2	8.5	4.7	3.7	4.2	5.0	5.5	-20.3
passenger motor veh. ex. buses	781	3.7	3.2	5.9	2.3	1.5	2.0	2.4	2.3	-38.1
goods, special pur. veh.	782	0.6	0.3	0.3	0.4	0.2	0.2	0.3	0.3	-46.7
road motor veh. n.e.s.	783	0.1	0.1	0.1	0.1	0.1	0.2	0.2	0.4	445.1
parts, bodies, tractors	784	2.3	2.2	1.9	1.5	1.6	1.2	1.5	2.0	-12.2

	SITC rev. 3	1995	1996	1997	1998	1999	2000	2001	2002	Relative change
Hungary										
road vehicles	78	6.1	4.8	6.3	6.6	9.5	9.3	9.6	9.3	50.8
passenger motor veh. ex. buses	781	1.7	0.5	1.9	2.6	5.7	5.4	5.2	4.6	174.3
goods, special pur. veh.	782	0.2	0.2	0.1	0.1	0.1	0.0	0.1	0.1	-67.5
road motor veh. n.e.s.	783	1.0	1.0	1.3	0.6	0.3	0.3	0.4	0.2	-76.3
parts, bodies, tractors	784	2.2	2.2	2.1	2.7	2.6	2.8	3.2	3.6	62.1
Latvia										
road vehicles	78	4.4	2.3	1.6	1.2	0.7	0.6	0.7	0.9	-79.3
passenger motor veh. ex. buses	781	0.4	0.2	0.1	0.1	0.0	0.1	0.2	0.2	-44.2
goods, special pur. veh.	782	0.5	0.3	0.2	0.2	0.1	0.1	0.2	0.1	-75.2
road motor veh. n.e.s.	783	2.3	0.6	0.0	0.0	0.0	0.0	0.1	0.2	-93.2
parts, bodies, tractors	784	0.7	0.7	0.8	0.6	0.2	0.1	0.2	0.3	-63.1
Lithuania										
road vehicles	78	4.4	7.4	8.6	8.6	3.7	4.3	7.4	10.2	128.7
passenger motor veh. ex. buses	781	3.2	5.7	6.7	6.7	2.0	2.8	5.7	7.9	148.8
goods, special pur. veh.	782	0.1	0.2	0.2	0.2	0.1	0.1	0.3	0.4	285.9
road motor veh. N.e.s.	783	0.1	0.1	0.2	0.3	0.3	0.1	0.2	0.2	142.4
parts, bodies, tractors	784	0.5	0.8	0.7	0.6	0.5	0.4	0.3	0.5	4.9
Malta										
road vehicles	78	0.1	0.1	0.2	0.2	0.1	0.1	0.2	n/a	n/a
passenger motor veh. ex. buses	781	n/a	n/a	n/a	n/a	n/a	n/a	n/a	n/a	n/a
goods, special pur. veh.	782	n/a	n/a	n/a	n/a	n/a	n/a	n/a	n/a	n/a
road motor veh. n.e.s.	783	n/a	n/a	n/a	n/a	n/a	n/a	n/a	n/a	n/a
parts, bodies, tractors	784	0.0	0.1	0.2	0.2	0.1	0.1	0.2	n/a	n/a
Poland										
road vehicles	78	5.5	6.0	6.4	7.6	9.0	10.2	9.6	10.0	80.2
passenger motor veh. ex. buses	781	3.2	3.5	3.3	3.8	4.4	4.9	4.2	3.7	13.8
goods, special pur. veh.	782	0.9	0.7	0.8	1.3	1.4	1.5	1.1	1.4	52.6
road motor veh. n.e.s.	783	0.0	0.0	0.2	0.1	0.2	0.4	0.3	0.4	893.6
parts, bodies, tractors	784	0.6	0.9	1.4	1.6	2.1	2.6	3.2	3.8	533.3
Slovak Rep.										
road vehicles	78	4.8	9.8	10.8	19.1	19.4	22.6	18.9	21.7	353.6
pass. motor veh. ex. buses	781	0.9	4.0	5.2	14.4	14.2	17.9	14.3	16.1	1755.3

	SITC rev. 3	1995	1996	1997	1998	1999	2000	2001	2002	Relative change
goods, special pur. veh.	782	0.5	0.4	0.7	0.2	0.2	0.1	0.2	0.2	-58.4
road motor veh. N.e.s.	783	0.1	0.0	0.0	0.0	0.0	0.0	0.0	0.0	-69.8
parts, bodies, tractors	784	2.5	4.4	4.3	3.8	4.4	4.0	3.8	4.7	87.1
Slovenia										
road vehicles	78	11.7	12.4	12.1	14.6	13.1	12.4	11.8	12.5	7.0
passenger motor veh. ex. buses	781	8.6	9.5	9.4	11.0	9.4	8.7	8.0	8.3	-2.7
goods, special pur. veh.	782	0.1	0.2	0.1	0.2	0.2	0.2	0.2	0.4	198.4
road motor veh. n.e.s.	783	0.3	0.1	0.1	0.4	0.2	0.1	0.1	0.2	-40.2
parts, bodies, tractors	784	1.8	1.7	1.7	2.1	2.3	2.4	2.4	2.5	41.5

Source: UN-Trade database, wiiw calculations.

Table 81. Road vehicles and sub-groups: world market shares[1] of the NMS, in % 1995-2002

	SITC rev. 3		1996	1997	1998	1999	2000	2001	2002
Cyprus									
road vehicles	78	0.00	0.00	0.00	0.00	0.00	0.00	0.00	0.00
passenger motor veh. ex. buses	781	0.00	0.00	0.00	0.00	0.00	0.00	0.00	0.00
goods, special purpose veh.	782	0.00	0.00	0.00	0.00	0.00	0.00	0.00	0.00
road motor veh. n.e.s	783	0.00	0.00	0.00	0.00	0.00	0.00	0.00	0.00
parts, bodies, tractors	784	0.00	0.00	0.00	0.00	0.00	0.00	0.00	0.00
Czech Rep.									
road vehicles	78	0,39	0.47	0.62	0.82	0.82	0.89	1.04	1.42
passenger motor veh. ex. buses	781	0.31	0.39	0.52	0.74	0.74	0.82	0.95	1.43
goods, special purpose veh.	782	0.39	0.40	0.60	0.54	0.35	0.34	0.19	0.18
road motor veh. n.e.s.	783	0.37	0.47	0.44	0.45	0.43	0.49	0.56	0.71
parts, bodies, tractors	784	0.41	0.55	0.71	1.00	1.12	1.17	1.52	1.81
Estonia									
road vehicles	78	0.03	0.03	0.05	0.03	0.02	0.03	0.04	0.04
passenger motor veh. ex. buses	781	0.03	0.02	0.06	0.02	0.01	0.02	0.03	0.03
goods, special purpose veh.	782	0.02	0.01	0.01	0.02	0.01	0.01	0.02	0.02
road motor veh. n.e.s.	783	0.01	0.01	0.01	0.01	0.01	0.04	0.06	0.09
parts, bodies, tractors	784	0.03	0.03	0.04	0.04	0.03	0.03	0.04	0.05

Hungary

road vehicles	78	0.17	0.13	0.24	0.30	0.46	0.48	0.53	0.53
passenger motor veh. ex. buses	781	0.08	0.02	0.13	0.20	0.46	0.48	0.48	0.44
goods, special purpose veh.	782	0.05	0.05	0.03	0.02	0.03	0.02	0.03	0.03
road motor veh. n.e.s.	783	0.70	0.72	1.46	0.68	0.45	0.56	0.84	0.49
parts, bodies, tractors	784	0.21	0.21	0.29	0.46	0.48	0.54	0.68	0.76

Latvia

road vehicles	78	0.01	0.01	0.01	0.00	0.00	0.00	0.00	0.00
passenger motor veh. ex. buses	781	0.00	0.00	0.00	0.00	0.00	0.00	0.00	0.00
goods, special purpose veh.	782	0.01	0.01	0.01	0.01	0.00	0.00	0.01	0.00
road motor veh. n.e.s.	783	0.15	0.05	0.00	0.00	0.00	0.00	0.01	0.02
parts, bodies, tractors	784	0.01	0.01	0.01	0.01	0.00	0.00	0.00	0.00

Lithuania

road vehicles	78	0.02	0.05	0.06	0.05	0.02	0.03	0.06	0.08
passenger motor veh. ex. buses	781	0.03	0.06	0.08	0.07	0.02	0.03	0.08	0.10
goods, special purpose veh.	782	0.01	0.01	0.01	0.01	0.01	0.01	0.02	0.03
road motor veh. n.e.s.	783	0.01	0.01	0.04	0.05	0.04	0.03	0.06	0.05
parts, bodies, tractors	784	0.01	0.02	0.02	0.01	0.01	0.01	0.01	0.01

Malta

road vehicles	78	0.0	0.0	0.0	0.0	0.0	0.0	0.0	0.0
passenger motor veh. ex. buses	781	0.0	0.0	0.0	0.0	0.0	0.0	0.0	0.0
goods, special purpose veh.	782	0.0	0.0	0.0	0.0	0.0	0.0	0.0	0.0
road motor veh. n.e.s.	783	0.0	0.0	0.0	0.0	0.0	0.0	0.0	0.0
parts, bodies, tractors	784	0.0	0.0	0.0	0.0	0.0	0.0	0.0	0.0

Poland

road vehicles	78	0.27	0.31	0.33	0.43	0.46	0.60	0.63	0.67
passenger motor veh. ex. buses	781	0.29	0.32	0.30	0.37	0.38	0.49	0.46	0.41
goods, special purpose veh.	782	0.41	0.33	0.34	0.64	0.68	0.81	0.67	0.89
road motor veh. n.e.s.	783	0.05	0.05	0.30	0.19	0.34	0.81	0.75	0.98
parts, bodies, tractors	784	0.10	0.17	0.25	0.33	0.41	0.57	0.81	0.94

Slovak Rep.

road vehicles	78	0.09	0.16	0.22	0.42	0.38	0.48	0.46	0.51
passenger motor veh. ex. buses	781	0.03	0.11	0.19	0.55	0.48	0.65	0.58	0.64
goods, special purpose veh.	782	0.09	0.06	0.12	0.04	0.03	0.03	0.04	0.05

road motor veh. n.e.s.	783	0.03	0.01	0.02	0.02	0.02	0.02	0.02	0.01
parts, bodies, tractors	784	0.16	0.25	0.32	0.32	0.33	0.31	0.35	0.41
Slovenia									
road vehicles	78	0.23	0.24	0.22	0.28	0.22	0.21	0.21	0.22
passenger motor veh. ex. buses	781	0.30	0.32	0.30	0.36	0.27	0.25	0.24	0.25
goods, special purpose veh.	782	0.02	0.03	0.02	0.03	0.02	0.02	0.03	0.07
road motor veh. n.e.s.	783	0.13	0.04	0.06	0.21	0.09	0.04	0.05	0.10
parts, bodies, tractors	784	0.12	0.12	0.11	0.15	0.15	0.15	0.17	0.17

1) exports of individual countries divided by world exports in the same SITC group.
n.e.s.= not explicitly specified.
Source: UN-Trade database, wiiw calculations.

List of Figures

List of Tables

References

ACEA (2003), *Annual Tax Guide 2003*.

ACEA (2004a), *ACEA Comments Regarding the Proposed Modification of Directive 98/71 on the Legal Protection of Designs – Executive Summary*, Brussels.

ACEA (2004b), *EU-15 Economic Report*, Brussels.

ACEA Auto Data (2004), Auto Data, *http://www.acea.be/ACEA/auto_data.html*, March.

Ashrafian, V. and X. Richet (2001), Industrial Cooperation in the Russian Car Industry, *Russian Economic Trends* 10 (3/4).

Assanis, D. (1999), An Optimization Approach to Hybrid Electric Propulsion System Design, *Mechanics of Structures and Machines* 27 (4).

Audretsch, D. and M. Fritsch (2002), Growth Regimes over Time and Space, *Regional Studies* 36 (2).

Automotive Resources Asia (2003), China Passenger Vehicle Market Sets Monthly Sales Record in September, Online document: www.autoresourcesasia.com/Mas_CASR_-09_2003.pdf.

autopolis (2000), *The Natural Link Between Sales and Service. An Investigation for the Competition Directorate-General of the European Commission*, Brussels.

Baily, M. N. and H. Gersbach (1995), *Efficiency in Manufacturing and the Need for Global Competition*, Brookings Papers on Economic Activity, Microeconomics, Vol. 4.

Balassa, B. (1965), *Trade Liberalization and 'Revealed' Comparative Advantage*, The Manchester School of Economic and Social Studies, Vol. 33.

Bartlett, C. and S. Goshal (1989), *Managing Across Borders: The Transnational Solution*, Boston.

Bartlett, C. and G. Sumantra (1987), Managing Across Borders: New Organisational Responses, *Sloan Management Review* (Fall).

Baum, H. (2000), Transport Intensity, Decoupling and Economic Growth, *Zeitschrift für Verkehrswissenschaft* 71 (2).

Beise, M. (2001), *Lead Markets: Country-Specific Success Factors of the Global Diffusion of Innovations*, ZEW Economic Studies, Vol. 14, Heidelberg.

Beise, M. and T. Cleff (2003), *Assessing the Lead Market Potential of Countries for Innovation Projects*, Discussion Paper Series No. 142, Kobe.

Beise, M., T. Cleff, O. Heneric, and C. Rammer (2002), *Lead Markt Deutschland – Zur Position Deutschlands als führender Absatzmarkt für Innovationen*, ZEW Dokumentation No. 02-02, Mannheim.

Berndt, E. R. (1991), *The Practice of Econometrics: Classic and Contemporary*, Reading.

Bingmann, H. (1993), Antiblockiersystem und Benzineinspritzung, in: Albach, H. (Ed.), *Culture and Technical Innovation: A Cross-Cultural Analysis and Policy Recommendations*, Berlin.

Bode, B. and J. van Dalen (2001), *Quality-Corrected Price Indexes of New Passenger Cars in the Netherlands, 1990-1999*, Rotterdam.

Breschi, S. (2000), The Geography of Innovation: a Cross-Sector Analysis, *Regional Studies* 34 (3).

Breschi, S. and F. Malerba (1997), Sectoral Innovation Systems, Technological Regimes, Schumpeterian Dynamic, and Spatial Boundaries, in: Edquist, C. (Ed.), *Systems of Innovation: Technologies, Institutions, and Organisations*, London.

Buckley, P. J., Ch. L. Pass and K. Prescott (1988), Measures of International Competitiveness: A Critical Survey, *Journal of Marketing Management* 4 (2).

Burwell, M. J. and P. Wylie (2002), Automotive Transaction Numbers Reach All-Time High in 2002, *PricewaterhouseCoopers Global Automotive Financial Review*, http://www.pwcglobal.com/Extweb/industry.nsf/docid/3690EA483AFBA6FA8525687 E00590EAA

Cap Gemini Ernst & Young (2003), *Cars Online 2003: Unlocking Hidden Value. A Cross-Channel Analysis of the Automotive Industry – From Consumer Demand Through the Aftermarket*, Stuttgart.

COWI (2001), *Study on Fiscal Measures to Reduce CO2 Emissions from New Passenger Cars, Consulting Engineers and Planners AS*, Brussels.

DG ENTR (2002), *Final Report on Emission Control Technology for Heavy-Duty-Vehicles*, Brussels.

Diekmann, A. (2001), The Impact of Transport on the EU Economy, *Zeitschrift für Verkehrswissenschaft* 72 (2).

Dodgson, M. and R. Rothwell (1994), *The Handbook of Industrial Innovation*, Oxford.

Dollar, D. and E. N. Wolff (1993), *Competitiveness, Convergence, and International Specialisation*, Cambridge.

Doran, D. and R. Roome (2003), An Evaluation of Value-Transfer Within a Modular Supply Chain, *Journal of Automobile Engineering* 217 (7).

Doz, Y. et al. (2001), *From Global to Metanational*, Boston.

Dr. Lademann & Partner (2001), *Customer Preferences for Existing and Potential Sales and Servicing Alternatives in Automobile Distribution*, Hamburg.

Dudenhöffer, F. (1997), Restrukturierung von Vertriebsnetzen, in: Belz, C. and T. Tomczak (Eds.), *Thexis, Marktbearbeitung und Distribution, Kompetenz für Marketing-Innovationen*, Vol. 4.

Dudenhöffer, F. (2001), Automobile mit Brennstoffzellen-Antrieb: Eine Zukunftslösung für den Individualverkehr, *Zeitschrift für Verkehrswissenschaft* 72 (2).

Dudenhöffer, F. (2003), Kann Deutschland vom Zulieferer-Wachstum profitieren? *Automotive Engineering Partners* (2).

Dunning, J. H. (1981), *International Production and the Multinational Enterprise*, London.

ECG (2004), Maintaining the Competitiveness of the European Automotive Industry by Supporting the Finished Vehicle Logistics Sector, European Car-Transport Group of Interest, January, www.eurocartrans.org.

Ekonomines Konsultacijos ir Tyrimai UAB (2002), *The Automotive Component Industry in Lithuania, a Study Prepared for the Lithuanian Development Agency*, Vilnius.

electronics (2002), *Driving Force for Innovation*, Engineer Centaur Communications *291 (7615)*.

Emanuel, I. (2002), The European Motor Vehicle Block Exemption: An Update, *PricewaterhouseCoopers Global Automotive Financial Review*, http://www.pwcglobal.com/Extweb/industry.nsf/docid/3690EA483AFBA6FA8525687E00590EA

Energy and Environmental Analysis Inc. (1995), *Automotive Technologies to Improve Fuel Economy to 2015*, Final Report, Virginia, USA.

Energy and Environmental Analysis Inc. (2001), *Technology and Cost of Future Fuel Economy Improvements for Light-Duty Vehicles*, Arlington, USA.

Ernst & Young (2003), Practical Solutions for the Automotive Industry, *Autobeat Daily*.

European Commission (1999), *High Level Group on Transport Infrastructure Charging*, Final Report 1999, Brussels.

European Commission COM (2001a), *White Paper, European Transport Policy for 2010: Time to Decide*, 370 Final, Brussels.

European Commission (2003), *Directorate-General for Energy and Transport, Energy and Transport in Figures 2003*, Brussels.

European Commission COM (1995), *Council Conclusion of 25.6.1996*, 689 Final, Brussels.

European Commission COM (1997), *Communication 97/358*.

European Commission COM (2001b), *Tax Policy in the European Union – Priorities for the Years Ahead*, 260 Final, Brussels.

European Commission COM (2002a), *Communication from the Commission on Impact Assessment*, 276 Final, Brussels.

European Commission COM (2002b), *Action Plan Simplifying and Improving the Regulatory Environment*, 278 Final, Brussels.

European Commission COM (2002c), *Taxation of Passengers Cars in the European Union – Options for Action at National and Community Levels*, 431 Final, Brussels.

European Commission COM (2003), *The Commissions Legislative and Work Programme for 2004*, 645 Final, Brussels.

European Commission COM (2004a), *Implementing the Community Strategy to reduce CO2 Emissions from Cars: Fourth Annual Report on the Effectiveness of the Strategy*, 78 Final, Brussels.

European Commission COM (2004b), *Towards a European Research Area; Science, Technology and Innovation*, Brussels.

European Commission Green Paper (1995), *Towards Fair and Efficient Pricing in Transport*, Brussels.

European Commission Staff Working Paper (2003), *Monitoring of ACEA's, JAMA's, KAMA's Commitment on CO2 Emission from Passenger Cars*, Brussels.

European Commission White Paper (1998), *Fair Payment for Infrastructure Use*, Brussels.

Eurostat (2003a), *European Business, Facts and Figures*, Luxembourg.

Eurostat (2003b), *Statistical Yearbook on Candidate Countries*, Luxembourg.

Farrell, D. (2004), Making Foreign Investment Work for China, *Business Times Online McKinsey Quarterly*, http://business-times.asia1.com.sg/sub/mckinsey/0,5318,00.html.

Fieten, R. (1995), Automobilzulieferer im Verdrängungswettbewerb, *Arbeitgeber* (15).

Freeman, Ch. (1994), The Economics of Technical Change, *Journal of Economics* 18 (5).

Frigant, V. and Y. Lung (2001), *Are the French Car Companies PSA and Renault the European Automobile Industry's Champions of Shareholder Value?*, TSER Project "Corporate Governance, Innovation and Economic Performance in the EU", Bordeaux.

VDA (2003), Anual Report 2003, Frankfurt/Main.

Govindarajan, V. and A. Gupta (2001), *Building an Effective Global Business Team*, Cambridge, USA.

Han, X. and B. Fang (1998), Measuring Transportation in the U.S. Economy, *Journal of Transportation and Statistics* January.

Hanzl, D. (1999), *Development and Prospects of the Transport Equipment Sector in the Central and Eastern European Countries*, wiiw Industry Studies, Vol. 4, Vienna.

Hanzl, D., P. Havlik and W. Urban (2002), *Competitiveness of Central and Eastern European Industries Now and in an Enlarged EU*, a study commissioned by Bank Austria Creditanstalt.

Havlik P. et al. (2001), *Competitiveness of Industry in CEE Candidate Countries*. Composite Paper; prepared for the European Commission, DG Enterprise, Vienna,

Head, K. and J. Ries, (2001), Overseas Investment and Firm Exports, *Review of International Economics* 9 (1).

Hein, C. (2004), Indien oder China – zwei Systeme wetteifern um die Märkte von heute und morgen, *Frankfurter Allgemeine Sonntagszeitung*, February 29.

Heß, A. (1997), *Aktuelle Entwicklungen der Vertriebsnetzgestaltung in der Automobilwirtschaft – Ursachen, Hintergründe, Zukunftsperspektiven*, Jahrbuch der Absatz- und Verbrauchsforschung, Vol. 1, Berlin.

Hild, R. (1998), *Die Brennstoffzelle*, München.

Hoon-Halbauer, S. K. (1999), Managing Relationships Within Sino-Foreign Joint Ventures, *Journal of World Business* 34 (4).

Huang, Y. (2002), Between Two Coordination Failures: Automotive Industrial Policy in China with a Comparison to Korea, *Review of International Political Economy* 9.

Inklaar, R., L. Stokes, E. Stuivenwold, M. Timmer, and G. Ypma (2003), Data Sources and Methodology, in: van Ark, B. and M. O'Mahony (Eds.), *EU Productivity and Competitiveness: An Industry Perspective. Can Europe Resume the Catch-Up Process?*, A Report for the European Commission, Brussels.

Jürgens, U. (2003), *Characteristics of the European Automotive System. Is There a Distinctive European Approach?* Discussion Paper SP No. III 2003-301, Berlin.

Kansky, A. (2000), Opportunities for U.S. Firms in the Russian Automotive Market, http://www.bisnis.doc.gov/bisnis/country/001026AutoISA.htm.

Kogut, B. (1985), *Designing Global Strategies: Comparative and Competitive Value Added Chains*, Boston.

KPMG (2003), Impulse in der Automobilindustrie. *Strukturelle Veränderungen in der Automobilzulieferindustrie*, Vol. 3.

Lambert, D. M., M. C. Cooper, and J. D. Pagh, (1997), Supply Chain Management: More Than a New Name for Logistics, *The International Journal of Logistics Management* 8 (1).

Larsson, A. (2002), The Development and Regional Significance of the Automotive Industry: Supplier Parks in Western Europe, *International Journal of Urban & Regional Research 26 (4)*.

Lepape, Y. and J. Boillot, (2004), *Le renouveau de l'industrie automobile dans les pays d'Europe Centrale et Orientale*, Etudes des Missiones Economiques, par le Reseau Automobile Elargissement, March.

Lessard, D. (2003), Frameworks for Global Strategic Analysis, *Journal of Strategic Management Education* 1 (1).

Link, H. et al. (1999), *The Costs of Road Infrastructure and Congestion in Europe*, New York.

Lohmueller, J.-D. (1997), *Transportation Applications of Fuel Cells*, Discussion Paper No. ISYE 6777, Georgia.

Lucas, R. and D. Schwartze, (2001), End-Of-Life Vehicle Regulation in Germany and Europe – Problems and Perspectives, Wuppertal Papers No. 113, Wuppertal.

Maibach, M. et al. (2000), *External Costs of Transport: Accidents, Environmental and Congestion Costs in Western Europe, INFRAS and IWW*, Zurich.

McKinsey Global Institute (1993), *Manufacturing Productivity*, Washington.

McKinsey Global Institute (1998), *Productivity-Led Growth for Korea*, Seoul.

McKinsey Global Institute (2002), *Reaching Higher Productivity Growth in France and Germany*, Washington.

McKinsey Global Institute (2003), *Improving European Competitiveness: MGI Perspective*, Washington.

McKinsey&Company (2003), *HAWK 2015 – Knowledge-Based Changes in the Automotive Value Chain*, Frankfurt.

Ministry of Industry and Trade (2004), *Panorama of Czech Industry*, Prague.

Moch, D., M. Almus, T. Eckert, D. Harhoff, T. Hempell, and G. Licht (2002), *Einsatzmöglichkeiten hedonischer Techniken in der amtlichen Verbraucherpreisstatistik*, Study on behalf of the German Statistical Office, Mannheim.

Monnikhof, E. and B. van Ark (2000), *New Estimates of Labour Productivity in the Manufacturing Sectors of the Czech Republic, Hungary and Poland*, Groningen Growth and Development Centre, University of Groningen 6 The Conference Board, Second Report for the wiiw Countdown Project, June

Moomaw, R. L. and E. Yang (2004). *Total Factor Productivity and Economic Freedom: Implications for EU Enlargement*, ZEI Working Paper No. B02-2004, Bonn.

Mulligen, P. H. van (2003), *Quality Aspects in Price Indices and International Comparisons: Applications of the Hedonic Method*, Ph.D Thesis, Groningen.

Murphy, J.J. and M. A. Delucchi (1998), A Review of the Literature on the Social Cost of Vehicle Use in the United States, *Journal of Transportation and Statistics* 1 (1).

Nayman, L. and D. Ünal-Kesenci (2001), *The French-German Productivity Comparison Revisited. Ten Years After the German Unification*, CEPII Working Paper, No. 1-14, Paris.

Neuner, A. (1993), *Die Wettbewerbsfähigkeit der amerikanischen Automobilindustrie am Ende der 80er Jahre*, Frankfurt/Main.

Nill, J. (2000), *Die Brennstoffzelle im Auto – Antrieb eines Umweltinnovationswettbewerbs mit Zukunft*, Diskussionspapier des IÖW No. 48, Berlin.

OECD (2001), *Measuring Productivity. OECD Manual Measurement of Aggregate and Industry-Level Productivity Growth*, Paris.

O'Mahony, M. and B. van Ark (Eds.) (2003), *EU Productivity and Competitiveness: An Industry Perspective – Can Europe Resume the Catching-Up Process?*, DG Enterprise, European Commission, Brussels.

OSEC – Business Network Switzerland (2003), *Russia Sector Report – Automotive Components Market*, Zurich.

Plunkett Research (2003), *Plunkett's Automobile Industry Almanac*, Houston, Texas.

Porter, M. E. (1990), *The Competitive Advantage of Nations*, New York.

Porter, M. E. (2000), Clusters and Government Policy, *Wirtschaftspolitische Blätter* 47 (2).

PricewaterhouseCoopers (2000), The Second Automotive Century, http://www.pwcglobal.com/Extweb/industry.nsf/docid/3690EA483AFBA6FA8525687E00590EAA.

PricewaterhouseCoopers (2002a), Prospects for the Russian Passenger Car Industry, *Automobile Financial Review*, http://www.pwcglobal.com/Extweb/industry.nsf/docid/3690EA483AFBA6FA8525687E00590EAA.

PricewaterhouseCoopers (2002b), *End of Life Vehicle Directive*, September, http://www.pwcglobal.com/Extweb/industry.nsf/docid/3690EA483AFBA6FA8525687E00590EAA.

PricewaterhouseCoopers (2003), *Supplier Survival. Survival in the modern automotive supply   chain.* http://www.pwcglobal.com/Extweb/industry.nsf/docid/3690EA483AFBA6FA8525687E00590EAA.

PricewaterhousCoopers (2004), *Wissen, Erfahrung, Innovation*, Frankfurt.

Prognos (2001), *Survey of Costs in International Road Goods Transport*, Basel.

Quinet, E. (1997), Full Social Costs of Transportation in Europe., in: Greene, D. L., D. W. Jones and M. A. Delucchi (Eds.), *The Full Social Costs and Benefits of Transportation*, Berlin.

RAND Europe/Institut für das Kraftfahrzeugwesen Aachen FKA/Transport&Mobility (2003), *Preparation of Measures to Reduce CO2 Emissions from N1 Vehicles*, Final Report.

Recordit (2003), Final Report: Actions to Promote Intermodal Transport.

Reger, G., M. Beise, and H. Belitz (1999), *Innovationsstandorte multinationaler Unternehmen: Internationalisierung technologischer Kompetenzen in der Pharmazie, der Halbleiter- und Telekommunikationstechnik*, Schriftenreihe des FhG-ISI, Vol. 37, Heidelberg.

Reinaud, G. (2001), *Hard Times for the Automotive Industry? Overcapacity and Downturn in the Markets*, Paris.

Rhys, G. (2000), *Report on the Economic Prospects for the Automotive Industry in the UK and Europe and Its Impact on Ford of Dagenham*, Cardiff.

Robinson, C., L. Stokes, E. Stuivenwold, and B. van Ark (2003), Industry Structure and Taxonomies, in: O'Mahony, M. and B. van Ark (Eds.), *EU Productivity and Competitiveness: An Industry Perspective. Can Europe Resume the Catching-Up Process?*, EU Commission, Brussels.

Roland Berger & Partners (2000), *Automotives Supplier Trend Study*, Detroit.

SAE International (2004), www.sae.org/fuelcells.

Scott, B. R. and G. C. Lodge (Eds.) (1985), *US Competitiveness in the World Economy*, Boston, Mass.

Smitka, M. J. (2003), *Adjustment in the Japanese Automotive Industry. A Microcosm of Japanese Cyclical and Structural Change?*, Lexington.

SPIEGEL-ONLINE (2004), Gebremste Erwartungen in China, http://www.spiegel.de/wirtschaft/0,1518,292119,00.html, March 24, 2004.

Standard&Poor's (2004), Mainland China's Auto Industry Prepares for More Competition, Publication date: 12-Feb-04, www.standardandpoors.com.

Stoneman, P. (1995), *Handbook of the Economics of Innovation and Technological Change*, Oxford.

Sturgeon, T. (1997), *Globalisation and the Threat of Overcapacity in the Automotive Industry*, Research Note 1, Globalisation and Jobs in the Automotive Industry, Boston.

Sturgeon, T. and R. Florida, (2000), *Globalization and Jobs in the Automotive Industry*, A Study by Carnegie Mellon University and the Massachusetts Institute of Technology, Final Report to the Alfred P. Sloan Foundation.

Takeishi, A. and T. Fujimoto (2002) *Modularization in the Auto Industry: Inter-Linked Multiple Hierarchies of Product, Production, and Supplier Systems*, CIRJE Discussion Paper, Tokyo.

Technopolis (2003), *Impact Assessment of Possible Options to Liberalise the Aftermarket in Spare Parts*, Final Report to DG Internal Market, Paris.

Terporten, M. (1999), *Wettbewerb in der Automobilindustrie*, Duisburg.

The Vienna Institute for International Economic Studies (2003), *wiiw Handbook of Statistics, Countries in Transition*, Vienna.

Tidd, J., J. Bessant, and K. Pavitt (2001), *Managing Innovation, Integrating Technological, Market and Organizational Change*, New York.

TIS Study (2002), *Study on Vehicle Taxation in the Member States of the EU*, TIS/PT.

Triplett, J. (1987), Hedonic Functions and Hedonic Indexes, the New Palgrave in: Eatwell, J., M. Milgate and P. Newman (Eds.), *A Dictionary of Economics*, Oxford.

Triplett, J. (2002), *Handbook on Quality Adjustment of Prices Indexes for Information and Communication Technology Products*, Washington D.C.

Urban, W. (1999), Patterns of Structural Change in CEEC Manufacturing, in: Landesmann, M. et al. (Eds.), *Structural Developments in Central and Eastern Europe*, wiiw Report, Vienna.

Van Ark, B. and E. Timmer (2002), *Measuring Productivity Levels – A Reader*, OECD DSTI EAS IND SWP (2002)12, Paris.

Verhoef, E. (1994), External Effects and Social Costs of Road Transport, *Transportation Research* A 28A.

Vernon, R. (1966), International Investment and International Trade in the Product Cycle, *Quarterly Journal of Economics* 80 (2).

Walsh, M. (2000), *Vehicle Emission Trends*, European Conference of Ministers of Transport.

WardsAuto.com (2003), Automobil Produktion – Begleitheft zu: Internationale Verflechtungen der Automobilhersteller.

Weidner, M. (2004), *China – Automobilmarkt der Zukunft?*, WZB Discussion Paper SP No. III (105), Berlin.

Weidner, M. et al. (2004), *Das Brennstoffzellen-Rennen, Aktivitäten und Strategien bezüglich Wasserstoff und Brennstoffzelle in der Automobilindustrie*, WZB Discussion Paper SP No. III 2004-101, Berlin.

Willeke, R. (2003), Nachhaltige Mobilität, *Zeitschrift für Verkehrswissenschaft* 74 (3).

Wolter, F. (1977), Factor Proportions, Technology and West-German Industry's International Trade Patterns, *Weltwirtschaftliches Archiv* 113.

Womack, J. P. and D. T Jones (1991), *Die zweite Revolution in der Automobilindustrie. Konsequenzen aus der weltweiten Studie aus dem Massachusetts Institute of Technology*, Frankfurt/Main.

Wong, D. (2003), Practical Solutions for the Automotive Industry – Ernst & Young Viewpoints in Autobeat Daily.

Yu, W. (2004), New Auto Policy Big Leap Forward, CHINAdaily, http://www. chinadaily.com.cn/english/doc/2004-06/09/content_337978.htm.

Zhang, W. and R. Taylor, (2001), EU Technology Transfer to China – The Automotive Industry as a Case Study, *Journal of the Asia Pacific Economy* 6.

Printing and Binding: Strauss GmbH, Mörlenbach